Praise for *StepWisdom*

I have known Eleanor Alden for many years, and I have frequently been impressed with her ability to relate to complex material from a depth of perception, and to express that perception with
clarity. Her book on stepfamilies is a fine example of this ability. It is
chock full of insight, compassion, and humor. She takes the reader
on journeys both mythical and concrete, showing us how these two
dimensions inform each other in that most "basic" social structure
that we know of – the family. It was C.G. Jung's strong belief that
we must not see our clients through a fixed theoretical lens, but
look at each person as a totally new image of the psyche, and Eleanor has brought this wisdom to her work with stepfamilies. In this
book, she brings *us* to an expanded and more flexible way of relating to the experience of family, and she does this through her keen
ability to recognize the archetypal imagery inherent in the multiple
and complicated patterns within stepfamilies, and her compas-
sionate way of recognizing the potential for growth that each pattern holds. I highly recommend this book to anyone interested in
better understanding the stepfamily experience, the challenges and
opportunities it brings to our lives.

Lara Newton, MA, LPC, Diplomate Jungian Analyst,
Author of Brothers and Sisters, The Psychology of Companionship

The understanding you seek for what makes a healthy family
and a healthy stepfamily has been available to you for thousands
upon thousands of years. In a very readable and compelling way,
Eleanor Alden has pieced together archetypal images, fairy tales,
biblical stories, historical figures and her own case studies to help
us gain understanding from the wisdom of the ages. As she states
"whether the stepchild is a historic, mythic, or biblical figure, the
courage to face the new and different and to believe that change

can be good is a common theme in the stories." And, it is a common theme in this encouraging work.

Eleanor's masterful work addresses the negative perceptions about stepfamilies that our society has fostered for far too long and allows us to see that these families have tremendous potential to support the development of strong, healthy and courageous individuals. We are invited to step back and accept the tremendous gifts that can come from brokenness. When we stand in judgment of brokenness, which our culture tends to do, we will miss the gift, and Eleanor gives us multiple examples to help us rework our thinking and to reshape our belief system.

She captures beautifully a central message of her book: "stepfamilies are not easy or simple family systems, but much in life that is the most rewarding is neither simple nor easy."

Thomas Long, M. Div
Pastoral Counselor, Minister, Stepfather

In *StepWisdom* Eleanor Alden makes a valuable contribution to the study of families by broadening our awareness that stepfamilies have been a part of our family systems since the beginning of family formation. By highlighting the wisdom that stepfamilies contain she brings to them the status they deserve. Her Jungian perspective brings new light to the uniqueness and commonness of stepfamilies highlighting both their positive and challenging aspects. She skillfully weaves the lessons from our rich history of fairytales and myths giving them modern interpretations that express both the conscious and unconscious beliefs in our families. This is a must read as we are all members of stepfamilies.

Mel Grusing, MSW, LSCW
Past President of StepFamily Association of Colorado

"This is a very important book, some chapters brought tears to my eyes and made me re-think a lot of my life, but each chapter should resonate with someone who has been in a step-family."

Anne Cole, MSN
Author, Psychotherapist and Stepmother

StepWisdom: Knowledge from the Ages for Successful StepFamilies is a book that will guide today's stepfamilies away from what they don't want and gracefully into what they do want—a healthy, loving family.

Dr. Patricia L. Bay, Psy.D., Redding, CA.
Psychologist, and author of Therapy in a Nutshell.

Stepfamilies and family therapists will find a deep reservoir of wisdom here. Even amidst the often-devastating fallout of divorce, there is the real possibility to create a successful and vibrant new family. Straightforward and inspiring, Eleanor Alden brightly illuminates the journey to a different kind of wholeness.

The Rev. Dr. Kenneth Plattner, Tucson, Arizona
Author, Pastoral Psychotherapist and Stepfather

Eleanor Alden has written a book that will help all of us to see step families differently. This is a perfect time to begin talking more openly about what is helpful in the therapeutic arena when working with step families. The book illuminates areas that are not often talked about in therapy. The careful attention to detail in areas for conversations with step families will help all of us to avoid pitfalls that can be destructive.

Wayne H. McCleskey, M.Th.,LMFT

StepWisdom

Knowledge from the Ages
for Successful StepFamilies

ELEANOR SPACKMAN ALDEN, MSW, BCD

StepWisdom: Knowledge from the Ages for Successful StepFamilies

Copyright © 2010 Eleanor Spackman Alden. All rights reserved. No part of this book may be reproduced or retransmitted in any form or by any means without the written permission of the publisher.

Published by Wheatmark®
610 East Delano Street, Suite 104, Tucson, Arizona 85705 U.S.A.
www.wheatmark.com

ISBN: 978-1-60494-444-0
LCCN: 2010928142

Cover Photo: The Great Wall of China by Mike Holtby,
DenverPhotography.com and
Back Cover Portrait by Alexandra Sheremet, 2009

WWW.STEPWISDOM.COM

This book is dedicated to my brother
David Spackman
whose presence on our joint journey of growing up
in stepfamilies made the experience
by far more joyous, and the difficulties easier

Contents

Introduction

Contemporary Americans tend to believe that stepfamilies are a relatively new phenomenon. In truth, these families have always been with us. In the days when disease was rampant, when women commonly died in childbirth and men frequently died young from accidents or warfare, surviving children were taken in and raised by others as a matter of course. Divorce may have been less common in the past, but it existed in most cultures. More than 75 percent of all cultures in history, and many even today, were polygamous, leaving the majority of children throughout history in a family in which they have a stepmother. Stepfamilies have always been an enormous percentage of all societies, and information collected from thousands of years has been handed down from generation to generation about the problems and the benefits of living in stepfamilies.

We know that dysfunctional marriages and destructive divorces are harmful to adults, and to children who will then become adults who have significant emotional problems. However, even in these less-than-ideal circumstances, creative healthy people, like the mythical phoenix, can arise from the ashes.

As a Jungian and family-oriented psychotherapist in both private practice and in hospital and clinical settings, I have seen hundreds of families and individuals, both adults and children, who struggle with issues arising from membership in families in which at least one parent or at least one child is someone they are not biologically related to. These families form when people marry into families following a divorce, a death of, or abandonment by a biological parent, sometimes also resulting in adoptive or foster families. In the process of forming new families, which include children from prior relationships, I have seen serious struggles, but I have also seen immense gifts, successes, and courageous growth of personality which otherwise might not occur. Change and adapting to the unknown are hallmarks of stepfamilies, and can be gifts. Stepparents and stepchildren alike can use this situation to grow as individuals in ways not often offered by intact biological families.

Our culture and the professionals in it have a good basis for stating that good marriages and happy biological families are the best foundations for confident, creative, relational people. In my experience, however, good stepfamilies can also produce happy, confident, relational people, and often these families raise children who have flexibility and a willingness to see other points of view.

In stepfamily formations, most nonbiological parents marrying into a family or caring for children who are not their own enter the situation with good intentions, but can find themselves embattled and overwhelmed. Even if both biological parents are present, supportive, and helpful to the newly forming stepfamily, difficulties that arise can be damaging and upsetting. Children in these circumstances might be bewildered by expectations and feelings they are ill equipped to handle. Acting out and sabotage, testing boundaries and rules, failing in school, truancy, drug and alcohol use, and other behaviors seen as disrespectful by adults can be ways in which children attempt to relieve pressure and pain. Many stepfamilies seek help in psychotherapy to understand their family's interactions and find better adaptations to the situations in which all members find themselves. Jungian therapy and analysis are options that many people who are in difficult, pain-filled times in their lives use to examine patterns of feelings, thoughts, attitudes, beliefs, and adaptations that sometimes serve them well but sometimes hinder personality growth. Jungians work with images reflecting archetypal patterns that can lead patients to increased consciousness of their thoughts, feelings, and behavioral adaptations. This increased consciousness can help them to resolve the issues they face.

Carl Jung (1875–1961), a Swiss psychiatrist and contemporary of Freud, developed theories about archetypes and their reflections in images appearing throughout the ages in every culture and civilization. Archetypes are immortalized in fairy tales, myths, and legends that children hear and internalize early in life. These ancient images originated in the dim past, before written language, and have survived through time to appear in familiar forms as diverse as nursery rhymes, Shakespearean plays, movies, and simple metaphors we use daily. Nearly a century of examination of archetypal theory by Jung and his students validates the assertion that these patterns show up in a wide variety of ways in human behavior and thinking. Jung understood that the images, stories, and myths that survive the centuries resonate in the human psyche in descriptions of patterns of psychic energy. He also saw how these patterns reflect and elucidate what happens when a natural adaptation to life is thwarted, blocked, or overdeveloped at the expense of balance and wholeness in each psyche as well as in the family as a whole. The majority of Jungian analysts, and much of Jung's writing, focused on understanding how these archetypal patterns described in stories acted in the inner, so-called subjective level of the psyche. Jung also acknowledged that these archetypes have a holographic quality and their patterns describe patterns between people and in families, called the objective level. When looking at these archetypal patterns between nations and groups, it is called the collective level. The focus of this book is to look at these archetypes on the objective level as they play out their patterns in family life, as well as look at some common sense wisdom developed over the thousands of years of human history.

In my practice, I interpret these archetypal images and tales with patients, using them as helpful "maps" to healthier steprelationships. These ancient guides contain wisdom about human experiences in families going back thousands of years, instead of seeing a stepfamily as a recent development, a deviation from the norm of human existence and cultures. These oral and written histories offer a wealth of gifts too valuable to ignore.

As in any situation that requires courage, the stepfamily not only presents the risk of failure, but also the positive potential for success beyond our hopes. The purpose of this book is to offer the possibilities of using Jungian archetypal theories and practices in helping stepfamilies become more successful and healthy, certainly better than a destructive biological family, and for recognizing the potential available in steprelationships.

As I was writing this book and working through memories of my own childhood as a stepchild and of the many stepparents and stepchildren who have populated my private and professional life, bringing the gifts of joy and sometimes suffering, I had a dream that stayed with me.

> In the dream, I am sitting with some older women at a large table, which seems incredibly ancient. We are working on some wonderful bowls or vases. Some are small, some larger, some appear oddly shaped, some are beautiful to look at, some look as if they need to be fired in a kiln nearby, but I am not sure why. Some of the lovely, but fragile vases shatter. I am horrified at first, and then I watch as the women seem to be quite calm and accepting of the loss and simply take the pieces of shattered glass and pottery and begin making the most beautiful mosaic. It seems wondrous and lovely as they work together doing this work, and one woman says, "Now that is something of beauty and will be stronger than the vases that broke." I awake feeling joy.

The image of the beautiful, fragile vases breaking and being formed into something strong and once again beautiful is my image of stepfamilies at their best.

Chapter 1

After Families Break Apart: Stepfamilies Can Succeed

When one door of happiness closes, another one opens,
but we often spend so much time looking at the closed door
that we miss the one that has been opened for us.

—HELEN KELLER

Stepfamilies are one of the most maligned and undervalued groups in our culture, while at the same time impacting almost every person in the United States. For perspective: The U.S. divorce rate is close to 50 percent; 80 percent of people who divorce remarry, and the majority of these remarriages involve children.[1] Other figures state that between thirteen hundred and eighteen hundred new stepfamilies are created each day.[2] If you then add the number of single-parent families where nonrelated adults function in the role of stepparent, the total grows exponentially. The resulting number of stepfamilies is enormous—probably close to half of all existing families. Some researchers believe that more people are part of a stepfamily than those who live exclusively in a so-called traditional nuclear family.[3]

If one adds into the above figures the number of grandparents, uncles, aunts, cousins, adult children, and stepparents of adult children, there is almost no one in this country who does not have a close familial bond to someone called "step." Society also has millions of additional foster-parent families; uncles, aunts, and grandparents raising relative's children; and adoptive families who often have stepparent figures in them, whether formally acknowledged or not. Therefore, there is practically no one who is not touched by these families and, therefore, engaged in the support, or disparagement, of this kind of family system.

Clearly, we are surrounded by such family structures, and most of the time they function quite well. Most of these are successful, not disasters as they are so often portrayed. The immense creativity, worthwhile challenges, and special gifts of these families are seldom described or examined. However, it is also tragically true that many of these families do not successfully negotiate the sometimes rocky path of building a happy stepfamily. Often their difficult stories are exaggerated and magnified, while those stepfamilies that produce gifted and successful members of our society are generally ignored and minimized. When a news report describes a member of society who has psychological and legal difficulties as being from a "broken family," the blame seems easily assigned. People nod their heads and assume they know the reason for the individual's deviant behavior. However, when a person who is from a "broken family" is enormously successful by society's standards, the contributions of the stepfamily in nurturing that exceptional human being are seldom described. In fact, this person's success is seen as an exception to the prevailing wisdom.

The premise of this book is that there are many examples of highly successful and functional stepfamilies, and that after the breakup of the original family unit, the creativity and loving resourcefulness of the stepfamily members can create a fertile ground for a flexible, successfully adaptive group of people in a new family structure. This book in no way means to disparage the immense gifts gained by growing up in a nuclear family in which the adults are one's biological parents who create a loving and dynamic family system. However, unique advantages and rewards can also exist in a stepfamily. Stories of exemplary people who became who they were due to the influence of stepparents, not in spite of them, abound throughout history. From the patriarchs of the Bible to more recent heroic figures such as King Arthur, George Washington, Abraham Lincoln, and Benjamin Franklin, personalities we admire and revere have been shaped by stepfamilies. These figures became who they were because of the stepfamily, not in spite of it. Their lives may also illustrate some of the reasons that successful stepfamilies differ from those described as deviant or dysfunctional. This book will attempt to begin the process of defining the unique qualities that many stepfamilies offer children and adults alike, which provide them with qualities less readily available in biological families.

Watching the 2008 election of Barack Obama to the office of President of the United States should cause people to rethink these stereotypes regarding stepfamilies, but most consider his success the exception rather than the rule. Obama has stepmothers and a stepfather, as well as step- and half siblings. His biological parents were divorced, and his father, described as an excessive drinker, remarried several times as he lived in a polygamous society.[4] Since one of the goals of a family today is to raise successful, creative, loving people, his stepfamilies cannot be called blatantly dysfunctional. They certainly do not fit tidily into the usual and customary framework of what society has erroneously come to believe is stereotypical for a stepfamily. The variety of parental figures and their varied ways of looking at the world, as well as varied family units that cross cultures, such as Barack Obama's families, can create an awareness for stepchildren of how differently individuals and groups of people experience and value the world around them. A unified and unexamined or unchallenged family viewpoint that often characterizes biological families is much less likely to be experienced by stepchildren, and the daily awareness of the varied rules, roles, and values of parental figures often results in a child with a more sophisticated worldview and an ability to explore new options with less fear.

Another stepchild, Abraham Lincoln, is almost always voted the most revered President of the United States. He had a stepmother and stepsiblings, but the unique qualities of their influence are seldom examined by biographers, even though Abraham Lincoln stated that his stepmother's influence made him who he was.

Since families with steprelationships have been with us since the dawn of time and undoubtedly will be with us as long as human beings form family units, looking at the richness of history and stories to see patterns that work and traits that result in success for those who grow up in step-relatedness might help us see this situation not as an anomaly, but as a pattern with its own wisdom and pitfalls. Mythology, biblical history, and fairy tales also have a wealth of stories of the consequences of not understanding and valuing the problems and dangers of these steprelationships, as well as a wealth of wisdom about how well these re-formed families work and the exceptional people they can produce. The stories of Moses with his stepparents, the myths of Greek gods and heroes, and the fairy tales of Cinderella and Snow White reveal the themes and patterns that describe the complexity of these relationships, as well as dangers and successes for people living in these systems. The path described in these tales is often fraught with difficulties, but the outcomes are positive, and only because of the path getting there.

If you have picked up this book, you are probably one of the many millions of people who have been impacted by being part of a family where all of the adults and children are not biologically related, or you care for someone who is, or work professionally with stepfamily members. Whether you are part of a stepfamily, contemplating becoming a stepparent, or involved in some other form of family other than the cultural ideal of a "nonbroken" family, then you have undoubtedly heard, since you first could understand language, the dire stories of the horror of stepparents and stepsiblings. No one wants a parent like the stepmothers of Hansel and Gretel, Cinderella, and Snow White, and no one wants to be identified with those figures and be called an ugly stepmother. In fact, while I have met children who wanted to adopt children when they grew up, or become foster mothers or fathers, I have never heard a person, adult or child, say that as a child she or he dreamed of becoming a stepparent or of raising someone else's biological children, sharing the parental role with their spouse's ex!

The phrase "blended family" was developed simply because our image of stepfamilies is so unpleasant. "Happy stepfamilies" sounds like an oxymoron; often those who are happily living in such a family decline to use the word "step" in referring to the parents or children. They pass in our society without anyone knowing that their family is anything other than a group of biologically related people. In fact, many happy stepfamilies go out of their way to hide this status, with keeping even close friends unaware that both parents are not biologically related to all the children. However, stepfamilies offer, both to their members and society, something that is different from the original family unit. Stepfamilies are here to stay, and guiding them into being the best they can be is more productive than giving judgmental lectures that increase shame or guilt.

Most of us will, at one time or another, be a stepchild or a stepparent, have stepsiblings or half siblings, or have a close relationship with someone who carries the title "step." Whether or not we use the term, the dynamics are there. Becoming conscious of the patterns, hopes, and pitfalls that storytellers have described for thousands of years seems to be a wiser attitude than bemoaning our fates.

Unfortunately, the narrowness of our present-day myths about family with the polarizing jargon of being dysfunctional and functional, the negative mythology concerning the outcome for children of divorce, and the horrors of having a stepparent exists. We need to reexamine these myths of family, determine whether the terms *dysfunctional* and *functional* are still useful, and reexamine what wisdom is to be found in the more than four thousand years of recorded history. Rejecting useless or outgrown attitudes and beliefs and replacing them with vital and supportive structures that serve stepfamilies is an immense task and beyond the scope of any one book. The rest of this book will attempt to describe the ways that these families support qualities that benefit all of us and are harder to develop without the experience of "step." A vital discussion, and a lot more research, is certainly needed in the arena of the emotional issue of families that bend, break, and re-form, sometimes with better outcomes than if they had stayed locked in destructive relationships.

Throughout history, most stepfamilies were the result of new families being formed after previous marriages ended in the death or disappearance of one of the spouses. War, disease, social and environmental upheavals, and financial strains caused most of the disruptions to previously intact families. Divorce now is the leading cause in the U.S., in an age with fewer orphanages, stronger child labor laws, no legally indentured children as servants, and an increasing life span, with death in childbirth becoming less common than at any other time in history.[5] Whether these nontraditionally structured families form because of the death of a biological parent or divorce, the initial break in the first family structure involves some degree of suffering and grief, as well as a loss of the idealized image of family by some of the family members. Thankfully, along with the losses comes the possibility of increased consciousness and human growth.

The reasons for the existence of stepfamilies in the past were:

- the practice of polygamy by the majority of human cultures;
- the death of the mother in childbirth;
- the death of a parent due to illnesses, accidents, and wars;
- abandonment of the family by one parent;
- divorce or annulment of marriages, which was acceptable in many cultures;
- a mistress with her own children, which was considered acceptable. (Mistresses in the past and in Europe and elsewhere have had their own family structure without the first family divorcing; the half siblings are often acknowledged and, therefore, have stepparent figures.)

Today, the vast majority of stepfamilies seem to be the result of prior marriages ending in divorce, but the other reasons still exist to a lesser degree.

Nuclear families in the traditional sense begin with a marriage between two people without children. The reasons people marry are complex and often unconscious, even to the people getting married, let alone to their families and friends who may or may not be totally supportive of the union. All of us carry within us images of the kind of person we hope to marry someday. I call this an *inner resume* for a partner, sometimes specific in its requirements and sometimes vague. For example, as children, the longing for a royal marriage and living happily ever after may seem an ideal fantasy, but as time goes on, human beings usually hope for someone who helps them feel loved and cherished, respected and protected, and who will not be interested in any other sexual or romantic partners for the rest of their lives. Some of these idealized images are unrealistic and bound to result in disappointment. Whether a marriage or family can adapt to the disappointments of reality, in order to live up to its desired image of lifetime commitment, is determined by each couple: the flexibility of the individuals, the external stressors on the family, and the ability of each person to self-regulate his or her own emotions, thinking, and behavior. Successful, lifelong marriages have many other attributes, and people are constantly looking for reasons why some marriages make it to the golden anniversary, while most do not.

Marriages that start when people are very young often involve people who have only a vague idea of who they are, what they can give, or do not want to give, to a commitment of this kind, and what their relationship needs are. These relationships are fragile and often break. Physical beauty, sexual attraction, financial security, and power are qualities listed on the "job description and resume" as items that can overwhelm and minimize other needs, especially in the early stages of dating. The shortness of the list, and its tendency to describe feelings and romantic states without concrete, descriptive items, dominates most young marriages. As the concrete realities of daily life, and the addition of children make idealized feelings less important, the tensions between what was really desired and longed for, and the situation in which the couple is really living, can lead to divorce.

Case Illustration

The couple sat quietly on the chairs they had chosen on either side of the conspicuously empty couch, while I waited for them to sort out what they wanted to tell me about their marriage and why they were separated. Both hoped they could "save" the relationship for the sake of their children, a pressure they were feeling not only from themselves, but from their families of origin. The woman had called to make the appointment after a tearful fight with her mother, who had also enlisted the help of the minister who had married the couple. Both older adults had admonished the young couple that they were being thoughtless of the harm a divorce would do to their children and that they were being selfish in separating and hiring divorce attorneys. The man brushed his right hand through his short hair while clenching and unclenching his other hand. He glared at the floor, and then looked away with tears brimming.

The woman's long hair hid some of her features, but her eyes never rested as they darted from her lap (where she had a pad of lined paper with her notes) to the man and then to me. She pulled herself up and stated, "Well, I guess I can begin. I brought some notes so I can remember what I want to say, since he hates it when I start to cry and lose my train of thought."

The woman then went on to describe a relationship that began in college, where both of them had been involved in the drama society. The woman described herself as quiet and shy, but said she enjoyed working behind the stage and designing costumes. The man loved the limelight and enjoyed acting, and as a student, he was enrolled in premed. By their senior year, they were engaged, and the man had been accepted at a medical school. The woman had always wanted to be a teacher, and she began student teaching while studying at night. They married after the man's first year as a medical student, and a year later, the woman was pregnant with their first child. Although their finances were strapped, with her being the sole breadwinner while the man attended medical school, they both reported this period of starting their new family as the time when they were the closest. The man's family provided babysitting help, and the woman's family helped with the finances. The man interjected that he had thought they were not going to have children until he finished his internship, but once his son was born, he couldn't imagine a world without him. The woman continued, saying she got pregnant again at the end of his last year of medical school, again unplanned, but she emphasized that she knew she wanted at least two children, and thought having siblings three years apart was best.

The man, who had not talked as much as the woman throughout the history gathering said, "That is it in a nutshell; it is always what is best for her, for the kids, for God, for her mother. I am never considered. We make a plan that might make my life easier, like when to have kids, and, surprise, she changes the plan for someone else's good; if I have wants or preferences, then I am being selfish." The woman began to sob and said to me, "See? It is always my fault, and we can't talk."

Neither of them had really entered marriage with any idea of who they were or why they loved each other. The woman began to tell of a childhood, which she thought was a good one, but in which the primary parenting messages were threats of punishment if she didn't behave well. Her longing for unconditional love, which she felt she had found when she met her husband, along with her own need to be "good" as defined by her parents and her religious views, had left her with little sense of who she was as a person of her own. The man had grown up as one of several boys in a home with two working parents, who were chronically exhausted and had little time for joy and fun. When he met his wife in an arena where he was on stage having fun and where he was the center of attention, he thought all his childhood longings were finally being fulfilled.

By the time they had been married for three years, they had recreated the same childhood hurts in their marriage. The woman was too busy with the kids and her work to pay much attention to her husband. Her role of earning money for the family left little time for "fun," something she didn't think was appropriate to want as an adult, and her husband began to sound like her critical parents in threatening her with punishment if she didn't change. The husband, in fact, no longer wanted to have sexual relations with his wife, as he was sure she would get pregnant again. He was now seeing a nurse at the hospital where he was a resident, enjoying the fun of being the center of attention again. He loved his children, but no longer trusted or loved his wife.

The woman's dream of being loved unconditionally had never included giving the same unconditional love to a husband, and she certainly didn't love herself this way. The undemanding love she felt from her children seemed more in line with what she had longed for than the love of a critical husband. Her childhood had taught her few skills in successfully negotiating the often conflicting needs and hopes of a group of individuals called family. The man's parents, too, had done what they could to survive, and while less punitive, had little energy left to pay much attention to a large group of kids. Therefore, both partners in this couple were locked in a relationship they had designed around unspoken requirements that the other one neither understood nor accepted.

The man fully believed he had found a much better partner in the nurse at work, and the woman did not want anything to do with a man who would "cheat." They agreed to divorce, even in the face of the hostile disapproval of both families. Both sought individual therapy and made the commitment to be more aware of their own needs, hopes, and personalities before marrying again and beginning the more complicated process of building two separate marriages with shared children. They learned that honoring the disruption their children would feel in a way that validated the children's feelings, and increasing the quality time spent by each parent with them, was not going to be easy while they dealt with the stress of moving to separate homes and dealt with the financial problems divorces create. They were bright and thoughtful people, whose first marriage was ending very painfully. Both loved their children, but they needed to know themselves more deeply before entering another marriage. They needed a more conscious awareness of what their own "job descriptions" for a partner were, as well as what the "resumes" they would bring to the table looked like. They would also need to add their children's hopes and dreams into the mix in order to consciously restructure a more mature stepfamily system in the future. Their children will grow up moving between two homes and two families, each different from the other; hopefully the experience will broaden their awareness of diverse ways of living, and allow them to become flexible and caring people.

This pattern has many variations, but the ending of a first marriage with children can be a working template for developing an awareness that will make a second marriage and a stepfamily a more conscious commitment with more potential to support everyone involved than the less aware arrangements made by younger, less mature people.

So what makes a second or even third marriage different from the first one, the end of which was characterized by the pain of expectations and unmet needs? From what I have seen in my practice, and from what the myths and stories tell us, there are many reasons, but the overwhelming characteristic of such a successful journey is loving respect and honesty, or as much honesty as any of us can muster, given that there are parts of ourselves we don't really know.

Respect for each other, an attitude of grateful admiration, and a tendency to give five pieces of praise for every criticism consistently predicts a good outcome. However, couples can't admire each other seven days a week, year after year, unless it is heartfelt. Therefore, mature adults need to find an awareness of what the commitment of marriage means, what the traps and snares are that they bring from their past, and what their needs and hopes are in order for a second or subsequent marriage to succeed. Sometimes this awareness between two adults, and the inclusion of the children in the recognition of expectations, feels far less romantic than believing one has found unconditional love with one's "soul mate." However, in the long run, the love and security of knowing one is loved, regardless of obvious flaws and limits, and the knowledge that the hopes and needs of all involved are being honored, allows one to feel more truly loved and loving than being loved by someone who does not see one's flaws, or one's humanity.

Understanding the ancient wisdom handed down to us in the forms of mythology, stories, and fairy tales is increasingly important as the sheer number of humans involved in nonnuclear, biologically related families increases with population growth. Fairy tales and myths have dealt with stories and patterns of family and romance since they were first told; and with each telling of the tale, the pieces that seem irrelevant to the listeners are discarded like out-of-date or ill-fitting clothing. What we are left with are centuries of stories telling of patterns of human interaction which rang true to countless generations. In addition, since so many ancient tales and myths include stepfathers, stepmothers, and siblings caught in rivalries or deeply loyal relationships that transcend blood, those stories say something familiar to each generation.

We are a storytelling species that remembers truths when told in story form. If you wish to test this, ask yourself how many biblical stories you know. Then ask yourself how many of the hundreds of rules and laws laid out in the Bible you can recite from heart. Because of our Judeo-Christian culture—Christianity being the dominant religion in the United States—even people of other religious backgrounds or people with no religious affiliation know of Moses bringing the children of Israel out of Egypt, of Abraham thinking he must sacrifice his favorite son, of Joseph's coat of many colors, or of Cain and Abel; however, most will be hard-pressed to recite all Ten Commandments in order, let alone name any of the many other rules. Stories that grab our attention and imagination flow the way our psyche's energy does; they describe reality as we see it in our daily lives. They describe archetypal patterns, ways human beings have developed structuring behavioral and social norms, and organized the world into meaningful experiences as they adapted to life on this planet. Stories about stepfamilies abound in the earliest mythologies, the gods of the ancient world often being stepparents and stepchildren, learning, growing, and relating in the extended family these systems provide. There are thousands of years of human experience and wisdom in these tales.

Chapter 2

Listening to Four Thousand Years of History with Its Wisdom about Stepfamilies

"You are the embodiment of the information you chose to accept and act upon. To change your circumstances you need to change your thinking and subsequent actions."

—CARL JUNG

The written records of families, their dynamics, and their development are among the oldest of written historical documents. Many biblical stories are about families, their conflicts, their emotional complexities, how they adapted to changing circumstances, and how they survived in what was often a hostile world. Egyptian, Sumerian, and Greek myths offer a wealth of material for understanding the emotional drama of family dynamics at their best and their worst. What is interesting in looking at stories that are three thousand to four thousand years old is that stories of stepfamilies are so common of many heroic figures in the Bible; and gods from Egypt, Sumer, and Greece had stepchildren or were stepchildren. The dissolution of first families and the forming again of another family constellation with a stepparent is clearly not a recent phenomenon.

Men and women today struggle with the meaning of family in a way that, although not new, is more complicated because there are more societal demands today than at any other time in humankind's history. In our present-day family mythology, we speak of *dysfunctional* and *functional* families as if we all had identical definitions and were in consensus about what the words mean. What these words do hold are powerful emotional associations, images, and personal and collective stories that drive our lives in ways that make it difficult to stay rational, objective, and calm. One of the stronger sets of images that I, as a therapist, hear time and time again is the idea that functional families do not have divorced parents. If a person has divorced parents or ends up with stepparents, he or she automatically belongs in the dark bin of families who are shamed by the collective imagination as being dysfunctional and somehow not a "good family." At the least, studying old myths and history allows people to identify with Joseph, Moses, King Arthur, Queen Elizabeth I, Abraham Lincoln, and a host of other historical figures whose families would be labeled dysfunctional by today's definitions.

This human need to divide society into opposites, those who are "in" and those who are "out" when it comes to families, is not new. Fifty years ago, the words "dysfunctional" and "functional" were not paired as readily with family, but "good families" and "bad families" were labeled with equal zeal. There was a societal readiness to shame and embarrass the members of "bad families" as not good enough for the vague image of what a family was supposed to be. "Good families" were praised with little specificity as to what their qualities were. "Good" was often paired with wealth and property, and the financial security of the family was more important than anything else.

The purpose of family has always been fluid and hard to define with any precision, rather like pinning down a bead of mercury. It is hard to pinpoint what makes a family good or bad, functional or dysfunctional. The parameters of family and whom this social structure serves is perhaps a good place to start.

Questions such as the following may not have any right and wrong answers, but they can open discussions between people who often find that they disagree on the answers, even when they are part of the same family.

- What is the meaning of "family" as it has evolved in present-day awareness?
- Who are its members?

- How extended is the family?
- What does a member have to do to be shunned and rejected by the family?
- What are the intergenerational obligations and responsibilities that are accepted or rejected by the family?
- What is the goal of developing a family?
- How does the family support or hinder the personal development of each of its members?
- If some resource is low in the family, who must sacrifice and who is entitled to it?

Popular media talks about family of origin, family of choice, "just like family," nuclear families, extended families, stepfamilies, alcoholic families, adopted families, abusive families, authoritarian families, patriarchal families, permissive families, families with poor boundaries, narcissistic families, enmeshed families, and the list can go on and on. Are stepchildren or in-laws family? Is the second cousin who runs a huge corporation and just won an international award for excellence part of the family? Is the second cousin who is spending his life in prison part of the family? Is the mother of your son's children still family, even though the couple is divorced? What if there are no children but you still love the ex-daughter-in-law? What about the mother of your daughter-in-law with whom you have become like "sisters" when your son and daughter-in-law divorce? You both share the same grandchildren and have spent every Christmas holiday in each other's company for twenty years. Do you divorce everyone related to your ex-daughter-in-law except the children, or do you not? All of these scenarios question the definition of family in modern times.

These complex questions become even more complex depending on which of the many subcultures in Western culture a person belongs to. All cultures have some idea of who is family and who is not, and how its individual members are supposed to behave toward family, and how that is different from those we define as being "outside" the family. For example, the image of the godmother or godfather as the person who will care for children if the parents die has evolved into someone who is a special addition to the family for some and into a religious role in the child's life for others.

Do aunts and uncles assume the care for children of a disabled or deceased sibling, or is this the role of grandparents or the state? Do adult children care for aging parents at home, in institutions, or at all? At what point does someone call Child Protective Services if they think a relative is abusing another relative? What do you do if your grandchildren are being neglected by your alcoholic daughter? At what age should children be asked to leave the parental home? How are the financial resources of the family spent: for the health of the aging or the education of the young? Some tribal groups have banned divorces, perhaps because determining who is "in" and who is "out" gets so terribly complicated; other groups have decided to accept divorces and only recognize clans and blood kin, or only matriarchal lines. Some tribes insist that a woman totally leave the family into which she was born and become part of her husband's family. A woman's family of origin is no longer hers. Others reverse this, and the man leaves his family of origin forever.

The word "family" brings up so many different images that people can never be sure that two people using the same word have the same definition in their heads. In truth, they probably don't. So while every culture has a word or concept for family, and there are some things that seem universal, a good deal of what defines family and what it is supposed to provide for its members varies from culture to culture, from century to century, and even within one "family" over time. Stepfamily members often feel as if they are accepted family in one grouping only to be "sort of family" in another branch of the family or not accepted at all by yet another.

Our use of the word *family* in present-day English is rooted in a Latin word *familia*. The "family" to the Romans was the term for the household servants, and it even included the furnishings and possessions of the adults who owned the property, servants, and slaves. Therefore, a concept of family that includes things and people who serve, support, and provide for the owners underlies our use of the word. Biological kinship is missing completely from the original word's meaning. Kinship relationships and people who support and serve the best interests of those in charge have certainly not always been synonymous. Bible stories from three thousand years ago tell us that kinship relationships were often conflicted, lethal, destructive, and fraught with jealousy and betrayal. Just as in today's statistics, homicides by those we know, many of whom are kin, are more likely than homicide by a total stranger.

Our present-day sense of family still contains some sense of property and ownership as well as a belief that part of the purpose of family is service to one another. Families in the same culture may differ in their views as to whether a family is to serve the adults, who often see children as belonging to them with a strong sense of passionate ownership, or whether it is to serve the community, a religion, or ancestors. Some families serve the children, who are seen as the hope of the future. Of course, mixtures of these elements occur and can vary from person to person and from time to time, often depending on the feeling of success that people experience in doing their jobs of service or the joy found in being served. Rules of obligation and responsibility abound, often without being discussed and sometimes with little consensus or conscious understanding.

Regardless of who is being served in the family, the language used for family ties reflects the connection to ownership or belonging. For example, family members refer to each other with first-person pronouns and often have trouble in divorce situations letting go of the phrases "my wife," "my husband," or "my house" long after the divorce is final and the ex-spouse has remarried. Likewise, the sense that property is family is often seen in the division of the family goods during divorces, upon the death of a family member, or when parents suddenly realize that their children have another mother or father who also sees them as "mine." The pain that this understandable possessiveness often causes to families, with or without steprelationships, is real and must be honored and acknowledged. Grieving or a sense of loss occurs when what one thought was owned exclusively needs to be shared or given up entirely. The stereotypical emotional intensity of relationships with mothers-in-law and fathers-in-law often has to do with the sense of ownership that a family feels towards its biological members and an unwillingness to relinquish that ownership to a new spouse. The conflicts around this sense of ownership, which is clearly defined in the Latin meaning of the word *'familia,'* is also portrayed over and over again in stepfamilies, with children emphasizing the word *my* in referring to their father or mother in discussions with stepparents, or the mother-in-law or father-in-law who again places the emphasis on the word *my* with more vehemence with their child's spouse than with any other person.

So while a mother of adult children may "forget" to include her daughter-in-law in her conversations about her family and may resent being replaced as the first lady in her son's life, her own daughter may be angry enough about her own issues with her biological parents to describe her idea of family to others with terms such as "family of choice" or to exclude her parents or siblings from her "family" vacation plans. Determining who is part of a perceived family is a fluid process with some rigid components that may or may not be healthy to family success. In some families, the boundaries between who is and who is not included are more permeable and flexible than others. Some have rigid definitions, and when "step" is added to this already rigid definition, the family needs to become more flexible if it is to survive intact. Problems can arise if some members of one family see stepchildren as outsiders, not really family, and others are more inclusive. The ability of an entire family of siblings, parents, and others to accept stepchildren and extended steprelationships is limited by the confidence and emotional adaptability of the individuals, and by the family's resources and ability to adapt to change. This ability may evolve and fluctuate over time and life-stage development because of the external and internal pressures of life.

One of the more painful differences between original family and stepfamily structures is in the area of the changes in preference and closeness. Loyalties are stretched and redefined. The word *step* is actually a fairly recent addition to the English language. It comes from a Germanic word *Steif,* meaning "bereft"; in any stepfamily there are feelings of bereavement. No one looking at their child for the first time longs for the time that child calls someone else "mother" or "father." The loss of a sense of specialness, of being the only mother or father, is intense and can at times lead to depression and rage in the parent now sharing the title with another person not of their choosing. The parents are, indeed, bereft as they now share the role with another. The child is also bereft of the original nuclear family, and most of those related to the original family also feel the loss of old patterns of relationships. There certainly may be pleasant feelings of joy, relief, and celebration by some members of a family as an old structure breaks and a new one forms, such as the happiness when a widow finds a new love, but Western culture all too often skips the rituals or rites of passage that deal with loss. Divorce and remarriage, no matter how happy or unhappy the members have been, contain experiences of both sadness and suffering as well as celebration. This grieving can also be intensely expansive and healing if honored and if all engaged undertake the new paradigms of family with the best interests of everyone concerned in mind. For example, the daughter who resents her divorced mother's new relationship because she sees it as a threat to the close bond her mother has made with her grandchildren can grow by recognizing that both her mother's and children's lives can be enriched by the new partner and stepgrandfather. This type of challenge can lead to immense human growth as new roles are negotiated and new bonds are formed.

It may seem a very simple thing compared to the other issues involved in remaking a family, but often the issue of choosing the name/label for the stepparents becomes an emotional experience for everyone. Sometimes the label/name given to the stepparent at the beginning of the dating relationship sticks, and Jeff stays Jeff even after the marriage to "Mom." Other times children seem to want to have their own acceptance ceremony and choose when to call a new parent "Mom," "Dad," "Pop," or "Mommy Z." Other times it is something that evolves naturally on its own. As a recommendation to lighten the potential for anger and territorial disputes, using a different name/label for biological parents and stepparents usually leads to less friction and fewer explanations. One mother can be "Mom," another "Mumzie"; one father can be "Daddy," another "Popesan" or "Dagda." I know a man who as a child called his new stepfather "S-dad," which initially stood for Stepdad. Years later at his wedding, he stated that somewhere down the line in his head he had changed the S to stand for "Super." His stepfather had become "Superdad." He wasn't sure exactly when the meaning had changed, but the relationship certainly had.

This differentiation in labels/names helps families psychologically. The stepparent has a different and unique relationship and role with the children, and a separate name/label recognizes this

and eliminates the need to explain which Mom or Dad one is talking about, which can be a painful experience for everyone. Just as
people do not name their children all the same first name, (unless
they are George Foreman), so each child believes the family sees
him or her as unique. This need for distinction applies to parental figures as well. Titles such as aunt, uncle, and grandparent help
define the roles these adult family members play in our lives: more
influential than those not in the family, but not as close as those in
the nuclear unit. However, when a child has two separate nuclear
units, the issues of uniqueness and identity need to be acknowledged even as they change over time. As an aside, acknowledging
this need to identify new family members is not a bad plan when
adding in-laws to one's family.

Part of this naming/labeling process often includes dialogues
among members of the family as to the meaning of their roles with
each other. Is "mother" just a biological descriptor, or are there
qualities of mothering that others may have provided for the child
that are important to the use of that term? How and when does
one include a new stepparent in decisions about the children that
are not his her biological children? There is tremendous potential
for conflict in so many areas of life in negotiating the new relationships. Holidays, joint custody arrangements, birthdays, vacations,
schools, and just simple household rules and chores can become
the focus of arguments and conflict. Therefore, discussing these
things is essential to building strong stepfamilies.

Case Illustration

When a young couple divorced, they split parenting time in a
way that met the needs of the two biological parents by honoring their unusual work schedules. The first wife was an emergency
room nurse, who worked a lot of evening shifts from 3:00 PM to
11:00 PM. The man had a more regular job schedule as far as hours
worked, but often he had to work weekends. Then the man married
his second wife, who was self-employed and had previously spent
several years teaching school. The first wife was initially accepting,
and although she found it painful to hear the children talk about

their new stepmother, she did her best to hide her hurt and anger from the children. Then the first parent–teacher conference was scheduled, at which the new stepmother, who helped the children with their homework more than any of the other adults, wanted to be included. The pain of knowing that the new stepmother knew more about her children's academic successes and problems than she did sent the first wife into a tailspin of depression, humiliation, and rage. Not only did she not want her children's stepmother to participate in the conference, she was furious at the idea of this stepmother meeting separately with the teacher. The principal was asked to intervene, but he stated that the school's policy was that the biological parents had the right to decide who was at the conferences, and that his staff did not have time to hold two separate meetings. The young husband dutifully took the notes that his second wife gave him and acted as a conduit for the questions and observations that were appropriate concerns for the parent in charge of the homework. This pattern went on for a few years until the first wife also remarried and stopped working, which enabled her to devote more time to her children and their homework, and she no longer felt as if she had lost a competition that was undermining her confidence as a mother.

As this case shows, courts and mediators, child advocates, and school counselors often find themselves caught in the middle between passionately enraged people. The unresolved conflicts and unfinished grief work of a prior marriage can spill into new marriages and new family structures with a poisonous vengeance that most often harms the children more than the battling parents. Proactively avoiding this kind of conflict can lead to tremendous growth of personality and to a highly developed sense of compassion and willingness to see life from someone else's perspective. It may take hours of discussions over weeks and months for all involved to feel heard and valued, and to feel that their positions and sacrifices are being honored, but it is well worth it in order to help prevent the hostile environment in which so many children live.

Favoritism issues are also more sensitive in stepfamilies than in nuclear families without steprelationships. In most such nuclear families, the pressure culturally is to not play favorites, in spite of the reality that children often feel that there are favorite children in their families, and parents bond differently with each of their children. In stepfamilies, however, there will almost always be closer ties between a parent and his or her biological children than to the stepchildren, and often the guilt and anger around this reality can destroy the stepfamily entirely. Accepting that one can't feel the same kind of love for one's stepchildren can be dreadfully hard on stepparents and a phenomenal disappointment to the biological parent, but if the best qualities of the stepfamily are to develop, this inequality needs to be understood and utilized. This difference in acceptance can be a strength. Stepparents often regard their stepchildren with a more objective awareness of how the rest of the world sees such children, and can be wonderful mediators and guides between the less objective and less critical world of biological parents and the much more conditional world of society at large. To ignore the more conditional regard of a stepparent, minimize it, or act it out without compassion is dreadfully dangerous to all. Even more difficult can be the comparisons between one's biological children and one's stepchildren, especially if the stepchildren are clearly easier and more successfully adaptive human beings. Also, the conflict that occurs when one set of children has a popular high achiever, and the other set has one that is constantly in trouble can be agonizing, especially for the parent of the difficult child. The competition can be difficult, and painful, but how it is handled and accepted can lead to a stepfamily developing stronger people or harming its members.

A "Case Illustration" from History

Imagine if you read a "case illustration" like the following:

In a news conference today at noon, the district attorney announced that arrests had been made after a long investigation of a wealthy couple who appear to have lived in several different countries in the Middle East before moving to this state. They are charged with attempted murder and imprisonment for holding an Egyptian woman as a slave for many years. The woman was hired as a personal servant, was never paid, and was forced to work seven days a week. The servant stated the wife demanded that she be sexually involved with the husband in order for the childless couple to have an heir.

The Egyptian-born woman stated that after being told that she was to bear the husband a boy, the wife became enraged and jealous, starving the servant for a period of time. A year after the servant's baby was born, the wife was able to become pregnant and have a son. At this point, the tension became intolerable to the wife, and she demanded that the servant and her son be abandoned in an isolated area and left to die. The servant stated that she was destitute and had no skills or papers, making it impossible for her to escape and care for her son and herself.

Prior to this investigation, the couple had been investigated for allegedly blackmailing a political figure in another state. The alleged blackmail victim, a well-known public figure, claimed he dated the wife for a period of time after having been told the woman was not married and that the pair were siblings. After he found out that the woman was married, he paid the couple to stay quiet and leave the area, where the scandal of his involvement with a married woman would have destroyed his career. Another well-known public figure stated he had also heard that the husband had told numerous people that the wife was his sister, and he had been heard to say that he had married his sister.

The ongoing investigation revealed that a sibling of the husband was accused of offering his daughters to a gang of men attempting to break into his house when he had guests. The two daughters of this same sibling claimed their mother died suddenly under mysterious circumstances and that their father was also the father of these daughters' children by an incestuous relationship.

In another piece of the investigation, even more disturbing, the husband was heard stating that a divine voice told him to kill his younger boy. At this time, several state agencies, including Children's Protective Services, have been involved in the ongoing investigation.

Although the above may sound like a recent case in the Boston area that received national attention and was on the cover of sev-

eral tabloid magazines,[1] it is actually a report using language that
a journalist of this century might use to describe the home life of
one of the most revered married couples in our cultural history:
Abraham and Sarah.

This sacred Bible story, told to billions of members of three different religions, sounds sordid through the perspective of modern
news reporting! Our cultural norms have certainly changed over
the thousands of years since this story was first told, let alone written down, but the issue of what is "family" when confronted with
the jealousy of a stepmother has not.

That Sarah and her "handmaiden" from Egypt were not involved in a loving relationship, bonding only for the sake of their
two sons, is not new news; however, that we think such behavior,
when it occurs today, is shocking and new to the modern era is
baffling. It is often from the same pulpits that those who speak
with reverence of Abraham and Sarah also tell stories like this in
the present day and say they are a sign of the decline of family. Actually, if one looks at the current attitude toward this kind of behavior, it would appear that our standards for family interactions
have become higher rather than lower, but the pattern has been
repeated millions of times over thousands of years, causing harm
to children and making outcasts of innumerable women. We have
come to a place in human society in which we struggle with the image of a God in Sarah's story, who is angry at her doubting that she
would have a child in her nineties. Being upset with a woman that
age for thinking she could not have children seems bizarre now.
Then being told that the same God was not upset at Sarah's driving a woman and child out to die is more challenging ethically, not
to mention that Sarah's and Abraham's behavior would be illegal
today. So have we had a change in moral perspective as to how we
cope with the age-old issue of how two women with children by
the same father relate to each other, or is this a vivid description
of a pattern of psychological feelings that we need to acknowledge
because it will always exist? Does this pattern play itself out in the
psychological lives of people today as it did back then? Are there
other ways to deal with these all-too-human feelings that will lead
to a more loving and inclusive family design? The interesting point
in the Sarah story, as it applies to the development of stepfamily

relationships, is that she is clearly responsible for encouraging the relationship between her husband and her handmaiden, reminding modern readers of the situation in which nannies become involved with their employers, and the public's view of these situations illustrates the betrayal of the wife.

The Greek pantheon also carried with it images of divine entities acting in ways that would result in scandal and incarceration if played out in any other arena than our active imaginations. In my practice I have heard many times about the desire to kill a mother and her child whom a husband had conceived outside the marriage, whether it applies to a former wife, a lover, or a one-night stand. Angry fantasies and imagery are understandable; acting on them destructively is not.

Hera in the Greek pantheon was constantly attempting to stop Zeus's philandering ways, although it was always clear he would not leave her. His offspring and their mothers were often on her list of those she wanted dead. Her many creative ways to attempt to destroy them were often prevented by Zeus's interference or by the protection from others who felt the child and mother were innocent and undeserving of such a fate. As a culture we still use metaphors of Hera when a wife describes a rival as a cow, one of the beasts into which Hera turned a rival. Another metaphor used today that Hera's actions described is the desire of the wife to have the mistress see the man in his true light, and then watch the relationship "go up in smoke," something which happened to Semele, whose pregnancy by Zeus elicited Hera's spite. Semele was tricked by Hera into wanting to see Zeus in all his divine glory. Hera knew such an experience would kill a human; Semele did not. Zeus knew what would occur, but he went along with the scheme. Perhaps he wasn't enthusiastic about it, but he did not refuse, and showed himself to Semele who immediately died from the shock of seeing Zeus in his fully divine state.

Similarly, in the Bible story of Abraham and Sarah, one must wonder at Abraham's passive response to all of Sarah's plans, and whether his willingness to kill his son by Sarah might have more to do with guilt about his treatment of his oldest son than any demand by a loving God.

Rather than dismissing Sarah's behavior as simply a story that has no connection to the actions of modern people, we can apply its lessons to the news we read and hear every day about illegal slavery, including sexual slavery occurring in the United States and worldwide. In 2008, a woman from Pennsylvania was arrested for allegedly drugging her own thirteen-year-old daughter so that the mother's boyfriend could get her pregnant and the mother and boyfriend could have a child. The mother of the girl stated she could not become pregnant, and wanted her thirteen-year-old daughter to bear a child for the boyfriend. The girl stated that the man attempted to rape her three times, but she got away and reported it to the police.

What modern society can learn from these biblical and Greek stories is to avoid repeating the jealous, rage-filled behaviors they portray, to understand the feelings and powerful imagery, and to grow into more conscious adults who can self-soothe in the face of jealous feelings. Adults must grow to the point where the needs of the children involved are considered in the decisions they make about their behavior toward a spouse's former wife or husband and the children that that relationship produced. It is generally far easier to go through a divorce without children, because unless one is close to the ex-spouse's family, the opportunity to cut all ties and walk away usually exists. With children involved, the ex-spouse and all of their future relationships become a part of one's life. With accepting and even embracing that challenge comes growth and compassion, if one strives for it.

In order to facilitate that growth, however, jealousy and envy—those emotions that have been at the root of wars and courtroom battles, and that play out in endless tales about stepfamilies—must be honored and mediated without eliciting behaviors that could harm everyone involved. The goal for adults is to use these emotions to grow into more mature people with a broader perspective and empathy for others with different viewpoints, rather than being completely self-absorbed with only one perspective on life. (Chapter 6 is devoted to the issues of jealousy and envy, and the positive role they can play in human maturation.)

Another lesson from these ancient stories is that the active role of the biological father, whose jealousy overwhelms reason, can have an immense impact on the safety and health of the children who are also stepchildren. Abraham appears in the story to oblige his wife's demands that he produce a male child from her handmaiden, but he is passive when she is unrestrained in her jealous behavior. Family members need to communicate about consequences, and anticipation of ugly feelings will help prevent those natural, but unpleasant, emotions from turning into actions that will later be regretted. Painful feelings are not an excuse for bad and inappropriate behaviors.

Case Illustration

The couple arrived for therapy in a state of emotional crisis, with the wife bursting into tears shortly after she sat down. They had been married for seven years before she discovered that he had another child from a short romance in college with a fellow student. The husband stated that he and the young female college student were no longer dating when she told him she was pregnant, and he had hoped that this ex-girlfriend would get an abortion, but when she explained that she would not have an abortion due to her religious beliefs and was going to put the child up for adoption, he agreed to help her with the medical bills so the baby would have the best prenatal care.

During that time, he found he enjoyed going to the medical appointments with the woman who would bear their child, and although both agreed they did not want to continue as romantic partners, he wanted to be there for her throughout the pregnancy and delivery.

In the birthing room, the new mother changed her mind and decided she would keep the baby and raise the little boy by herself. The man stated he was stunned, but found he was glad he would not have to lose the child, as he held the baby shortly after his birth. The ex-girlfriend dropped out of college and returned home to live with her parents with the new baby; and the man continued with his college career, graduated, earned a master's degree in engineering, and shortly after starting his first job, met the woman he would eventually marry. He stated he was immediately aware that this relationship was different, and he could imagine a long life with this new love in a way he had not imagined possible. They were married after a year of dating, and two years later had their first child, a second son for the man.

The ex-girlfriend and mother of the oldest son had married years before, about the time that the man had started graduate school. Prior to that time, he had maintained some contact with her and his son, but since his son's new stepfather was so jealous, the child's mother decided to ask the biological father to stay out of her life. The man continued to get an occasional letter with pictures of the boy, but it was not until six months before his wedding that the old girlfriend wrote asking for financial help for herself and the boy. Her first marriage had ended with a great deal of drama as the man had both a drinking and a drug problem, and she had to get a restraining order at one point and had spent several nights in a battered women's shelter.

The man stated that for the first time he really felt as if he needed to be involved in his first son's life, and he made several trips to see his son and the child's mother. He began to make monthly child-support payments and agreed to continue to do so. He felt his earning potential as an engineer would not make this difficult, but he found himself resisting telling his fiancée about the boy, whom he had never acknowledged publicly. Now with the wedding plans consuming their time, he did not want to "rock the boat," or truth be told, risk losing his wife-to-be. As time went on, it became harder and harder to feel comfortable bringing up the subject, and he did not.

The man admitted he felt awful not telling his fiancée, and she never seemed to notice his monthly trips to see his oldest son, which were timed with business trips and did not interfere with the time the busy, dual-career couple saved for themselves. The fact that the new wife traveled more than he did prior to their son being born made his ability to manage this dual life absurdly easy.

The truth of this arrangement was revealed one evening when the man's cell phone rang while on the charger and his new wife picked it up. The old girlfriend's mother was on the phone crying. The ex-girlfriend and her son had been in a car accident, and both were in the hospital. The new wife, at first, was sure that the woman had a wrong number, but stated she finally realized that the woman on the phone knew her husband quite well, and that the father of a child was needed at the hospital as soon as possible. There was little time for discussion, and although the young wife wanted to hear some explanation that made sense to her, the look on her husband's face and his immediate need to get to the hospital left little doubt that there was a son about whom she knew nothing.

The young wife stated with embarrassment that she was not proud of how she handled herself during the next fifteen minutes. She screamed at the man that if he left the house he should never return, and that she didn't care if the "slut" and her bastard child died. Her feelings of jealousy, betrayal, mistrust, and humiliation had left her unsure of their marriage and her own perceptions about who her husband really was. The fact that she still hoped there was some way to continue the marriage and heal her family said an enormous amount about her ability to forgive.

What began the long journey back to trust and intimacy was the woman's recognition that the quality that would not allow her husband to abandon his first son and that made him insist on going to his son's bedside, even when his wife was in so much pain— knowing he might be destroying his marriage, was one of the qualities that she loved about him. His fear of losing her, and his lack of confidence in being honest about the complexity of his life, had led him into making a dreadful decision to withhold a very important piece of that life.

The healing process was slow. It took months before they were able to laugh and truly relax with each other, finally confident that if they could survive this trauma, they could make it through anything. The husband increased his connection with his first son, who recovered quickly from the accident, and this boy now visits his father, stepmother, and half brother every other weekend. The young wife never thought she would be a stepmother; and though she has the usual difficulties in adapting to both the image and the logistical problems of joint custody arrangements, she finally met her new stepson's mother and was able to develop a friendship based on the love of their sons, and the desire for them to have the best childhoods possible.

The ex-girlfriend had never realized she and her son were a secret, and had been hurt by the man's refusal to let the older boy

meet his brother. Once the secret was out, however, she offered to
take both boys for some weekends so the couple could have some
time free of children, partly since she felt that having a weekend
off from parenting was fun for her, and that it was not fair that the
couple didn't get the same benefit.

This situation has not been an easy journey for any of the
adults involved, but as the woman stated a year after finding that
her family was larger than she had known, "I can see why Abraham
was considered the wise patriarch! Going through all of this, I feel I
have grown ten years in maturity and stretched myself further than
I felt capable of ever doing. I have learned to forgive what I would,
two years ago, have thought was unforgivable, and I can't imagine
my life now without both my boys." It has helped tremendously
that the older boy was a sweet child who looked like his father,
and that the younger boy idolized his big brother at this stage in
his life. This family could have gone down the path outlined in the
Bible and in Greek stories, acting on the rage and pain, so that the
older, illegitimate son would have been considered a threat, not
a welcome addition. Instead, they chose another path, and all are
grateful for the outcome, aware there will still be difficulties to
overcome, but confident they can get through them. The husband
now has a maturity and confidence that he never had before he
battled through this chaotic situation of his own creation. He states
he never felt fully loved by his new wife as long as she didn't know
his secret, and now he feels like the luckiest man alive, to be loved
by someone who has seen him at his "weakest and stupidest" and
continues to love him.

The story of Abraham and Sarah offers us wisdom, not in terms
of guiding a modern couple in how to act in a situation similar to
theirs, but in the story's willingness to describe the emotions and
longings, good and ugly, which go with the intensity of the relationships we call family. The story not only illustrates jealousy toward
the children fathered by the husband with someone else, but parts
of the story with Abraham's brother, Lot, and his daughters, as well
as Sarah's ambiguous relationship with Abraham (sister and wife),
contain the element of incest, another dark side of family dynamics, step or not.

Although the story of Sarah being billed as Abraham's sister sounds like some norm from ancient Egyptian culture, rather than something acceptable today, many couples do separate over the sense that their relationships with their spouses feel more like a relationship between siblings rather than romantic couples. Today, as it was four thousand years ago, this incestuous feeling can lead to the dissolving of marriages, which plants the seeds for the possibility of future stepfamilies. Sibling-like marriages often end up celibate, and while affectionate at times, they can leave the door wide open for romance and passion to wander into the home uninvited, with the marriage often resulting in divorce.

There are hundreds of stories from dozens of cultures, describing the passions and dangers of stepfamilies, and the rage and jealousy which can impact them severely. But at the same time, these stories also contain examples of exceptional human beings, biblical and mythological leaders, and pioneers, illustrating that it is possible for people who grow up with changing family patterns to succeed. And, as in the examples of Moses, Joseph, and others, it is in the process of adapting to these difficulties that the leadership potential developed. Moses would not have been given an audience by Pharaoh without the steprelationship he had to the royal family; Joseph would never have gone to Egypt. Perhaps it is the instability itself that produces the flexibility and absence of a firm status quo for these children, that produces people willing to explore a world of possibility. Whether the stepchild is a historic, mythic, or biblical figure, the courage to face the new and different, and to believe that change can be good, is a common theme in these stories.

Chapter 3

Functional and Dysfunctional: The Present Myths We Live By

If you ever start feeling like you have the goofiest, craziest, most dysfunctional family in the world, all you have to do is go to a state fair. Because five minutes at the fair, you'll be going, "you know, we're alright. We are dang near royalty."

—JEFF FOXWORTHY

Over the past four decades, I have listened to thousands of clients, all of whom had one thing in common: They wanted to feel better about their lives. It is healthy and human to want to feel joy in work, play, and relationships. The specifics of what people hope will happen in their lives are unique and individualized; but increasingly I hear something in the first session about the family of origin, an unquestioning acceptance that childhood attitudes and patterns are interfering with their ability to achieve the kind of life and relationships, success, and joy my clients had hoped would fill their adult lives.

One common theme clients have is the willingness to live by one of culture's present myths: If their parents are no longer married, then my clients came from a "broken" and, therefore, "dysfunctional" family; if their parents are still married, they are baffled about their current problems because they think they came from a "good" and, therefore, "functional" family. It is often a source of pride for them that their parents are still married after decades in order to "raise a family." This paradigm of functional and dysfunctional family patterns has taken on a mythological quality: images and beliefs infused with meaning, emotion, and rules that drive people and groups.

Why do I refer to our present images of family as mythological? Humans are storytelling beings who appear to have an innate need to find meaning in life, to create living myths that describe our reality. The present-day myths of family are all the more powerful, because we see them as objective fact and reality, and they influence our attitudes and decisions as to how to judge and relate with others. When we are living in a myth, we do not see it as a paradigm, one of many from which we may choose, which then may fuel our emotional lives and give us a sense of purpose. These images may not, however, have any more objective, observable reality than the gods of ancient Greece with their mythology. However, when living in a myth that seems objective and factual, people seldom challenge the pieces of information that support it. The danger for those of us working with families and living in families is that we can be dominated by a myth and a set of nearly religious laws and taboos, which have the potential to restrict our capacity for relating openly and with feeling, both lovingly and creatively with those in our intimate social system.

Understanding the power of myth is important, because the myths around our present-day social arrangement called family are increasingly influential, and they can also drive politics, religions, courts, and our sense of self-worth in complex and complicated ways. This is a mostly unconscious process, and sometimes to society's benefit, but they also sometimes cause the people who are not members of society's model of the ideal family to sacrifice their emotional, psychological, and spiritual well-being. The guilt and shame accompanying divorces, being a single parent family, and living in challenging steprelationships can restrict many people from living creative lives and from being as genuine and loving as they could be without the emotional baggage our mythology about stepfamily systems delivers to our awareness.

For example, I have certainly listened to men and women from self-labeled "broken" or "dysfunctional" families, who describe families that clearly functioned successfully, filled with people who like each other and who have, to varying degrees, made the transition from dependency in childhood to more independent lives, with careers and families of their own, while still enjoying each other's company. Then in the next hour, I begin to hear of violent, abusive, and neglectful behaviors of the parents, who were initially described as heading a good family. It seemed at times that the only quality that could be labeled as "good" was that the parents were still married. All too often, the litmus test for whether a family is good/functional or bad/broken/dysfunctional has to do with the marital status of the parents.

So what is functional and what is dysfunctional? Why have we divided and labeled families with these judgmental images? Why is it so hard to define these terms in a way that doesn't illicit high emotion and distorted thinking? Can a stepfamily function as optimally as a family without steprelationships? Are the goals different? Are the tasks more complex, or simpler? In order to answer these questions, we have to come to some conclusion about what are reasonable goals for families, and about what we are trying to achieve when we commit to a marriage and have children.

Determining these goals is essential, because it is useless to talk about functional and dysfunctional families without asking what the function of the family is and what it is supposed to provide for which members. The joking that often goes with this discussion often indicates that 97 percent of families are dysfunctional, and yet the explanations for this attitude are foggy and vague. For example, we speak of divorce as the failure of a marriage, even when the divorce leads to increased personal growth for all people involved. Is a divorce really a failure if the divorce results in happier and more successful adults and children, who are then able to fulfill themselves and serve society in a more functional way? We hold up the ideal of the golden anniversary as a gold-medal prize, even if the couple wouldn't honestly marry each other again if they could go back in time or if there is no warmth and love left in the marriage. Our culture also sifts its information to support its view of reality, so when someone from a "broken home" commits a crime, we shake our collective heads, assuming immediately why the person did the crime. However, conversely, if the person came from an intact family, we look for other causes and assume the ongoing marriage of the parents could not have caused the delinquency. This is the emotional reasoning of a living myth. It feels objective, but no solid researcher should tolerate the bias. Yet research in the area continues to focus on proving the myth no matter what bias the samples have.[1]

Professional psychologists and counselors often assume problems will exist in stepfamilies and judge them as "dysfunctional" before evaluating any of the relationships. The words, "The parents were divorced," conveyed with a wise nod of the head, can seemingly justifiably lead us to all-too-clear images of personality damage. With almost religious zealotry, media and health professionals describe our families with labels that sound like illnesses: narcissistic families, abusive families, incestuous families, enmeshed families, single-parent families, violent families, addictive families, alcoholic families, polygamous families, child-focused families, and parent-focused families. All these family illnesses have a host of priestlike therapy specialists trying to label, define, and sometimes heal the alleged illnesses that prevent such families from being "functional." However, families are messy; they don't stay rigidly the same, if for no other reason than because people grow and age, and the more rigid the definitions of what is "in" and what is "out" in terms of families defined as successful, the less likely that the descriptors will be useful for more than a few people.

As a culture, what is and is not a functional family becomes less clear than the boundaries we put around our "sick" families. Because our myths around family seem to have merged with the medical imagery we use in our physical and mental health mythology, we think we can define illness with textbook precision, but health and who is healthy becomes fuzzier when applied to the health of a family or relationship.

People have told me that no matter how violent the family, no matter how socially disabled the children, if "all were saved in the Lord," then the family was successful and healthy. Others have told me the family is healthy because no one has ever been divorced, even though affairs were a permanent part of the system. For others, being functional has to do with the level of education achieved, where they live, what financial success they have, or whether they are members of an exclusive country club where only the "best families" are accepted.

The problem this paradigm presents for modern families is illustrated in the following story of a couple struggling with the definitions of function.

Case Illustration

A young woman came into my office stating that she never felt connected with anyone, could not seem to keep friends for any length of time, and had found herself unable to make any lasting relationships with the men she dated until she met the man she was now hoping to marry. He came from a "broken" family and was divorced with joint custody of two young children.

The woman, an attractive and eloquent thirty-two-year-old, stated she always felt that something was wrong with her, but she had no idea what it was. She wondered if she was so attracted to a man who came from a "dysfunctional" family, because there was something wrong with her. She could not imagine being a step-mother, let alone dealing with an ex-wife, but for the first time in her life, she was "head over heels in love."

She began to talk about her own large extended family, and repeatedly stated that she thought she had a "normal" childhood and that her family certainly was "not dysfunctional." No one ever divorced, and she knew everyone in her family would see her as a "black sheep" if she married a man with children from a former marriage.

The woman's extended family of uncles, aunts, and cousins from both family sides gets together on the Fourth of July for a barbecue each year at the family farm where she had grown up, and "They all get along. No one gets drunk or fights." Throughout the past, the family got together once a year and at weddings and funerals, acting as if they were in a polite, dramatic play about the "happy" family, which left her mother with a migraine. Her father always paid the large bill in silent martyrdom, until he died suddenly of a heart attack in his early fifties. Later she realized her fears of intimacy were based on a family rule that no one ever talked about feelings, disappointments, infidelities, or anything else that might cause conflict. No one got close enough to irritate anyone.

[Does this describe a functional family? Should this family be labeled with some medically defined term, as if they had a social or psychiatric illness? Or should other perspectives on what families do and don't do well be examined?]

> The couple eventually married, starting their stepfamily with two children with a lot of fear and a lot of courage. They learned that life can be messy and emotional, that sometimes ex-spouses fight with each other, and that her family culture of being "conflict avoidant" actually made her a good mediator. She was able to develop an alliance of sorts with the children's biological mother when she approached her using skills learned through her family's tendency to stay "cool." In this situation, reticence began to look more like diplomacy. She was able to convince her husband's ex-wife that all everyone wanted was what was best for the children, and that they all would be happier with less conflict between the parents. She insisted on utilizing the biological mother as the expert on the children's needs for mothering, and found by calling her to ask for help with ideas and for the children's history, she readily assuaged the other woman's fears that her primary place as the mother was in danger. The two women now do most of the scheduling of the various shifts back and forth between homes, and they have found they can enjoy the same elementary school events sitting next to each other. The children are thriving with their two mothers, one called "Mom" and one called "Merrymum," and the husband is relieved to have less interaction with his former wife.

In a different situation the new stepmother's reluctance to share feelings openly might be seen as "sick." She continues to work on being able to identify what her emotions are, as she struggles with her inability to know her own emotional states as a deficit from her family inheritance. True to her family code, she has been able to appear calm in difficult situations, which allowed what could have been a fragile or hostile alliance for the purpose of raising the children to develop into something strong and supportive of both families, showing that our wounds can also be our gifts.

Is this stepfamily functional? One could label the woman's birth family as cold, conflict avoidant, emotionally detached, full of secrets, and superficial. The woman sometimes found her family reunions to be just that and loved the messy, emotional, boisterous atmosphere of her husband's family. However, at times she found his family's tendency to "call it like it is" created a lot of hurt and angry feelings she thought served no purpose. In contrast, the couple has created a loving, warm home for their children, who will grow into adults with their own gifts and wounds, and hopefully create a family system that works for them.

If wounds can help us, as well as hurt us, and flaws can be gifts in different situations, can we judge any qualities as always being family enhancing, or damaging? What might be more productive is to list qualities that serve the goals of a family, and ones that clearly do not. Yet we need to use these guidelines with caution. Each family has a blend of traits that either serve the growth of the members or hinder that growth, and sometimes what serves the growth of one hinders the development of another; it is messy. Recognizing the differences, the costs, and the benefits of the patterns and attitudes in a family is not always simple, for it is in the hindering, the suffering, and the sacrifices, that the personal qualities that may ultimately have value are developed. It is in response to those "dysfunctions" that the greatest gifts of a personality often emerge. Life is not about having a perfect childhood or being a perfect parent; it is about facilitating growth; and, within limits, some suffering and hardship can enhance our growth into more empathic and complete adults. When everything is pain free and without suffering, few people challenge themselves to grow and explore new options. It is often in our failures and struggles, when an attitude, belief, or relationship is no longer comfortable, that our personalities and sense of self are pushed to grow and change, often helping us become wiser and more adaptive.

Some qualities labeled "dysfunctional" may actually assist stepfamilies in meeting the goal of most families. Healthy family goals include providing a physically and emotionally safe place to raise children to become adults who are happy, well-adjusted members of society. Simultaneously, the family strives to support the parents in their partnership, careers, leisure activities, and friendships outside the family, and relationships with their own families of origin. It is easy to see why this goal becomes so complex and for each family a unique experience. As stepfamilies form, they have an opportunity to look at the past marriages or relationships and redesign a way of living that may serve everyone's needs more successfully than the past family structures did. The suffering in the failure of the first marriage often leads to a determination to not repeat the mistakes of the past and to have a more fulfilling relationship in the next one. Problems in either family labeled "dysfunctional" can lead to increased insight and problem-solving skills.

Although no one would disagree that "functional families" are *not* families in which there is violence, addiction, incest, poorly defined roles, poor boundaries, a lack of respect, or children who find it difficult to abide by the social and legal limits in society at large, some of the above terms are complicated to define when applying them to your own family.

For example, arguments about what is and is not violence go on endlessly in our society. Most of the research is no longer focused on violence between spouses, which society has recently defined as illegal and "dysfunctional." This is a new cultural norm, as only a few decades ago beating a wife was legal and by some considered a necessary part of a good marriage. It was illegal to treat an animal with the same violence before domestic violence laws gave adults the same rights and protections as their pets. When I was a child in Pennsylvania, the legal system in one of the cities nearby always recorded a woman's death due to a beating by her husband as an "accident." Now that kind of behavior by a husband usually hits the national news, and the man is arrested. Our tolerance for some kinds of behavior has certainly diminished. Yet even today, assaulting a child with a degree of violence that would result in an arrest if it was perpetrated on an unrelated adult, or pet, is still acceptable to many people in many places.

The function of family has evolved over time and will continue to change and grow. Any attempt to rigidly define that function will elicit valid exceptions, and some attributes may become obsolete over time. All definitions have limits, and each family or individual may take exception to some or add their own, or both. Discussing the following lists can help people more clearly define their "unique" family.

A GUIDELINE FOR FAMILIES

"Functional" Families:

1. Support the growth of individuals without the inappropriate sacrifice of other members' goals. (Some personal sacrifice by members of a group is normal for the benefit of other individuals or the benefit of the whole system, as long as the sacrifices are understood, appreciated, and acknowledged appropriately.)
2. Are flexible, able to adapt to new changes and to external and internal stressors.
3. Have creative responses to problems; the family teaches its members to solve problems thoughtfully and empathically.
4. Are free of chemical and behavioral addictions.
5. Are violence free.
6. Have appropriate roles for mother, father, and children that are age appropriate.
7. Support relationships within the family and outside the family. (Families encourage friendships, hobbies, and activities that involve individual members of the family as well as the entire family.)
8. Cherish the cultural identity of family without intolerance of others who are different.
9. Support some form of spiritual or transpersonal ethic and awareness.
10. Encourage members in being creative, relational, and successful at achieving social and personal goals that serve community and society as a whole. In present-day Western culture, this usually means supporting educational successes and career goals.
11. Enjoy each other's company individually and as a group without splitting behaviors. (Not encouraging hostile or demeaning attitudes or behaviors toward others; this can include gossip, sharing confidences inappropriately, and connecting with one person at the expense of another's confidence and security or self-esteem.)
12. Act respectfully and with awareness of each other's needs and boundaries, respecting emotional and physical privacy and space.

13. Define emotions, thoughts, and behaviors as separate aspects of human awareness, which are expressed appropriately, with constructive behaviors.
14. Work happily and play well together.
15. Encourage and support intimacy rules:
    a. Tell the microscopic material truth (truth that shares important information which, if withheld, results in behaviors that would be different if the truth were known.)
    b. Feel your own feelings.
    c. Keep your commitments.
16. Actively supports the individual and group commitment to physical, spiritual, intellectual, and psychological journeys.

"Dysfunctional" Families:

1. Do not acknowledge or address addictions to chemical substances, gambling, work, sex, spending, etc.
2. Use addictions or compulsive behaviors to mood alter and avoid genuine expression of feelings.
3. Use passive-aggressive communication.
4. Are plagued by violence: physical, verbal, or emotional abuse used to control.
5. Use fear- and shame-based control methods on each other.
6. Have inflexible and rigid rules, or chaotic or inappropriate rules and boundaries.
7. Have confusing rules, roles, and role reversals.
8. Use a merged sense of self that uses mind rape (someone insisting they know what you are feeling or thinking in an aggressive and uninvited way that causes pain.)
9. Are characterized by emotions expressed inappropriately (sexual, hostile, or feelings used to produce shame and guilt).
10. Are characterized by secrets: the more secrets, the more dysfunctional.
11. Are hostile to outsiders: relationships outside the family that support individual growth are taboo or discouraged.
12. Are intolerant of other cultures or one's own culture.
13. Are strictly authoritarian without earning respect or trust.
14. Have chaotic authority or no authority.

15. Are characterized by an inability to play well or work well to-gether.
16. Have inappropriate rules around communication:
    a. Don't feel or express unpleasant emotions.
    b. Don't talk.
    c. Don't trust.
17. Emotional or physical incest is present.
18. Poor and inappropriate boundaries and role confusion.

No family is without some traits from both lists; none is 100 percent in either direction. Some characteristics such as incest are far more damaging than some blurring of roles at times, or a tendency to insist that one knows what another is feeling or thinking. Some families are stronger than others in some areas and may be weaker in others. There is no black-and-white, functional–dysfunctional paradigm that has a real-life example.

Although our labels are black and white, dysfunctional, or functional, there is a lot of gray in the dysfunctional area. Perhaps if we used a full-color model, rather than a black-and-white one, we could honor strengths, gifts, weaknesses, and areas that need growth in all families. In addition, it is true that sometimes the gifts of a family at one stage of a child's or adult's development become stifling and harmful at another period in the life cycle. Families are immensely complex and complicated, rewarding and invaluable people-growing systems, but their very power to serve can also result in tremendous harm. To further add to the complexity, as society has become more complicated, so have the demands on families, with many new pressures on families.

In the past, when families depended solely on their members for their basic needs of survival, including food, shelter, protection, and safety, the present-day demand for emotional intimacy, companionship, and intellectual stimulation may have seemed absurd. Until fairly recently, because many marriages in the past were formed for financial reasons or were arranged by parents rather than by individuals in love with each other, the demand for the kind of bonding we expect in a "good marriage" and a good family was seldom expected; those needs were met elsewhere, if at all.

Divorce and desertion could become death sentences, and orphanages were filled with children who were left by women and men who could not feed them. Historically, to leave a wife and children could risk assigning them to poverty, if not death. The careers for single women trying to support children were extremely limited, as is still true in most of the world where literacy is the exception and not the rule, government support for single mothers is negligible or nonexistent, and prostitution is often the only viable option for a woman to make a living.

The demands we have placed on the institution of marriage, which includes the expectations of perfection and happiness, have given people reasons for dissatisfaction, coupled with an increasing freedom to successfully and happily end marriages that are making one or both of the partners miserable. The divorce rate may be increasing because of this transition from one set of expectations, which required that marriage enable survival by meeting minimal physical needs, to a set of expectations for personal happiness: emotional, intellectual, and sexual compatibility, and common interests, including hobbies, lifestyle, and vacation choices. Clearly, expectations have changed.

My great-great-grandmother was proud of her marriage to a sea captain, and stayed married to him for almost fifty years. The fact that he was often gone for many years (as many as seven) at a time, and then was home for only a short period before going to sea again, seemed irrelevant to her. A letter or two every six months, a steady income, and a warm home in which to raise her children left her feeling lucky. I doubt that her pride in her relationship would be heard with anything but skepticism by any modern woman or man. However, she certainly considered herself to have a good family and a good husband. The fact that they saw each other only a few months each decade until he died was not part of the equation.

Although I doubt that anyone would challenge that the function of family still includes basic survival needs, our culture has added so many more expectations that it is no wonder that what might have sufficed even one hundred years ago is no longer acceptable. Even forty years ago, many men might have hoped to find a woman with a college degree, but it was often to his shame and embarrassment if the woman worked. In contrast, the young men I see in my practice daily expect their wives and partners to work and often want someone whose income matches or exceeds theirs. To be the sole provider is now something about which some men and women seem apologetic rather than proud; young children are an "excuse" for one spouse to stay home until they are grown. Young women in college forty years ago knew that their primary job was to find a spouse, not a career; those who reversed that order in priority were met with comments that suggested they were compensating for their lack of attractiveness to men. Whether their attractiveness had anything to do with it or not, the myth that a single working woman was somehow deficient as a woman was only one of many issues to be challenged by the feminist movement, and women are only beginning to find new confidence in their ability to enjoy life without men to support them. This change in women effects changes in relationships and marriages. The expectation of gainful employment by either or both spouses differs from socioeconomic groups, cultures, and from family to family.

As I work with couples forming their first family, or constructing stepfamilies, the richness of human experience and the diversity of goals and images for family, marriage, and parenting become increasingly apparent. Not all contingencies for the human dilemmas that develop in complex relationships will ever be addressed in a premarital counseling forum—and they should not be—but the discussion of what each person wants, hopes, needs, and expects in this social construct called "family" can certainly be discussed more calmly and with some depth when the couple is not in the midst of an emotional crisis. Role-playing conversations and problem solving around anticipated conflicts can make the experience of them less traumatic. Role playing around the sensitive role of relating to an ex-spouse, a newer and challenging role in stepfamilies today, can avoid crises and minimize the emotional pain this interaction can create.

In stepfamilies, the difficulties caused by problems of relating to ex-partners can seem endless. People who are prone to jealousy, to the point at which a romantic partner's ex-partners are seen as off limits, would do well to avoid getting involved with a person with children. Learning to be coparents with your husband or wife's ex-spouse can test the strength of anyone's sense of self, as well as lead to enormous growth of personality and confidence for all concerned. The opportunities for personal growth in a stepfamily situation are endless, as is the potential for disastrous outcomes if the people involved do not have the ego strength to self-regulate their emotions and monitor the behaviors that they choose to exhibit in situations often fraught with jealousy, conflicting loyalties, and complex responsibility patterns, not to mention scheduling issues.

Therefore, for those who find it hard to share responsibilities, negotiate differences of perspective and opinion, relate in a civil and cordial manner to an ex-spouse or ex-lover, or who do not wish to accept the fact that at times the children will seem to hate you for existing, no matter how nice and kind you are, the role of stepparent will be a real challenge. It will either expand your personality in ways undreamed of, or the chances of the stepfamily surviving will be dramatically jeopardized. Being willing to share a beloved with children can be difficult for some people, but sharing that person with children who don't like you very much, and having to accommodate one's schedule, due to an ex-spouse or other persons, may seem more than most people can tolerate. This is one reason why second marriages with children so often fail quickly, and why couples should enter into these relationships with mature commitments. The good news is that when stepfamilies survive the first three years and work through the issues with as much compassion and love as one can humanly muster, they often have a better chance of surviving and lasting longer than any other group of marriages, first or second.

Chapter 4

Unconditional Love and the Reality of Life

*"Anyone can give up; that is the easiest thing in the world to do.
But to hold it together and keep going when everyone would understand
if you fell apart, that is true strength."*

—CARL JUNG

The disappointments that occur in relationships are often the result of expectations, many times unreasonable ones, that cannot be met, because some part of every love relationship has hopes that exceed the human condition. It is heady stuff and the ambrosia of the gods; however, archetypal patterns are encoded in our makeup in the patterns of human behavior, emotions, and thoughts that have been experienced by billions of people throughout the history of humanity. Wanting to be loved unconditionally is one of the most universal longings, and, unfortunately, is an expectation that can't be fulfilled.

The longing to return to the Garden of Eden, where little would be required of us in order to feel loved and accepted, appears in the mythologies of many cultures. That is probably why the story of Adam and Eve, which in so many ways does not fit with the rest of the Bible, still holds so much power over our imaginations. But even in the Garden, there were two conditions required in order to receive love and acceptance; those conditions could not be met then, and few would want to meet them today. There is an innate curiosity in mankind to discover more about the knowledge of good and evil, to find out why something is forbidden, and to know if there truly is eternal life. There is endless fascination with these topics, and they are things about which all humanity dreams and has written endless laws, movies, stories, and philosophy and ethics courses.

The number of times I have heard people longing for unconditional love is poignant, and I often feel tremendous sadness at my less naive, perhaps cynical, belief that there is no such thing in this real world. At times, it is amusing that those people who long to be loved unconditionally are also those who have the firmest conditions as to what is and is not acceptable behavior, feelings, or thoughts from their spouses or romantic partners. The myth in the Bible is totally accurate when it states that we won't die if we learn the difference between good and evil, right and wrong, but we will no longer live in a world in which we feel accepted no matter what we do. Life is often difficult; the suffering, fear, and pain seem to be prerequisites in order to develop the courage needed for rewarding, conscious living.

The amount of energy often expended in insisting that romantic love is at its best when it is unconditional seems to be enormous in present-day culture at this time. Often, when clients are asked what conditions must be met before they could truly commit to a new partner, people become upset and angry, as if their capacity for loving a spouse is being belittled. The common belief that spouses should love unconditionally and that a marriage needs this unconditional love is an immensely powerful witch, one that looks like a beautiful princess, a glorious and innocent idea that has little wisdom or staying power. When the fantasy of unconditional love is challenged and examined, it begins to look very ugly, and it can be a setup for victimization and abuse. The princess can be a lovely idea, but living without conditions is something neither nature nor humanity can tolerate. Yet, as in the myths, when the awareness of our conditions for genuine love and companionship is totally embraced and accepted, the special qualities of the relationship seem more beautiful and permanent than the initial longing to return to a juvenile psyche that wants to be loved simply because we exist.

Some of the longing for this unconditional love may be a residue of our first memories of being loved by parents who appeared to have no conditions on their love and acceptance of us. We could nurse, weep, and soil ourselves without the threat of the loss of love. The terror in a panicked baby crying triggers in most people the wish that someone would soothe the child or the strong desire to be the one doing the soothing. Sigmund Freud was undoubtedly correct in considering the experience of toilet training to be an early awareness that being loved has conditions, and this conditionality became a cornerstone for a large section of his psychology of early childhood. Parents may love their children with fewer conditions than any other love, but children often do not interpret this love as being unconditional.

How often do we hear a child say, "My Mom (or Dad) will kill me if I get caught!" On some level, most children do not live in terror of such an event. Sadly, however, there are some who do, and abused children never feel out of imminent danger from a parent whose love is never perceived as being without conditions, and is often unreasonable and unpredictable. Parents who are not abusive as caregivers, feel there is nothing a child could do that would make them stop loving that child.

But healthy parent–child relationships demand more than just being loved. Self-respect, the ability to be successful in the world, courage, and self-esteem are all conditional, and parents need to guide children through a minefield of conditional relationships at home and in the world. In the world outside the home, respect and admiration, companionship, and friendships all impose more conditions than those which a child receives from a good parent. Therefore, in addition to the love of biological parents, a healthy stepparent relationship can actually be an immensely important bridge to the outer world, which is so much more conditional than the safer and less challenging world of being loved by one's parents.

Romantic love is probably the most conditional love there is, and the loving of stepchildren is a close second. Romantic love usually has conditions of monogamy, respect, honesty, commitment, and varying levels of support: financial, emotional, and physical. When a man or woman loves his or her spouse so unconditionally that she or he does not, or cannot, leave when violence, incest, or drug abuse occurs, we consider that person mentally ill or, as is often the case, charge him or her with being an accomplice to the illegal activity. A plea of "I loved him or her unconditionally!" goes nowhere. Besides, it is often quite hard for prospective stepparents to be truly honest with themselves about what they can and cannot tolerate until it is too late. Most stepparents hope they will be able to love their stepchildren with the same devotion and minimal conditions that they have for their biological children or for the children they plan to have. This is a lot harder to accomplish than it is to talk about.

Humans are undoubtedly hardwired to feel more loyalty toward and to bond more intensely with their own offspring than with others. This is certainly true in the animal world, and it appears to be true with humans as well. One client, who was terribly disappointed in his behavior and feelings toward his adolescent stepson, stated with some humor that sometimes he felt like the man in the following off-color joke:

> A man sat down next to a young, obviously stoned kid with a purple Mohawk, tattoos, and piercings. When the kid saw the horror on the older man's face, he asked, "What are you staring at?" The older man said, "I had sex with a parrot once and thought maybe you were my son!"

The client felt alienated from this child in a way he never felt with his own boys, even though they too had gone through periods of rebellion and looking like fringe dwellers. He was worried that he was just too old to be a father and knew his wife was tremendously disappointed in his attitude toward the child, who the man felt was an intruder on his life, his finances, and his home. The boy's sullen hostility could not elicit anything vaguely resembling the love he felt for his own sons. He was aware that his own boys had not been that different from his stepson's teenage persona and attitudes; but he found his own anger and annoyance was more intense, and while he had never doubted that he loved his boys, even when they were at their most difficult, he could not bring himself to feel anything but disgust with his stepson. He had opted for a cold detachment and relinquished his role as any kind of parent in order to avoid conflict, but this was not helping the family or the boy.

In truth, what we find amusing or at least tolerable in our own children, we find harder to accept in other people's children. Just as many people tolerate in-laws with whom they otherwise would not spend two minutes because one's spouse comes with the unchosen baggage of relatives, so stepchildren often show up because two people fell in love. Most in-laws do not move in immediately, if ever, but stepchildren not only move in at least part of the time, but they often indicate in all kinds of ways that they liked their life better before the stepparent arrived. This is not even a close copy of the love with the fewest conditions that most parents and children feel or want to feel.

Unfortunately, as stated earlier, too many marriages and stepparenting relationships begin with a longing for unconditional love, or if not unconditional, then at least the same love reserved for a parent, biological child, and, sometimes, an adopted child. Therefore, the number of second marriages in terrible conflict because of a lack of clarity and perspective concerning the challenges of this situation is tragic. Although some people can and do love children who are not biologically theirs, the relief I see in the faces of my clients when I suggest that it is unreasonable to expect a stepparent to love a stepchild with the same kind of devotion that she or he might have given if the child had been theirs from birth amazes me. Their gratitude at being relieved of an impossible burden is apparent each time. Once free of expectations that can't be met, the pleasure and rewards of genuine relationships, although fraught with the complexity of conditionality, demands, hopes, boundaries, and restrictions, can be explored creatively. The conditions for children need to be reasonable, however, and to reflect the conditions of society at large, if children are to succeed in negotiating the path between dependency as children, and less dependency and a mature interdependency in adulthood. The conditions between adults also need to be defined and be reasonable things that can be accomplished, even if difficult, by the people engaged in the relationship. I often think that those who are the most resistant to the idea that unconditional love is a fantasy are those who in their own childhoods were so wounded by unreasonable expectations, and punitive reactions in their failure to meet these expectations, that the longing for unconditional love as an adult becomes an addictive quest and an unquenchable thirst.

For example, when I work with couples who are thinking of creating a stepfamily, I start with the same set of conditions I ask other couples without children to consider, and then add a list of conditions about the children, the ex-spouses, or in-laws. Thinking through and discussing these things is often uncomfortable, painful, and difficult when in the throes of the initial hormone surges of new love, which make people blind to prejudices and needs. About half the time, the very idea of making conditions seems to bring on an argument with me, until I ask if the love is so unconditional that sleeping with one's best friend is just as unconditionally acceptable as bringing home roses. The majority of my clients then get to work. Sexual behaviors, honesty, drug use, income, weight and staying in shape or not, and smoking may all become topics of discussion.

The resistance to looking at the reality of our conditional love for others paired with the longing to be loved unconditionally may be related to the hormone surges that accompany falling in love. When people first fall in love, choosing a single person out of all the people on the planet, the hormones seem to push people to explore the world with new eyes, as well as make them appear more attractive and alive to everyone around them. However, these hormone surges can also lead to shattering pain after they diminish, leaving the person trying to relate to a real human being whom he or she either will learn to love, flaws and all, or who will become boring, revolting, or infuriating once the blinding power of Eros's arrow has left.

I often ask clients to develop resumes and "job" descriptions for themselves and a partner or spouse before they fall in love. These are the aspects defining who a person is and identifying the qualities he or she feels are necessary in order to develop a long-term loving and committed relationship. Once people fall in love, the boundaries and clarity become diluted and fuzzy, at least initially. What they eventually find annoying or completely unacceptable actually can seem endearing at first, whether it is something as major as being unemployed while searching for life's meaning or as minor as leaving the toilet seat up or leaving unrinsed coffee cups on the sink. Habits that seem adorable while dating can cause irritation, if not divorce, three years into the relationship.

All people, semiconsciously or consciously, have things they want in a relationship. Many of these things are very individualized, and not just attributed to love and lust. Most people want to enjoy, respect, and honor their partners, as well as have their partners enjoy, respect, and honor them. I very unromantically call what one wants from a partner, the "job description." There may be hundreds of items on this list if people are honest. Some items are what I label "deal breakers," and some are preferences, which may be insignificant in the long run.

All people have attributes they wish appreciated, and these are described in one's personal resume. When I start work with new clients, I often find that those who are feeling lonely and desperate can't think of many things to list. The job description for a spouse for one client only had that she wanted to be loved unconditionally, and the resume of what she had to offer sounded like the generic sound bites on some dating ads: "I have a good sense of humor and love to cook and listen to music." However, once most people have really explored their own dreams and know what did and did not work in past relationships, the lists get longer and longer. Men are often more aware of the physical attributes necessary for them to be attracted to a partner and more forgiving of other attributes. Woman are often more aware of a need to feel secure, based on a man's career or education, but that is not always the case. When stepchildren are added to the list of wants and considerations, the process of finding a relationship that fulfills a person's needs and meets the needs of the entire family becomes increasingly complex.

How tolerant and accepting a person is of the emotional, psychological, and intellectual makeup of children, who often show signs of instability after their initial family dissolves, is often unknown until tested after the marriage has taken place, when the children feel their loyalty has been divided and may be jealous and envious of the position in the parent's eyes that this new spouse holds. They may also feel displaced, angry, and still hopeful that their parents will get back together. Minimizing or ignoring these feelings is a setup for the high rate of divorce when stepchildren are involved, because the children have their own resumes and job descriptions, mostly unconscious, defining whom they will or will not accept as a member of the family. Initially, their job description for a stepparent may be NO ONE, or a mirror image of the original parent. But children can come up with amazing things. One child said he wanted a new mother who was like bluebirds singing. He was only five, but his new stepmother held that image through many hard times when this stepson was anything but a lark.

Beginning therapy sessions by addressing the large number of conditions each man and woman has, which are often masked with hormonal feelings of unconditionality, has been successful in my work. This is followed by adding the issues involving children. Initially, the couple usually finds enough material to work on just between the two of them so that the issues of their children's needs must be addressed later, once the couple has defined their own needs and wants, hopes, and preferences. For most people, starting with the resume or job description for a partner can be significant to the success of the person's relationships by making him or her aware of the qualities he or she brings to a relationship and the things for which he or she longs.

The lists created for the resume or job description need to include, but are not limited to the following:

1. Lifestyle
   a. Work hours
   b. Play hours
   c. Friends and family involvement and needs
   d. Hobbies
   e. Values connected with travel, work, play, etc.
   f. Religious attitudes, values, beliefs, and practices
   g. Pets
2. Financial obligations and standard of living
   a. Income levels
   b. Life insurance and retirement planning
   c. Importance of savings, debts
   d. Spending patterns on vacations, home, recreation, etc.
   e. Budget issues
3. Dreams for the future
   a. Will any of the things under the lifestyle section change as you age?

   b. Plans for children, aging parents, retirement

   c. Continuing education or career paths of partners

4. Family interactions and demands
   a. Holiday rituals
   b. Vacation rituals
   c. Involvement with in-laws (socially and financially)
5. Use of leisure time
   a. How much money does each person plan to spend in this area, and how passive or active is each person?
   b. Time together and apart
6. Needs for space and intimacy in a home environment
   a. This may include needs for private office, garage, yard, pets, and space for visitors, or no visitors at all.
   b. Hobby space
   c. What can't be shared?
7. Career demands
   a. Hours devoted to work and commuting to work
   b. Social expectations of career
   c. Costs assumed by the couple related to their jobs
   d. Needs for spousal support or need for noninvolvement
8. Education level and aspirations
   a. Partners' values and hopes for self, spouse, and children
   b. Continuing education in field of hobbies or career path or change
9. Sexual Compatibility
   a. Monogamy or open relationship
   b. Past lovers as friends or honest acknowledgment of their existence
   c. Openness to discussing sexuality
   d. Sexual behavior, including pornography and Internet sex
   e. Physical attractiveness and fitness and its importance or lack thereof
10. Issues that go with having or not having children
    a. How many children to have and if adoption is an option
    b. How to fund costs and what costs to fund
    c. Family involvement with children
    d. Education costs, health costs
    e. Lifestyle changes; what will be sacrificed?

f.   Impact on careers
g.   Child-care responsibilities
h.   Abortion, surrogates, sterilization reversal

For those planning to merge families and to include stepchildren in a new family, the items in a job description and resume for the parents concerning parenting issues must be added to the above lists. An understanding of the developmental ages of the children, their birth order, and their relationship with the biological parent and their household are all important factors. Issues of goals, homework, chores, hobbies, sports, camp, family vacations, and sharing financial resources with children not one's own all complicate the picture, but can evolve into a dynamic and worthwhile exploration by the couple of the areas in which they feel comfortable with the new partner in shared parenting and those in which they do not.

For many children, any person other than their biological parents are not going to be accepted in the parental role, and a strategy to help children deal with their worldview in this regard needs to be developed. Without some strategy and forethought, a tug of war is likely to ensue, with the stepparent being the one who will most likely either lose the battle or harm the child. Ex-spouses can play havoc with this strategy implementation, and the relationships that are most likely to survive with stepchildren often require an acceptance of the new relationship by an ex-spouse and a gradual introduction of the new partner to the child at a speed that the child can accept.

This is an area in which the resume and job description of a stepparent need to be discussed in an age-appropriate way with the children involved in the creation and development of a stepfamily. Some children have a fear of what might happen, rather than a hope for an improvement in their lives. Gently encouraging a change can be immensely powerful. Instead of saying, "Now you won't spend holidays with both parents," the parent could say, "You now will have two Thanksgivings each year." If the parents value traditions, such as going to church as a family on Easter, these occasions will be harder to duplicate, but parents can assure the children that these celebrations can be shared on alternate years and that some special event will be added for the years when the valued tradition cannot be shared. Having two rooms and being able to decorate one in each home can be really fun for kids, but more importantly, having a say in how "their" rooms look will make them feel as if they belong in both homes.

Children do not have veto power over many of the decisions that go on in a family, just as they don't have veto power in most decisions in a home with their biological parents. They do not get to choose whom a parent loves or chooses, but there are ways to reduce obstacles and ways to prevent the whole process of bringing a new person into a child's life from becoming a nightmare.

In order for this change to happen comfortably, each family's needs must be addressed individually. The ages and number of the children and their level of emotional development are important. Another consideration is whether two families who each contain children are merging or if only one person has children. Still another question that needs to be addressed is if more children are desired in this new marriage, or if the number of children the couple wants has already been conceived or born. How accepting ex-spouses are, and how involved they are in the lives of the children, and, therefore, in the life of the new couple are also important considerations. Each child may have different fears about what a new partner will bring to his or her life, and these fears need to be addressed and never minimized, mocked, or dismissed.

Still another issue the new family has to deal with is whether the financial situation will change for the better or worse. One of the most difficult adjustments, which often breaks up new step-families, is the situation in which financial resources are stretched thinner by the new relationship. Alimony may cease, bedroom space may be compromised, children who had their own rooms may now find themselves sharing not only rooms, but their toys, space, and parent's time. The complications may seem endless, and sometimes it is best to delay marrying or living together until the complications are addressed. If children experience the arrival of a stepparent as a demotion in lifestyle and a restriction of valued time with a parent, the likelihood of disaster is increased.

Another consideration for new families is that a child's birth order is psychologically important; and what is not usually under-stood or addressed is the difficulty a child who has always been the oldest or only child may experience when he or she suddenly finds him- or herself as the youngest or middle child. Families who are not aware of these dynamics can suffer needlessly as children respond to the displacement. Teenagers who otherwise would see each other as peers and possible dating partners may find the forced intimacy that is normal for siblings, but not for unrelated children, unbearable or uncomfortable. Sexual abuse of younger children by older stepsiblings is reported at a much higher rate than among biologically related siblings, and it often happens in house-holds in which there is other sexual acting out of inappropriate behaviors.

Often a new couple, head over heels in love, wants alone time and naively makes the situation with their children's discomfort in the home worse by having both sets of children on the same weekend so they can have the next weekend without any children. A compromise needs to be reached so that the children don't expe-rience the arrival of the new stepparent and his or her children as a complete loss of valued time with their own parent. Being creative about the needs of all members of the family can feel like a travel agent's worst nightmare, but some families have found that hav-ing one weekend alone a month, one with the whole family, and one during which only one set of children is present is possible. Others have the biological parent spend one day alone with his or her children each weekend and have the whole group together on another day. Special one-on-one time with each child, such as do-ing projects, playing, or going out to breakfast, may be an added experience that makes the new arrangement easier for the child, and, therefore, for everyone.

Issues of financial responsibility and inheritance can also be immensely painful when families re-form. Prenuptial agreements may be needed. Often divorce decrees spell out financial obligations toward children that create immense inequality in the resources stepchildren have for education and health. The arguments that can ensue between spouses about this are often endless, painful, and destructive, and need to be anticipated, so that the financial responsibilities are spelled out before the wedding day, not afterward. There may be a need to plan around situations in which one set of children may have the financial resources to go to college without having to borrow any money, while their stepsiblings will have to pay for everything on their own. The tensions that can result need to be addressed and discussed openly, without rage and without victimizing anyone.

This issue of financial disparity between the financial resources of the children needs to be addressed, even when creating a new stepfamily involves adult children, because the probability of a happy marriage decreases when children are not engaged with the new stepparent, no matter how old they are. Inheritance issues may replace issues of space and college funding when the children are adults. The choice of life insurance beneficiaries can be a practical way to assure grown children that the inheritance they had expected, and most likely consider their right, is not vanishing; especially since they may have concerns that their children, the grandchildren of the couple, may no longer be a part of the family financial plan when a late-in-life marriage is planned. If the persons designated to inherit know that their inheritance will be similar to what it would have been without the marriage, or even financially larger, the ugly feeling of being abandoned, and the worry that even expressing a fear of abandonment will be seen as mean and selfish, is eliminated. This amount may not be possible, but a discussion of the issues is still important. Other alternatives may be found, such as the payment of a life insurance policy by the children who realize that the death of their parent would leave them with no inheritance if their parent's estate is left to a new stepparent. Solutions such as this can go a long way to calming angry waters.

When there are personality disorders and other psychiatric problems, or a child or adult child has disabilities, planning ahead becomes even more difficult. Walking into this forest with no map or compass, but with only a conviction that all will work out because two people are in love, is a prescription for disaster, no matter how well intended.

Imagine that you are in an office listening to a couple talking to a therapist over a period of months, telling their story.

Case Illustration

A woman states that she had spent her whole life hoping she would eventually fall in love and raise a family. She had pursued her career with more focus and daily enthusiasm than she had her social life, which often consisted of short-term relationships with men who were, in her words, "unavailable and commitment phobic." She enjoyed the freedom her financial success gave her, but increasingly felt lonely on Sundays and holidays as she spent time with family and with friends who were willing to share their family time with her.

She met a man at a girlfriend's house on a Sunday afternoon when she had been invited to join a large family gathering to watch football. The man brought his two girls, ages eight and ten, from his first marriage, with him and seemed to enjoy playing croquet with them while most of the group watched football games. As the woman was not a huge fan of watching sports, she wandered out to watch the croquet game, something she had not played since she was a child, and was soon invited by one of the man's daughters to join in. The man asked her out by the end of the evening, and soon they began dating.

The woman was soon enthralled by this man and by the family unit she lacked and longed to have. The girls stayed with their father every other weekend, and he stated to the woman that he had never dated on his weekend with them. But, since his daughters had enjoyed having her join them in the croquet game, he felt comfortable including her in their activities on his weekend with his children. As his girlfriend, she enjoyed feeling special and did everything she could to impress the man with her bonding attempts with his young girls.

The couple continued seriously dating; the weekends without the girls became romantic interludes during which they shut the rest of the world away and enjoyed with each other what seemed to them to be days far too short. The cost of child support and alimony was never discussed in detail, but they both began to comment to each other how much they could save if they shared a household and did not have the hours of commuting between each other's homes. The man was fearful of losing his children to their mother, if he lived with a woman without being married, and within eight months they were engaged. They married a year after they met.

Within three months the woman was finding herself increasingly angry and hostile with both her new husband and the girls, resentful of the alimony money which supported three other females, and even more confused at the loss of what had been their romantic weekends of carefree fun. Weekends seemed to alternate between sharing her new husband with his daughters and sharing household chores on weekends when the girls were with their mother.

In retrospect, both members of this couple felt they had married too quickly, and each hoped time would enlighten them on things they had not discussed before the marriage. Both had images of married life that were driven by cultural expectations and their own family myths. The woman firmly believed that she had been looking all her life for unconditional love, and that the man's love for his girls, with all the sacrifices of money, career advancement, and time he was willing to make for them, proved he would shower her with the love she had always longed for. The man, who had come from a deeply religious family, thought he had found his soul mate and an ideal coparent for his girls, and would now be able to live a more normal family life, closer to the dream family he had hoped to create with his first wife. Their personal myths about marriage, love, and family were drastically in conflict; and as is true with all myths, they seemed so real and so much a part of the worldview in which each lived that the idea that the other person with whom they were sharing their living and emotional space was living in an "alternate reality" was not even imagined by either.

The woman slowly began to realize that the love her husband had for his daughters was triggering jealousy related to childhood-perceived rejection in a home with a cold, dominating, and distant father from whom she longed for unconditional love. What had attracted her to this man was the quality of commitment and caring she now resented when she saw it focused, not on her, but more appropriately on his children. She began to demand that the girls earn her respect by sharing the household chores, so her alternate weekends alone with her husband could have some of the old romantic freedoms. The father found himself protecting his girls from their stepmother's demands. His desire to let them have a chore-free weekend was in direct conflict with his wife's demand to have a couple-centered weekend without chores, which could only be accomplished by including her stepdaughters in the everyday household maintenance. The ground was set for a battle of mythic proportions as these two attempted to meld into a family unit that provided for the emotional support of all of its members and the development of two children. Both girls were "regressing," in her words, and they loved watching and reading fairy tales, many of which included an evil stepmother. They had their own mythologies about what was happening in their universe, and as they increasingly saw their stepmother as a critical taskmaster, the stories of evil stepmothers and the ways young women coped and became victorious over them allowed them some hope for a way out of the increasing tension in the household.

As the couple struggled between their worldviews, expecting that these differing worldviews would allow them to organize their lives in meaningful and fulfilling ways, they began to understand that the problem was not the lack of time in their courtship, but the lack of consciousness in their assumptions about each other, and the lack of awareness of the diversity of personal and family myths that each brought into the home they had established.

For the woman, her first task was getting out of the competitive rivalry with her stepdaughters and acknowledging that as intense as her childhood longing for unconditional love felt, it was an unrealistic demand in a marriage. Unconditional love was not something she could give to her husband, or even to herself. Her love for him had endless conditions, one of which seemed to include desiring him to be unreasonably critical and harsh towards his daughters.

As the woman began to let go of her longing for a loving father, her jealousy of her stepdaughters did not vanish, but became more centered on resolving her own grief at not having had the kind of loving father she wanted, rather than focusing on her envy of her stepdaughters. She no longer attempted to block her husband from giving to his daughters the same kind of attention and affection she had wanted from her father. Her husband began to see that some of his wife's demands on his daughters' time, and some of her criticism of their lack of involvement in the day-to-day sweeping of the ashes of daily household life, was not only fair, but also good parenting, working toward the goal of creating responsible children who can become responsible adults.

Eventually the woman was able to state that her favorite fairy tale had been the one about Cinderella (see Chapter 8). Although not a stepchild herself, she often felt ignored by her father and felt that his work was the evil stepmother who demanded the best that he had to offer. She realized that she had begun to recreate her childhood drama, only this time putting herself in the role of the stepmother and her husband in the role of the passive and detached father. Her sorrow and grief at what had happened to her, and what she had tried to do with her stepchildren was a release, allowing her to develop a new paradigm with her husband. The man saw that his myth of being the "Disneyland dad," who was seen as a "fairy godfather" to his children, was trapping all the females he loved in an untenable position if they were to get along, and he was being neither a good father nor a good husband by "spoiling" his daughters.

As the family evolved, each member made a commitment to having one "chore day," during which they all scrubbed the debris from the hearth and home of an active family, and one "fun day" together. This also allowed the couple to have one day each week when the romantic fun of their first few months together could be relived, and the girls could look forward to one family day with their dad and stepmother. They seemed to also enjoy learning to work together with their father and stepmother, whether it was grocery shopping, ironing, or cleaning the garage, and they all worked together with music blasting.

The paradox of this situation was that the man felt that the one thing that had attracted his new wife, his love and commitment toward his family, was now something he was supposed to give up. The ability of a myth to allow one to live comfortably with contradictions that on a rational level are absurd, such as demanding unconditional love but being unable to give it, is a hallmark of powerful myths. Those standing outside of the myth seeing its fantastical qualities may label it a pure fantasy, but all of us live in these spaces, unaware of our own inner perceptual discrepancies.

The family now has a new shared paradigm about who the family is, and how it organizes itself; and as with all paradigms that have a mythic quality, which is hard to describe while living in it, it is functioning to allow the family to enjoy life with each other, as well as support the individual and family growth in a way that may still hold difficulty, dramatics, and suffering, but does not threaten the structure of their family.

Chapter 5

Naiveté and Innocence: How to Lose the Former and Save the Latter

Love all, trust a few. Do wrong to none.

—William Shakespeare, *All's Well that Ends Well*, Act I, Scene 1

As an original family shatters and those who are left with the shards of a family container try to develop a new family, or two new families with some shared members, the image of putting together a mosaic is useful in a variety of metaphors. Care needs to be taken with each piece; sharp edges can cut and cause pain. Reconstruction of the container is a slow process of sorting shapes and looking at what fits in the new container created from the original one. Each piece needs to be examined for its individual shape, to fit in a place pleasing to the whole, and then missing pieces need to be added from another source. Putting a stepfamily together takes more care and thought than most people imagine, and usually there are more people involved than just a husband and wife. Sometimes all of these people are angry, resentful, and fearful, something a couple without children don't need to consider as seriously. The naiveté and innocence with which so many in-love and hopeful couples approach this process often ends up with the first few years of the new marriage being fraught with disappointments and struggles that often break the marriage and family.

So many couples seem to be unaware of the care and difficulties in this restructuring process of developing a new family from the pieces of a broken one. Their naiveté does not help this process. Naiveté is a lack of knowledge. Not knowing that a snake is poisonous, or a tornado is coming, or that you have built a house on an earthquake fault may be naive, but this ignorance does not prevent natural consequences, often disastrous, from happening. Nature does not forgive naiveté. We are all born without conscious knowledge of how the world and society works, and much of maturation is an ongoing process of gaining knowledge and losing naiveté. All too often I hear in my practice, among my acquaintances, and in my own mind the longing to believe that if I don't see something, or don't know about it, it won't cause harm. In premarital counseling, the longing to stay unaware is often the root of endless expectations that will never be met without awareness and work. The statements that often are indicators of this longing for naiveté include:

"I turned a blind eye!"

"What I don't know can't hurt me," or with less innocence, "What she or he doesn't know won't hurt them."

"See no evil, hear no evil, speak no evil."

To act like the three blind, deaf, and silent monkeys of the Eastern fable leaves one senseless and vulnerable to the consequences that might be avoided or prevented with some knowledge. Just as a person may decide to not tell the truth to others to avoid dealing with the consequences, justified or not, the pattern of avoiding asking the right questions and thereby avoiding a truth that is painful or upsetting exists. This is one reason that psychotherapy, psychoanalysis, or marital counseling is hard work, and not for the faint of heart.

Naiveté and denial may appear to the observer to be the same process, but denial implies some awareness or knowledge that is ignored, minimized, or conveniently forgotten in the service of maintaining a false sense of security, a false sense of identity. Naiveté, in the sense I suggest using it, means the knowledge or information was never presented or searched out.

Fairy tales are very clear on this need to do the work necessary to become aware and not naive. "Snow White," "Little Red Riding Hood," "The Princess and the Pea," "The Emperor's New Clothes," and countless others warn that one of life's goals is to become less naive while maintaining innocence or lack of evil intent. Wisdom and knowledge have often been associated with power, and power can be used for good or ill. Innocence indicates a lack of guilt; wise innocence is perhaps the moral goal of a well-lived, conscious life. Being able to see the truth clearly in the stories and in life does not involve covering our eyes or ears, but does involve listening and watching, being detached from our dreams and longings enough to have some modicum of accurate knowledge about what is going on that impacts our lives. Yet staying innocent, neither wishing others excessive or inappropriate harm nor wanting to seek vengeance or lash out at those who have disappointed us, can be a challenge. The courage to refuse to hide behind a longing to stay unaware, and yet maintain one's innocence, is an immensely difficult task for all.

The desire to protect ourselves by remaining naive is particularly evident when men and women meet and wonder if they dare to try again to have a relationship. If they have children, the concerns they have need to be more complex than just whether the couple gets along. Thinking that "we love each other so much that all obstacles will disappear," or believing that because most children will be loving if you love them, so consequently being a stepparent will be easy and rewarding, is naive. Thinking that stepparenting is easy and always rewarding is naive. It certainly is helpful to believe you can become a great stepparent; loving the children and being a kind and understanding listener is helpful. Being head over heels in love with one's spouse does make things more tolerable when things are difficult. Both traits will make the hard times easier, but the hard times will be there. A positive attitude is a great start, but thinking that nothing more than love and good intentions are needed to create a happy family has led many people into angry disappointment, and often another divorce. When the painful recognition that stepchildren may resent new parents no matter how good and kind they are, both parents and children need to develop new coping skills, and love and good intentions get a real workout.

Children can get caught in the naive assumption that their parent's new mate will not have any power to impact their life, especially if they attempt to ignore the unwanted parent or sibling additions to the family and try to get their biologic parent involved in siding with them against all real and imagined insults. Children sometimes think that screaming "You are not my mother/father" will somehow allow them to avoid responsibility for behaviors unacceptable in any family. When biological parents think that empathic support without guidance to more appropriate responses is helpful, their naiveté is damaging. Likewise, refusing to correct disrespectful actions, mean comments, or outright defiance will not improve the situation. I highly recommend choosing one's battles, but avoiding them at all costs in the name of "getting along" does nothing to make parents or children feel safe in their new families.

In many fairy tales and myths, the sudden introduction of a new spouse, without any development of a relationship with the child prior to identifying the new partner as a spouse and stepparent, is a stage set for disaster. This is also true in modern life, yet many people assume that if they see their new love as wonderful and loving, then their situation will be the exception to the rule of painful problems. They imagine the original family will easily accept and integrate new people into the system that has been evolving over years. In reality, everyone gets to stretch and grow, hopefully not at a rate that tears emotional muscles. It will pay off for people to see dating as an interviewing process, and introducing someone to the kids as part of that interview for which the couple prepares in order to proceed with caution and wisdom.

This does not mean that the children have the power to negate adult decisions, but that the romantic relationship between adults is given the support and time needed to allow its potential to grow into the varied, caring relationships that define family. The nurturing of relationships between adults and children is a process deserving of respect before the word "marriage" is brought into the picture. That does not mean introducing every date to the children, but at some point, it is important to make the children aware of a new friend, and then let the relationship between the new person and the children develop. This lays the groundwork for the possibility of a healthy stepparent–stepchild relationship. As stated before, one does not need to love one's stepchildren with the feelings one has for one's own offspring, but some form of mutual respect is absolutely necessary. No one, adult or child, is safe in a living environment in which respect for each other is not present. Fondness and joy in each other's company may develop from that respect.

In contrast, hostility, fear, and disrespectful behaviors unchecked leave everyone feeling unsafe.

Abandoning the false security of naiveté in order to build secure families is particularly challenged, because the longing for knowledge and the conflicting fear of what the truth might tell us is one of the oldest dilemmas humans must endure. The story of Adam and Eve in the Old Testament portrays this so well:

Adam and Eve

And the LORD God planted a Garden eastward in Eden; and there he put the man he had formed.

And out of the ground made the LORD God to grow every tree that is pleasant to the sight, and good for food; the tree of life also in the midst of the garden, and the tree of the knowledge of good and evil. (Gen. 2:8–9 KJV)

And the LORD God commanded the man, saying, Of every tree of the garden thou mayest freely eat:

But of the tree of the knowledge of good and evil, thou shalt not eat of it: for in the day that thou eatest thereof thou shalt surely die.(Gen. 2:16–17)

Now the serpent was more subtil than any beast of the field which the LORD God had made. And he said unto the woman, Yea, hath God said, Ye shall not eat of every tree of the garden?

And the woman said unto the serpent, We may eat of the fruit of the trees of the garden:

But of the fruit of the tree which is in the midst of the garden, God hath said, Ye shall not eat of it; neither shall ye touch it, lest ye die.

And the serpent said to the woman, Ye shall not surely die:

For God doth know that in the day ye eat thereof, then your eyes shall be opened, and ye shall be as gods, knowing good and evil.

And when the woman saw that the tree was good for food, and that it was pleasant to the eyes, and a tree to be desired to make one wise, she took the fruit thereof and did eat, and gave also unto her husband with her; and he did eat.

And the eyes of both of them were opened, and they knew they were naked; and they sewed fig leaves together, and made themselves aprons.

And they heard the voice of the LORD God walking in the garden in the cool of the day; and Adam and his wife hid themselves from the presence of the Lord God amongst the trees of the garden.

And the LORD God called unto Adam, and said unto him, Where art thou?

And he said, I heard thy voice in the garden, and I was afraid, because I was naked; and I hid myself.

And he said, Who told you that thou wast naked? Hast thou eaten of the tree, whereof I commanded thee that thou shouldest not eat?

And the man said, The woman whom thou gavest to be with me, she gave me of the tree, and I did eat.

And the LORD God said unto woman, What is this that thou hast done?

And the woman said, The serpent beguiled me, and I did eat.

And the LORD God said unto the serpent, Because thou hast done this, thou art cursed above all cattle, and above every beast in the field; upon thy belly shalt thou go, and dust shalt thou eat all the days of thy life:

And I will put enmity between thee and the woman, and between thy seed and her seed; it shall bruise thy head, and thou shalt bruise his heel.

Unto the woman he said, I will greatly multiply the sorrow and thy conception; in sorrow thou shalt bring forth children; and thy desire shall be to thy husband, and he shall rule over thee.

And unto Adam he said, Because thou hast hearkened unto the voice of thy wife, and hast eaten of the tree which I commanded thee, saying, Thou shalt not eat of it: cursed is the ground for thy sake; in sorrow shalt thou eat of it all the days of thy life. (Gen. 3:1–17)

And the LORD God said, Behold, the man is become as one of us, to know good and evil: and now lest he put forth his hand, and take also of the tree of life, and eat, and live forever:

Therefore, the LORD God sent him forth from the Garden of Eden, to till the ground from whence he was taken. (Gen. 3:22–23)

This Bible story echoes so often in our language and metaphors today thousands of years after it was first told. If the story did not have some powerful and true messages, it would never have survived the centuries. Many of the themes in the story of Adam and Eve speak to naiveté. The number of myths and fairy tales that refer to those who are naive as being naked and not knowing it are far too many to list here. The person who tells the cold truth about a situation is often referred to as a "snake" or "a snake in the grass." Truth tellers, ranging from the biblical Serpent to Cassandra to Spartan runners who brought news of defeat and were killed for speaking the truth, are often not rewarded for their honesty. This is because many people would prefer to remain in a cozy Eden, not knowing what on earth is going on and thinking they will die if they investigate the truth. The number of times I have heard people say, "It would kill me if I found that out" or "I would rather die than find out" reveal how prevalent this theme is. Another belief is that one can't tell the truth because he or she "can't handle it" or "it would kill them" or "he (she) would kill me if he (she) knew," or "curiosity killed the cat." There is a fear about sharing the truth, ending someone else's naiveté, which is sometimes justified in the responses of rage and fear that sharing truth often brings.

Children carry this image with them even without violent parents, and the metaphor of "My dad or mom would kill me if" resound throughout every school building, often providing appropriate protection to the young child who wants to refuse drugs, sexual advances, or risky behaviors being encouraged by some teenage "snake" who is convinced that skipping school will not result in anyone's death. Probably no one will die, but sometimes Eden is a not bad place when it involves staying safe and not experimenting with good or evil things that we are neither old enough nor wise enough to handle.

In stepfamily formation, this Garden of Eden scenario plays out endlessly: that eternal longing to stay both innocent and naive, to not have to do the hard work that knowledge of reality brings. Most people do not want to know that the love of their lives, the person they love most in the world, has children who truly do not like them and they do not want to believe that if pushed, most parents will love their kids permanently and as close to unconditionally as they will ever love anyone, and that the romantic love that has the couple in its powerful grip is actually more fragile than they realize and may not last. How many times have the words, "I am a good mom/dad, and just want your kids to love me!" been met with silence or false assurances: "They do love you" or "They will love you once they get to know you."

In these families, the serpent will probably offer up the fruit once again. Will anyone say the truth: "Actually, my kids think they hate you and that you are ruining their lives, and they wish you would go away." Truths like that are seldom met with gratitude, and the inhabitants of Eden once again get kicked out of the garden, and women must do the hard work of giving birth to children, and sometimes people have to do the hard work of giving birth metaphorically in suffering to a stepfamily, and one in which not all of its members will like or love each other.

However, whether in Eden or exiled from it, what is often the most difficult task of a newly forming stepfamily is to accept that any attempt to avoid knowing what is good and bad, or right, wrong, or somewhere in between with any of the relationships in the family can't be avoided. Sticking your head in the sand and staying naive may bring a temporary sense of peace and relief, but in the long run we don't live in a world where we can avoid being impacted by problems; and creating a stepfamily is hard work, which can also be rewarding if one is willing to suffer some bruises on one's heel along the way. How many times has a step-parent tried to put his or her foot down and stand firm on some principle only to find themselves standing in a very painful spot from which they cannot accomplish what they wanted to achieve? I have repeatedly heard parents and stepparents set up rules and consequences for bad behavior that are difficult to enforce, and often more work or aggravation for the adult than the children. One parent ruefully stated that, having grounded his teenager for offenses that had resulted in poor grades, he and his wife then seldom got to go out for their weekly "date night"; in addition, they missed the evenings when their son had been gone with his friends, evenings in which they were now consumed with supervising his homework.

When forming a stepfamily, maintaining innocence can be just as big a struggle as rejecting the naive position. The ego strength and psychological growth required in facing difficult situations, painful moments, and angry and hurt feelings that occur in families without resulting in outright hostility, while also restraining the desire for vengeance and one-upmanship, is hard. Being aware of feelings of rage, anger, jealousy, envy, and betrayal while still choosing to act in the best interest of all concerned is a call for objectivity and innocence combined with wisdom. Most of us can't answer this call all the time, but learning to discriminate between feelings, thoughts, and behaviors, and attempting to be objective about balancing everyone's needs is a Herculean task, but one worth the work.

Experiencing this kind of thoughtful monitoring of feelings, checking thoughts, and modifying behaviors to serve all is one of the gifts of growing up with stepparents. Diplomacy, listening skills, ability to acknowledge differences of perspective, values, family culture, and diverse goals occur daily in stepfamilies as in no other family system. Because these families form with children who already have a family culture with which they are familiar, and the need to adapt to the needs of an ex-spouse and their social system is by far more complicated than what an original, nuclear family experiences, these skills will either develop, or scheduling and discipline disasters will follow.

One teenager, Cheryl, who was beginning to appreciate this skill in her stepmother, stated that watching her stepmom make endless phone calls to relatives trying to arrange a Thanksgiving and Christmas schedule that attempted to make everyone somewhat happy was like watching some political figure running back and forth between Egypt, Israel, and Lebanon via Washington and London. Her stepmom had to contact Cheryl's mother, who talked with her new husband, who needed to talk to his ex-wife, who needed to check with the grandparents, and so on. Cheryl laughed at one point and stated maybe the twelve days of Christmas were designed for stepfamilies as the number of celebrations was multiplying so all grandparents, step, and biological parents could spend some time with their children and grandchildren. These nightmares of scheduling are complicated, and become even more difficult if an emotional war is going on between ex-spouses.

Case Illustration

A couple in their midthirties had been dating for two years when they began to discuss making their living arrangements more permanent. Both had been through divorces, which they described as "bitter and destructive" because of spouses with alcohol and drug addiction problems. They each had two children from their prior marriages. When they met, the woman's two boys were ten and eight, and the man had one girl, fourteen, and one boy, ten.

They met at a soccer game, where each had a son playing, and became friends around their shared joy in watching the boys play and in sharing their stories of divorce. Soon they were dating casually, and each was cautious enough that the romantic part of their relationship blossomed slowly out of the friendship.

Independently they had each decided they would not remarry until the children were out of the home, as they had so many friends who had horror stories about "blending families"; both felt that the addictions of the ex-spouses had harmed their children enough so that it was "unfair" to add a stepparent to the bad memories the kids already had.

They came in for counseling six months after they had changed their minds about marriage, had married, and had begun the task of creating a stepfamily. Both were so fearful of reenacting the horrors of the mythological imagery of the "evil stepparent," which they were constantly being warned about by friends, horrors that matched the fairy tale nightmares they had been told as children, that they were unable to develop their own family. They knew what they did not want, but were uncertain as to how to proceed.

Both husband and wife each thought the other played favorites with their biological children and were acting like an evil stepparent with the children who were not their biological ones. The demand for "equal love" was destroying the family with its impossible paradigm.

Spending time with the imagery of the word "step" and its origins in the meaning of "bereft" (as explained in Chapter 1) began the movement psychologically toward a more conscious awareness of what they could and could not offer their stepchildren as opposed to their biological children. The husband stated he was also grieving the loss of his own personal belief that he could find his daughter a mother who would love her as her own, because the young girl had never experienced that from her own mother whose true "love" was cocaine. He also was aware of defending his own son from any perceived slight his new stepbrothers gave him, doing this in a way that was not empowering the three boys to sort out their relationships in an environment made safe by adults but not directed and controlled by them.

As both experienced their grief that they had not met earlier and that these four children were not mutually theirs, they began to appreciate the positive values in being "bereft." The man could bring the more conditional love of a mentor and teacher to his stepsons, giving them a more objective guidance as they grew and matured into the world of adults. The woman was also able to begin to love the stepmother role, since the role of an adult female guiding a young woman into adulthood suited her well, and she truly began to enjoy her times with her new stepdaughter. The young girl was starved for, but at the same time scared of having a female adult nurturing, guiding, and supporting her, and she tested her new step-mother's limits and strength by doubting her love and acceptance every time it began to blossom. The young girl not only doubted the stability of mothers (and older women in general because of all the betrayals and abuse she had experienced from her own mother), but she was sure that all stepmothers were evil. As they battled and danced around the mutually projected family myths and their own fears, the two females began to admire and respect each other's strengths. Amy did not gain the mother her father wanted her to have, but she gained a loving relationship with a woman she knew loved her and would train her to enter the world of adult men and women with confidence, a role not even a biological mother can fill without support from others. Her stepmother was by far more objective than she found her friend's mothers were of their daughters, and certainly more objective than her father was. The stepmother's assessments were loving, while also matching the way the rest of the world experienced the girl, and the older woman's guidance was rock solid.

The girl also gained a doorway into her future in a way she may never consciously acknowledge. She knew her father's world revolved around his children before his new wife's arrival. Under-standably, and to the children's benefit, this child-focused priority of his began when his first wife vacated her position as mother and spouse. What was less obvious to the girl was that, until her father committed himself to another woman, she was playing the roles of daughter and an emotional support person in a way that bordered on emotional incest. She, like so many children in single parent homes, felt guilty about growing up and leaving the parent alone. This results in a distorted extension of the family into future generations. Children who love their parents and do not have a sense that there is something emotionally worthwhile and mean-ingful for those parents after they leave home carry massive guilt about leaving and major ambivalence about choosing partners for their own lives. Knowing that her father was happily married gave the daughter a sense of freedom to leave and move on with her own life without guilt, and a better role model for finding a healthy adult relationship of her own in the future.

In addition, the man began to appreciate the difference in his relationship between his son and his stepsons. He could feel the strength of knowing he would love his own son, no matter what the child did or did not do, and that his respect and love for his two stepsons was a lot closer to what the rest of society would and would not tolerate, in terms of manners, social behaviors, and even chores around the house, and therefore equally beneficial to the development of the boys.

This family's willingness to approach their problems with open-ness and to deal with the loss of naive hopes and dreams, while maintaining an innocent desire to do what was best for everyone served them well, and left all of the children stronger and wiser than many of their peers. Rather than do what some families do and pretend that there is no differences between the love of a step-parent and a birth parent, they acknowledged the differences and worked with them to everyone's benefit.

Some families try to avoid the issue of being seen as a stepfam-ily by moving into new neighborhoods and even to other states, not letting any of their new acquaintances know they are a stepfamily. This can work in the short term, but all too often children feel they are betraying their biological parents. They also know and can see the differences between their new family and the previous one, even if the parents want to believe they have presented to the public a credible appearance of a nuclear family with no steprelationships. This tendency to try to appear as if one is different than one really is, is universal and often necessary for survival in many social situations. Jung called our public personalities, which may vary from situation to situation, *personae*. Stepfamilies can be very good at looking like biological families in many places, but the differences are there. "The Emperor's New Clothes" is a fairy tale about a king who thought he had a wonderful set of clothes, and yet was naked and visible to the entire world.

The Emperor's New Clothes

Adapted from Han Christian Anderson's Collection of Fairy Tales

An emperor of a prosperous city cared more about clothes and fashion than he did about governing his empire and paying attention to the needs of his subjects. He loved dressing up and holding balls and impressing his friends and family with how sophisticated he was and how pleasant his dinners and balls were for all who attended. Two men arrived in the kingdom who claimed that they were the finest of tailors, and the emperor immediately sought them out. The two promised him the finest apparel from the most beautiful cloth. This cloth, they told him, was invisible to anyone who was either stupid or unfit for his position. The Emperor could not see the (nonexistent) cloth, but pretended that he could for fear of appearing stupid; his ministers did the same. When the tailors reported that the suit was finished, they dressed him with great fanfare. The Emperor then with equal fanfare ordered a parade and a party to celebrate the new wardrobe and went on a procession through the center of the town showing off his new "clothes." During the course of the procession, a small child cried out, "But he has nothing on!" The crowd, no longer fearing they were unfit to see the clothes, realized the child was telling the truth. The Emperor, however, held his head high and continued the procession, refusing to believe he had been duped (or had duped himself).[2]

This story echoes the metaphor of not knowing who you are and how others see you. Being naked and exposed inappropriately was first expressed in the Garden of Eden story. Here the cost is not as dire, but the result is humiliation. Families that pretend that they are just like others, or that they have no problems, are likely to be seen by others for what they are. The wife who is the last to know of her husband's infidelities, and the parent who is stunned when she finds her daughter pregnant, in spite of the fact that all the neighbors knew the girl was intimate with her boyfriend, are examples of people who behave like the emperor with no clothes. In hindsight, they may recognize that they colluded in not wanting to see what was going on, and hoped that by acting as if all was well it would be so. Only the innocence of a childlike quality in someone or in themselves, which is honest enough to recognize "nudity," can dislodge the intentional blinders, and sometimes even that does not work.

What I find the most difficult for many stepmothers and stepfathers are the endless suggestions given by naive non-stepparents about how to be loved by stepchildren. The judgment of some of these well-meaning friends is painful, useless, and becomes even more ludicrous from those whose own children are not exactly as angelic as their parents think they are. All families have the same issues of jealousy, envy, preferences, and naiveté that stepfamilies have; the families who self-righteously preach against stepfamilies are acting like the emperor. They will continue to amaze and entertain others with their circuslike hypocrisy that suggests that staying in destructive marriages solves problems, or that not engaging in serious relationships while the children are still living at home will make their decisions less difficult than those of stepfamilies. Their issues may be different, but may also have long-lasting damages of their own. None of us can afford to insist that our transparent clothes are gorgeous, and that we don't want to be told if we are making fools of ourselves by believing it.

Chapter 6

Stories of Jealousy and Envy:
The Unavoidably Steep Learning Curve

*"You can never cross the ocean unless you have the
courage to lose sight of the shore."*

—Christopher Columbus

The emotions of jealousy and envy are a part of everyone's life, and most people do not categorize them as pleasant emotions. Some people think that because of the unpleasant quality of these feelings, and the tendency of those experiencing them to behave badly, that the feelings themselves are "bad" or "wrong." Many try to avoid feeling them, sometimes by attending classes and meditating or praying, in an attempt to remove these emotions because they are uncomfortable. This may not be a wise course of action, as unpleasant feelings and sensations are healthy in some situations, and can lead to greater insight and awareness if one is willing to tolerate and examine them while not acting in ways that are destructive to the self and others. In our culture, emotions, thoughts, and behaviors are often intertwined, making it easy to blame a feeling for a resulting inappropriate action. For example, people sometimes say that they hit someone because they were angry or lied because they were frightened, as if there are no alternative actions more appropriate available to their feelings. However, in the close quarters of a family, especially a stepfamily, the opportunities for poor behavior and the contrasting opportunities for strengthening one's ability to examine feelings before acting are innumerable. In the stories about these emotions as they applied to the Greek gods, such as Hera, Zeus, Apollo, and many if not all of the others in the Greek pantheon, and other mythological characters from Egyptian and Celtic cultures, jealousy and envy certainly can elicit behaviors that are murderous and frightening and that need to be addressed by modern culture.

People in Western culture have a difficult time accepting emotions as neither good nor bad in and of themselves. Like colors of the rainbow, the moral value assigned to them depends on how and why one feels the emotion. Love is considered good and divine, until a person "loves" harming animals, children, or other humans, or states that he or she loves doing things that the culture and religion describe as immoral. Then love becomes "sick." Feeling joy, taking pleasure, and being thrilled watching dogs fight in an arena is not only illegal in this society, but seems depraved by the standards of this culture. Humans seek happiness, and it is only when that seeking seems to be at the cost of another another's well-being or when it harms the animal world or the planet's health in some avoidable fashion that the question of the morality of following one's bliss becomes suspect.

Jealousy and envy are two emotions that are often used interchangeably, and although they seem to have a similar "feel" to them, they can perhaps be differentiated in a way that allows their benefit rather than their negativity to be experienced. They are dangerous only when felt by people who have little ability to self-soothe and delay gratification or reduce the intensity of these unpleasant emotions without harming others. They exist because they serve a purpose and further humanity's ability to survive and adapt. In stories about stepfamilies, both their destructive and life-fulfilling roles are portrayed repeatedly.

In this book, envy and jealousy are used not as synonyms but as feeling states that are different from each other. Jealousy has a possessive quality about it, an awareness of scarcity; when humans know there is not enough to go around, they "jealously" guard their treasures, their relationships, and their lives. In this sense, the unpleasant feeling of jealousy pushes us to stand guard over what can be taken, lost, or stolen. It is a guarding emotion, implying a need to guard or protect, and accompanying it can be thoughts and behaviors of violence.

In contrast, envy does not indicate scarcity. Humans can be envious of other person's skills, achievements, freedom, and knowledge. People can destroy that which they envy in order to remove the source of the unpleasant feeling, but that serves only as a temporary relief. However, envy can be seen as a beacon, telling people what is missing in their lives. If someone envies another person's ability to be able to vacation in Italy, it does no good to steal that person's tickets or make sure they can't go. A positive use of the emotion is to determine if Italy is an appropriate goal for a future vacation, or whether a vacation somewhere is overdue, or if envy rises because of not fulfilling other dreams. If you envy someone's fitness, destroying that person's health will not get you into shape. It would be better to acknowledge the envy and start exercising. It is better to acknowledge the envy of someone's talent or the gifts they have while learning to self-soothe, because no one gets everything he or she wants in life. Reality is a hard taskmaster, but one that results in ego strength and a more aware and wiser personality.

Jealousy tells us when there is not enough, or helps ask that question. If a person is jealous of the time his or her partner spends with another person, job, or hobby, then the question to be asked may be whether that person or activity takes away needed time from the relationship, harms the qualities of intimacy, or dishonors the importance of the relationship. Jealousy at its best may tell us when we are in danger of losing something special or that someone's focus, time, or energy is being lost to someone or something else. If a person is not jealous when a friend or spouse focuses most of his or her time and attention elsewhere, it may be an indicator that the person wants to get out of the relationship, is taking the relationship for granted, or is in danger of losing it. Just like a temperature gauge, the jealous feeling tells us something is not well. If you have a fever over 100 degrees Fahrenheit, something is wrong and needs to be explored. The feeling can be very useful as a warning that either someone is neglecting a relationship, or that we are focusing too intensely on getting our needs for validation and support met through other human beings when we need to do some of that for ourselves, or with the person feeling jealous. However, jealousy, like all emotions, can also be extreme and pathological. A man or woman may be jealous to the point of feeling threatened by almost any close relationship his or her partner has, or he or she may be jealous to the point of being unable to tolerate calmly the needed coparenting roles that ex-spouses need to develop. People who are so disabled by jealousy need to heal this disease and work on feeling less threatened. They also should not marry someone with children.

Greek mythology abounds with stories of jealousy and envy that can be the driving emotions behind acts of incredible creativity, bravery, and commitment, as well as murderous rage and dreadful behavior.

Hera: Queen, Goddess, and Stepmother

Hera was the wife of Zeus in the Greek pantheon. She was considered the goddess of matrimony, and her role as the wife of Zeus dominated the mythology about her. In her positive aspects, she is seen as the energy that drives and supports long-term marriage commitments "through thick and thin," for "better or worse." She can suffer, experience humiliation, betrayal, and abandonment, and yet stay loyal to her husband. Pre-Greek history probably described her as a more complete trinity of a woman independent of marriage (or a virgin), a married mother, and then an elder, sometimes referred to as "the crone." Her roots may go back thousands of years prior to Greek civilization.

By the time the Greeks described this pattern of psychic energy as a goddess, she was more specifically defined by her role as a wife. Being a wife was her passion and her identity, her blessing and her curse. She was the energy that allowed deeply committed women to be blinded to their husband's faults, immaturity, and even affairs. She may have been committed to her children as part of the marriage protocol and could play the role of devoted mother and wife, but the role of wife was where she excelled. Divorce, in many ways, was not an option for her. Even in a separation, she would still see herself as Zeus's wife, and her separation was not about involvement with another. For her, it was Zeus or no one.

Hera's relationship with Zeus was her central driving force. She was described as intensely jealous of all of her husband's dalliances, and endlessly sought to attack the other women, even if they were victims of his deception or rape. The relationships with her husband's offspring could often be just as murderous and filled with rage. Her loyalty to her marriage focused her pain and rage on the "other woman" and on any offspring. When her pain and rage with Zeus could not be contained, she punished and harmed her own offspring rather than harming Zeus. It is only at the end of her rule that she became Hera unto herself and was able to make a richer and calmer way of living without her obsessive need of a male who would be monogamous.

Hera's center as the queen of Mount Olympus, wife of Zeus, matriarch, and goddess of marriage interestingly does not include images of what we might call family. As a mother, she was not nurturing and, in fact, is described as being so disgusted that her son Hephaestus was not perfect that she threw him out of Mount Olympus. Her focus on her marriage to Zeus and her inability to define herself outside of this relationship has made her both an object of the ideal wife for many women and, for others, an object of fear for being so foolishly obsessed.

Hera's only son by Zeus was Ares, the god of war, called Mars by the Romans. Zeus was not fond of this son, and the son was not a popular god in most of Greece. The Roman culture worshipped this god of war with more devotion; the Greeks never were that fond of him outside of Sparta. Ares was the lover of Aphrodite, who was married to his brother, Hephaestus. This was an energy triangle pattern known to wreak havoc on a regular basis long after these gods no longer had temples of worship in Greece.

Hephaestus was a child born out of jealousy. When Zeus gave birth to the goddess Athena without Hera's help, Hera decided to have a son without a father, and gave birth to Hephaestus, who was born with a clubfoot. This so enraged Hera that she cast him out of Mount Olympus, as previously mentioned. The mythology describes him living inside a volcano (the Romans called him Vulcan) and being the most creative of the gods in terms of artistic creativity. He became god of the forge and was known for being able to make beautiful things, but he was not loved by his mother.

Both of Hera's sons had fiery temperaments, were not favored by loving parents, and were marginalized in the pantheon. Yet both were intimately connected with Aphrodite, the goddess of passion and love.

As poorly as Hera treated her own offspring, most of her step-children were the target of the worst of her wrath, as were their mothers. She turned one of Zeus's lovers into a bear; another was turned into a cow by Zeus to protect her from Hera's wrath, which she did not escape. Hera tricked another lover, Semele, into demanding that she see Zeus in his true form. The radiance was overpowering and killed Semele. Her son, Dionysius, was raised by Zeus himself, and Hera's jealousy of this love child led her to order him torn to pieces and boiled. However, Rhea, Zeus's mother and Dionysius's grandmother, collected the pieces and reassembled them, restoring Dionysius to life. One of the many recurring images from religious history is that of a god who is killed and brought back to life.

Heracles was a child of Zeus and Alcmene, a woman married to a king. Zeus tricked her into thinking he was her husband and made time slow down so one night lasted for three days, so he could intentionally father Heracles. Alcmene, who feared the wrath of the jealous Hera, abandoned Heracles in a field after his birth. Hera found the baby and nursed him. When she discovered he was Zeus's son, she began an endless pattern of harassment. Hera at one point sent a two-headed serpent to kill the young boy, but he was able to strangle both heads. Ironically, his name contains "Hera," in spite of the fact that no biological relationship between them existed. As a stepmother, Hera has few equals, both in the number of stepchildren and in the number of negative ways she responds to them. The sophistication with which the Greek story-tellers seemed to know the darker complexities of the stepmother and stepchild relationship is unparalleled in any other ancient images of which I am aware.

The story of Medea, a Greek tragedy, is another rendition of the pattern described in the myth of Hera. Medea loves Jason and commits to him with an intensity and loyalty that lead her to betray her father and brother in order for Jason to get the Golden Fleece. She is so devoted to Jason that she kills her half brother and others to promote a marriage to Jason. Medea then is jilted by Jason, who marries a princess. Medea, in her jealous rage, destroys Jason's bride with a poison cloak that burns her up, and then Medea kills her own children to keep them from their father. The jealousy and intense commitment to marriage, not to children or individuality, is a hallmark of the stories of both Hera and Medea.

Recognizing this kind of energy in men and women and preventing the overt violent expression of this kind of rage and jealousy is just as important today as it clearly was to the Greeks who described these eternal dynamics in steprelationships. The kind of commitment that a woman makes in a marriage where Hera's kind of energy pattern dominates leaves little room for other feminine energies. This woman may not be that involved emotionally with her children, and if she is, she must find another way of viewing the world, as Hera energy has little to do with mothering. The energy described in the goddess image of Demeter and other more nurturing goddesses needs to be accessed and developed. Our Western culture has an immensely ambivalent attitude toward this kind of commitment. We hold it up as ideal and rage at our leaders when they behave as Zeus did, having affairs or children out of wedlock, often with more collective rage and anger than the wife of the offending public figure feels.

The women who most strongly exemplify this pattern may sacrifice the well-being of their children in their rage at a husband who has betrayed them sexually or by passionately engaging in some activity, work, or sport. Although few will actually murder their children, these women are likely to tolerate emotional, sexual, and physical abuse of their children by their spouses. Their loyalty to their spouse is blinding. If their husbands have other passions, the women rage at the children, not at the spouse. The tendency to be seen as a nag seems to go with this, along with obsessive jealousy, and to be critical or to attack the reputations of a husband's friends or the worth of a hobby or sport if these things draw the man away from her. The ability to express the loneliness behind the wrath is often one of the things these women must learn in therapy.

Women who exemplify the Hera pattern have other characteristics that apply to modern relationships. They may call the
woman with whom their spouse had an affair "a cow," in line with
the mythology of Hera. They may poison and burn her reputation,
as Medea did, and when ultimately left for another woman, they
may do everything they can to kill the father's relationship with his
children. These are often children who may have seen little of a father who worked and ruled a bigger kingdom than a home. Before
the separation or divorce, there may have been little involvement
or deep attachment with the children. The children of these relationships are often conflicted and feel they are being used by their
mothers as weapons to attack the man who has left.

Yet the involvement of the mother, when not focused on her
unfaithful husband or divorced spouse, may not be deeply attached
or focused on her children. These children often show damaging
psychological stress during a divorce. The father may have been out
of the house a lot prior to the separation and behaved much like
a detached god who appeared and disappeared according to his
own plans. The mother, while happily being the wife, may have de-
fended his absence. Actually, the whole family may have financially
benefited a from the father's drive and work ethic. Men who often
attract women with strong connections to Hera energy are often
focused on their careers and are competitive and driven.

Today, as in ancient Greece, children of this kind of union need
other more nurturing energy patterns to be engaged in the family
through a divorce and remarriage. Otherwise, the children's mental health can be negatively impacted. Children may express their
pain and confusion with regressed behaviors, such as setting fires,
truancy, poor scholastic performance, drug abuse, and other symptoms of their sense of abandonment, despair, depression, and grief.
The mythology of Zeus describes an energy pattern in men that often makes them better at fathering solo. Zeus is a doting father to
Athena, Artemis, and Dionysius, among others. Hera has no such
history. She dominates and diminishes the two daughters she has
by Zeus. Women like her may see their daughters as competitors
for her husband's attention, and treat a daughter who continues to
love her father after a divorce like the hated "other woman."

The tendency of Hera- and Zeus-like relationships to lose their sensuality is epic, and the seriousness with which Hera takes the role of wife, and her distrust and hatred of Aphrodite, her promiscuous daughter-in-law, plays out daily in many people's lives. On a biological level, our hormones seem to dance with this. The hormones that are engaged when we are in the moment and in love or lust, such as phenylethylamine, or PEA, and pheromones derived from DHEA, seem to only be elevated in new relationships. Some can become addicted to the high they produce and move from relationship to relationship in search of this hormone luster. The hormones, such as oxytocin and others that need to be present for long-term relationships to continue to have sexual passion, also involve a maturity and seriousness of commitment. If dominated by the patterns of Zeus and Hera, however, mature sexuality never occurs. The result is all too often celibacy in human marriages and affairs outside of the marriage bonds.

Celibacy seems to be tolerated by women who are overwhelmed by Hera's archetype, but is not part of a man's behavior if he follows Zeus-like patterns. The clash that ensues is epic, dramatic, and experienced by millions. The story of Catherine of Aragon, from British history, is one that replays this myth. She refused to ever accept that Henry VIII was no longer her husband, no matter how many times he remarried, and was reported to have lived a celibate life after he left her. In popular culture, Spencer Tracy's long relationship with Katherine Hepburn is legendary, partly because his wife refused to divorce him and they remained married until death, although his obvious commitment was to Hepburn. Some women seem to actually prefer that their husband's sexuality be focused elsewhere, but women with Hera energy react with rage and anger, not at the spouse, but more frequently at the lover and her children, and at times toward their own children, as a way of punishing the absent spouse.

When Hera-like behavior is the dominant pattern in a new stepmother's life, she may treat her new husband's first wife with disparagement, and react to his children by his earlier relationship with the same hostility. This is often passively or actively supported by the man in this kind of relationship. As stated before, Zeus-like men often prefer to be solo parents, or may have little interest in parenting at all, and may encourage the hostility between the stepmother and the children. In any situation, whatever gives them a lot of solo parenting time with their children will be supported. Some men will not have any serious relationships with women until their children are grown and out of the home. Some fathers who are less interested in their children may passively allow the new wife to destroy their relationship with their children. It is very hard for men who identify with this kind of Zeus energy to share in parenting decisions and to make cooperative decisions that help keep everyone's needs in balance. If one of the children is disabled in some way, as was Hephaestus, the drive of a stepfather, who identifies with Zeus's energy, to develop a relationship with him or her may be nonexistent. Imperfect children often end up rejected by both parents and stepparents.

A girl who is independent and relates well to the world of business or sports may engage a Zeus-like father to the exclusion of any stepmother. For her, women can be tolerated or rejected in her life with her dad. Athena, Zeus's daughter, exemplifies this kind of energy. Born from her father's head, she knows, unlike Hera women, that there is no need to compete for her father's attention when she needs it. She will ignore, accept with some amusement, or dislike her father's mates. She is comfortable in the world of men and confident there. Her jealousy will only be aroused if one of her jobs is taken or some power usurped by the intruder. Then her wrath can be severe, and even a young child with access to that energy pattern can freeze others "dead" with her Medusa-like stare. Athena carried the gorgon head of Medusa as her shield, and the very sight of it turned others into stone. One stepmother stated, "When his daughter is angry with me, she can glare at me in such a way I feel speechless and as if there is no way I can move freely in the house; her stare freezes everything in the room."

Stepchildren who fantasize that they will have a warm new mother in a woman for whom Hera's energy patterns dominate are often confused and hurt by what they see as coldness and rejection at its most benign, and outright hostility at its worst. The images of the double-headed snake being sent by Hera to kill her young stepson are certainly blood curdling, and hopefully this murderous intent is not acted upon other than metaphorically, but the energy can be activated in women and men who can be immensely cold blooded in their "attacks" on their stepchildren. Additionally, it is seldom that the attack is based on only one characteristic. Instead, it is often cold-bloodedly focused on at least two character flaws in an attempt to poison the child's relationship with his or her parent. It takes a very heroic child to be strong enough to withstand such venom and symbolically strangle this two-headed serpent. Once again, the anger that ensues in Heracles' life of mayhem makes him look more like his stepbrother, Mars, than any of the other members of the pantheon. Modern children in these roles often develop enough ego strength to know that their stepparent's view of them is inaccurate, but this strength is seldom developed without embedding a kind of warrior hyper vigilance to any slights, real or imagined, in their adult lives.

The value of understanding these mythic types and emotional behaviors associated with them is great, because jealousy and envy both play havoc in the development of any family; and the spoiled envy a parent can feel for the time and devotion that his or her spouse spends on children, work, friends, and hobbies can be difficult enough without the added level of feelings of disruption to a family system that a new steprelationship brings. Using the wealth of information creatively in the family cauldron created by these emotions can teach adults and children a great deal. This knowledge can be used to increase the clarity as to what amount of time and quality of involvement parents need with each other and with their children individually and as a family. Determining these things involves a complex set of tasks and increases the need for acknowledgement of emotions, examining patterns of behavior, increasing communication, and developing patterns of cooperative interactions, which will serve all members of the family, not only in the home, but in the rest of the world.

Case Illustration

A couple entered therapy at the advice of their pastor, after telling him that they were on the verge of divorce and that they felt that their stepfamily situation was untenable. The man was tan, well-groomed, and dressed in an expensive polo shirt and slacks.

The woman had on an expensive sweat suit and stated, as she sat down, that she had just come from her exercise class. Just setting up the first appointment had taken several days of phone calls due to what appeared to be an extremely busy work schedule with a lot of traveling for the husband, and an endless round of classes and fundraising events for the wife. Both stated they wished they had just continued to date until their children were grown, or at least out of the house, and felt the degree of anger and hostility in the home was not healthy for anyone. The couple sat on the couch close to each other, and the wife moved closer to her husband, often reaching her hand to touch his arm or leg as she talked.

They repeatedly told me that they still loved each other, but were ruining their marriage with the constant fights with and about the children. The woman stated she had married her childhood sweetheart right after high school, and had worked to put him through college and medical school before having children. She laughed rather bitterly and stated she was the typical medical school wife, adding that her first husband had left her for a nurse he became involved with during his internship. She was pregnant with their son at the time, and moved across the country to be with her parents and to get away from the humiliating situation before she delivered the child. The boy was diagnosed early with a mild autism, and had to be in special education classes off and on for most of elementary school. The young single mother found this disappointing and embarrassing, but worked her way through college while raising the boy, although she admits that her mother and sisters were invaluable in helping her with this, as she found her son's difficulties overwhelming. The child's father never expressed any interest in seeing his son, and in fact, expressed resentment at the extra cost the boy's disabilities incurred.

The woman stated she often despaired of ever finding a good man who could accept her son when his own father didn't want to deal with him, and when she found it so hard herself. She felt that meeting her present husband had been a blessing she could scarcely believe; he didn't seem to mind the difficulties that the boy's autism involved and treated him like he would treat any boy.

The man stated he too had married "too young" the first time, although in his case he married a woman who worked in the country club he joined shortly after graduating from business school. He stated that he loved how socially connected she was, and that her father had a huge law practice. The father's desire to have his daughter safely married and his willingness to provide important business contacts were very seductive for the ambitious young man. They married within a year of meeting, and she became pregnant immediately. Their second child, a boy, was born two years after their oldest child, a daughter. The second pregnancy had been difficult, and the birth itself was complicated. He stated that after the birth, nothing was ever the same again. The boy needed constant medical care for several months after birth, and his wife began using prescription drugs for pain, then to sleep, then to get up. Within two years, she was so badly impaired that she was hospitalized for her addictions. The next few years went by rather peacefully as he worked endless hours at his new position at the firm he had joined. He stated that he didn't realize that his wife was back on prescription meds and was drinking heavily until he came home late, which was not unusual, to find that she was not home, and that the two young children were trying to fix their own dinner at 9:30 at night. They had not seen their mother since breakfast, and at age seven and five, were scared and confused. For the next twelve months, his wife went in and out of treatment and to AA and NA meetings. Nothing seemed to help for very long, and the children were clearly being harmed by the instability in the home.

The man stated he was furious with his first wife, because his rising position at the firm he had joined did not allow time for this kind of melodrama, and he often came home late to a house in chaos: dishes not done, children alone and sometimes not fed. His mother came to stay for a while, and that helped, but she and his wife fought constantly, and he finally decided he needed to divorce his wife and take the kids. Before the divorce was final, both he and his wife had begun dating other people, and the household was increasingly unstable. The ensuing battle was vicious, but his ex-wife's bouts with addiction and depression, and then a fairly serious suicide attempt in the middle of the legal wrangling, left the court deciding he was the fit parent. She still saw them occasionally since they lived in the same town, but she continued to abuse alcohol and drugs, and often did not show up at appointed visiting times.

The man stated that his daughter had to grow up fast with an unreliable mother, and she often acted like the little wife and mom in the house. His admiration and affection for "my girl" was stated repeatedly in many ways, and although he claimed he loved his son equally, he talked about the boy with less intensity and fewer stories or descriptions.

As the couple sat calmly holding hands, the husband stated that he had purposefully kept his dating life private from the children; he never brought any of the women he dated home and had his children stay with their grandparents at times if he needed a night out. However, when he met his present wife, she seemed the perfect companion. She was smart, fun, sexy, and loved to do things with him. Her son's medical problems and her ability to manage her life without needing drugs and alcohol were impressive to him. He did not want to live with her and his children without being married. He was sure that would trigger another legal battle with his ex-wife, and he was not sure he wanted to set up such a model of behavior for his children.

The couple married quickly, since they both found dating with two homes while meeting the needs of separate children daunting, and believed they had found the perfect love. They were young, attractive, socially and financially successful, and neither expected the difficulties they now were facing. Both felt the reactions of the children to the marriage were causing their problems, but both felt that the solutions each came up with were unacceptable.

The husband believed that his daughter felt displaced and uncomfortable as her new stepmother became the female director of the home, and that he needed to spend more time with "his girl." The woman pulled away from her husband as she stated that she believed that the girl was constantly challenging her role as wife and matriarch of the family, and she needed to be allowed to be a girl, not a "surrogate baby wife." The man was also disgruntled that his son now wanted to spend more time with his biological mother and was withdrawn from him. The woman was disappointed that her husband did not spend as much time with her son as he did with his own, even though his son was spending more time with his mother now. The man felt that his son was leaving him because he now had to share his father's time not only with his sister, but with his new stepmother and stepbrother. The father wanted the boy to feel sure that he was still his "best son ever," and as a result, often seemed to be supporting the mockery of his new stepbrother in which his children sometimes engaged, not overtly, but through smiles and snide remarks. Both members of the couple agreed on this.

This couple was caught in patterns older than our Western civilization with its divorce courts and therapists. The woman wanted to be a wife first and foremost, and being a mother, let alone a stepmother, had never been of primary importance. She jealously guarded her private time with her husband, and resented the time he spent not only with his children but even with her own child. She envied women who had problem-free children, the help of nannies, and who went on vacation in exotic places without their children. The man was envious of couples who seemed to find a balance between couple time and time with their children. He also was envious of families in which the father's authority was not challenged, but he had a harder time admitting this feeling of envy that he judged as sexist than he had expressing his fear that if he spent more time with his new wife and her son, he would lose his children, specifically his son, to their mother.

The man's ex-wife had her own soup of fear and jealousy, envy and fury cooking as well. She resented the lifestyle her ex-husband could now afford with a two-income family, whereas most of her income was spent on drugs and recovery from drugs. She was jealous of any time her children spent with their new stepmother, feeling it took something away from her, and she was envious of her ex-husband's ability to provide a lovely home for them. The children were caught in this mess of unspoken feelings and destructive behaviors. They, however, had their own agenda.

When the three children came in for several sessions, they were able to articulate some of their fears, but found it much harder to talk about feelings of jealousy or envy. At one point the man's son was able to articulate his feelings of envy (without calling it such yet) of his new stepbrother's freedom from the stress of a biological parent demanding his loyalty in aligning against a new stepparent. He stated that at least his new stepbrother wasn't constantly being told by his father that his new stepfather was a jerk, and he didn't have to betray anyone by liking his new stepparent. The mildly autistic boy's awareness of anyone feeling any envy of him was new, and this confused and astonished him. He said that he was baffled that a guy with one-and-a-half mothers and a whole father could be upset that he only had one mother (who didn't like him much) and only half a father in his new stepfather. This boy saw himself as scoring 1.5 in the parent department and the other boy as 2.5, an interesting observation about steprelationships. In the charming way that some autistic children see the world, he saw a stepparent as a half parent (0.5) and a stepchild as a half child (0.5), but at least better than a 0, the way his biological father treated him. Ryan saw the issue of a half parent as triggering issues of disloyalty and betrayal in his relationship with his mother, which was already difficult. Both boys on some level envied the other's position.

The daughter was in a totally different position. She was in open conflict with her new stepmother, and stated repeatedly that she hated her. Her jealousy of the woman's position with her father was not overtly sexual jealousy, but it had tinges of emotional incest with its negative consequences. In his attempt to keep his children out of his dating life, the man had left his daughter feeling as if she were center stage, as if she had won the Oedipal conflict. She wanted to marry someone like her father, and in many emotional ways, she had. She wanted his attention and her position as number one in his life back, and was not aware of the damage that doing this would do to her ability in the future to develop a marital relationship of her own. She hadn't yet learned that girls need to lose the first love of their life and the desire to marry their father in order to become an adult woman, available for marriage and their own family. Girls go from jealousy of their mother to wanting to be like the woman who won out over them for their father's love; then they eventually move on to an adult relationship of their own.

However, when a first marriage has not gone well, even without divorce, and it is clear that the father loves his daughter more than he loves her mother, or the mother sees her son as "her little man of the house," it is very hard for these children to have a healthy, adult-committed relationship. One must "dump" or "divorce" one's first love, the parent, in order to go on to find adult fulfillment in marriage. A child who feels like the head of the household and is the primary emotional support for the parent often finds the needs of the adult parent overwhelming. This scenario does not need a divorce in order to activate the emotional wounding. It is not nearly as severe as sexual incest, but is often confusing to those who experience it; they don't understand why they can't find mates, or find the right mates.

Sigmund Freud admitted that he understood he had "ruined" his own daughter and that she would never marry or accept any other man, because their relationship had been so close. His own relationship with the girl's mother was impoverished by comparison. Freud's analysis of the relationship between Oedipus Rex and his daughter Electra, who spent her life caring for the father she adored to the point that she had no real life outside of pleasing and caring for him once Oedipus went blind, is as tragic and darkly fascinating as the same myth played out in Freud's life. Freud lost his voice due to his smoking; his own daughter became his voice. The two of them had a closeness, not physically sexual, but in all other ways resembling a marriage relationship. The longing for unconditional love that a child has and the unconditional love that a parent comes close to giving is not the basis for a truly strong marriage. The contrast between the conditionality of romance and the less demanding love of parent–child bonds get blurred and confused when children become surrogate spouses.

Jealousy and envy are not pleasant feelings, and it is a natural wish to avoid or resolve them and to feel "better." We need to look at what these emotions tell us about ourselves, our need to grow, and how our situation and needs can be different. They are feelings that demand that something be different in our lives and our relationships, and in our maturity levels, inner security, or attitudes. The difficulty is in distinguishing which arena, internal or external, is being asked to adapt, and how that change can best serve our growth as people and help the family to serve its members more effectively.

Chapter 7

When There Is Not Enough: Hansel and Gretel and Redefining Home

"Our greatest glory lies not in never falling,
but in rising every time we fall."

—Confucius

The story of "Hansel and Gretel" is one of the most frequently told fairy tales in our culture. Although it may have gained popularity during the centuries when many children grew up in economic poverty without enough food to eat, it also continues to speak to children brought into families with emotional impoverishment. Worldwide there are still millions of children on the streets, in orphanages, and in slavery conditions because parents can no longer feed them. There are also millions more who are emotionally and psychologically abandoned by parents and stepparents whose own psyches are impoverished, making them unable to nurture. The story of Hansel and Gretel has both physical reality as well as psychological realities for families that lack emotional wealth, no matter how large the financial bank account.

There are several versions of this story. Some refer to the birth mother as having died and being replaced by a stepmother, and the other more bitterly describes a situation in which the birth mother demands the boy and girl be abandoned. In the real world of twenty-first century news, we hear of both situations. Some of the imagery of the award-winning movie *Slumdog Millionaire* resonates through our psyches partly because the fear of being abandoned as children, of being captured and seduced by false security, and the longing to go home echoes in each of us.

Hansel and Gretel

Hard by a great forest dwelt a poor woodcutter with his second wife and his two children. The boy was called Hansel and the girl Gretel. The poor woodcutter had very little to feed his family, and they often did not even have bread to eat. Now, when he thought over this by night in his bed, and tossed about in his anxiety, he groaned and said to his wife, "What is to become of us? How are we to feed my poor children, when we no longer have anything even for ourselves?"

"I'll tell you what, husband," answered the woman. "Early tomorrow morning we will take the children out into the forest to where it is the thickest. There we will light a fire for them and give each of them one more piece of bread, and then we will go to our work and leave them alone."

"No, wife," said the man, "I will not do that. How can I bear to leave my children alone in the forest? The wild animals would soon come and tear them to pieces."

"Oh, you fool," said she, "then we must all four die of hunger, and you may as well plane the planks for our coffins."

Then she left him no peace until he consented.

"But I feel very sorry for the poor children, all the same," said the man.

The two children had also not been able to sleep because of hunger and had heard what their stepmother had said to their father. Gretel wept bitter tears, and said to Hansel, "Now all is over with us."

"Be quiet, Gretel," said Hansel, "do not distress yourself. I will soon find a way to help us." And when the old folks had fallen asleep, he got up, put on his little coat, opened the door below, and crept outside. The moon shone brightly, and the white pebbles, which lay in front of the house, glittered like real silver pennies. Hansel stooped and stuffed the little pocket of his coat with as many as he could get in.

Then he went back and said to Gretel, "Be comforted, dear little sister, and sleep in peace. God will not forsake us." And he lay down again in his bed.

When day dawned, but before the sun had risen, the woman came and awoke the two children, saying, "Get up, you sluggards. We are going into the forest to fetch wood."

She gave each a little piece of bread, and said, "There is something for your dinner, but do not eat it up before then, for you will get nothing else."

Gretel took the bread under her apron, as Hansel had the pebbles in his pocket. Then they all set out together on the way to the forest. When they had walked a short time, Hansel stood still and peeped back at the house, and did so again and again.

His father said, "Hansel, what are you looking at there and staying behind for? Pay attention, and do not forget how to use your legs."

"Ah, father," said Hansel, "I am looking at my little white cat, which is sitting up on the roof and wants to say good-bye to me."

The wife said, "Fool, that is not your little cat. That is the morning sun which is shining on the chimneys."

Hansel, however, had not been looking back at the cat, but had been constantly throwing one of the white pebble-stones out of his pocket and onto the road.

When they had reached the middle of the forest, the father said, "Now, children, pile up some wood, and I will light a fire that you may not be cold."

Hansel and Gretel gathered brushwood together as high as a little hill. The brushwood was lighted, and when the flames were burning very high, the stepmother said, "Now, children, lay yourselves down by the fire and rest; we will go into the forest and cut some wood. When we have finished, we will come back and fetch you away."

Hansel and Gretel sat by the fire, and when noon came, each ate a little piece of bread, and as they heard the strokes of the wood-axe, they believed that their father was near. It was not the axe, however, but a branch which he had fastened to a withered tree which the wind was blowing backwards and forwards. And as they had been sitting such a long time, their eyes closed with fatigue, and they fell fast asleep. When at last they awoke, it was already dark night.

Gretel began to cry and said, "How are we to get out of the forest now?"

But Hansel comforted her and said, "Just wait a little, until the moon has risen, and then we will soon find the way."

And when the full moon had risen, Hansel took his little sister by the hand, and followed the pebbles, which shone like newly coined silver pieces and showed them the way.

They walked the whole night long, and by break of day came once more to their father's house. They knocked at the door, and when the stepmother opened it and saw Hansel and Gretel, she said, "You naughty children, why have you slept so long in the forest? We thought you were never coming back at all."

The father, however, rejoiced, for it had cut him to the heart to leave them behind alone.

But the stepmother still felt there was not enough food to feed four people, and told her husband that the children must go.

She said, "We will take them farther into the wood, so that they will not find their way out again. There is no other means of saving ourselves."

The man's heart was heavy, and he thought, it would be better for you to share the last mouthful with your children. The woman, however, would listen to nothing that he had to say, but scolded and reproached him.

The children, however, were still awake and had heard the conversation. When the old folks were asleep, Hansel again got up and wanted to go out and pick up pebbles as he had done before, but the stepmother had locked the door, and Hansel could not get out.

Nevertheless he looked at his little sister and said, "Do not cry, Gretel, but go to sleep quietly. I will figure this out."

Early in the morning came the stepmother and took the children out of their beds. Their piece of bread was given to them, but it was still smaller than the time before. On the way into the forest, Hansel crumbled his in his pocket, and often stood still and threw a morsel on the ground. Little by little, Hansel threw all the crumbs on the path. The stepmother led the children still deeper into the forest, where they had never in their lives been before.

Then a great fire was again made, and the woman said, "Just sit there, you children, and when you are tired you may sleep a little. We are going into the forest to cut wood, and in the evening when we are done, we will come and fetch you away."

When it was noon, Gretel shared her piece of bread with Hansel, who had scattered his by the way. Then they fell asleep and evening passed, but no one came to get the poor children. They did not awake until it was dark night, and Hansel comforted his little sister and said, "Just wait, Gretel, until the moon rises, and then we shall see the crumbs of bread which I have strewn about; they will show us our way home again."

When the moon came they set out, but they found no crumbs, for the many thousands of birds, which fly about in the woods and fields, had picked them all up. Hansel said to Gretel, "We shall soon find the way," but they did not find it. They walked the whole night and all the next day too, from morning till evening, but they did not get out of the forest, and were very hungry, for they had nothing to eat but two or three berries which grew upon the ground. And as they were so weary that their legs would carry them no longer, they lay down beneath a tree and fell asleep.

It was now three mornings since they had left their father's house. They began to walk again, but they always came deeper into the forest, and if help did not come soon, they must die of hunger and weariness. When it was midday, they saw a beautiful snow-white bird sitting on a bough, which sang so delightfully that they stood still and listened to it. And when its song was over, it spread its wings and flew away before them, and they followed it until they reached a little house, on the roof of which it alighted. And when they approached the little house they saw that it was built of bread and covered with cakes, but that the windows were of clear sugar.

"We will set to work on that," said Hansel, "and have a good meal. I will eat a bit of the roof, and you, Gretel, can eat some of the window; it will taste sweet."

Hansel reached up above and broke off a little of the roof to try how it tasted, and Gretel leant against the window and nibbled at the panes.

Then a soft voice cried from the parlor, "Nibble, nibble, gnaw; who is nibbling at my little house?"

The children answered: "The wind, the wind, the heaven-born wind," and went on eating without disturbing themselves. Hansel, who liked the taste of the roof, tore down a great piece of it, and Gretel pushed out the whole of one round windowpane, sat down, and enjoyed herself with it. Suddenly the door opened, and a woman as old as the hills, who supported herself on crutches, came creeping out. Hansel and Gretel were so terribly frightened that they let fall what they had in their hands.

The old woman, however, nodded her head, and said, "Oh, you dear children, who has brought you here? Do come in, and stay with me. No harm shall happen to you."

She took them both by the hand and led them into her little house. Then good food was set before them: milk and pancakes, with sugar, apples, and nuts. Afterwards two pretty little beds were covered with clean, white linen, and Hansel and Gretel lay down in them and thought they were in heaven.

But the old woman had only pretended to be so kind. She was in reality a wicked witch, who lay in wait for children, and had only built the little house of bread in order to entice them there. When a child fell into her power, she killed, cooked, and ate it, and that was a feast day with her. Witches have red eyes, and cannot see far, but they have a keen scent like the beasts, and are aware when human beings draw near.

When Hansel and Gretel came into her neighborhood, she laughed with malice, and said mockingly, "I have them. They shall not escape me again."

Early in the morning before the children were awake, she was already up, and when she saw both of them sleeping and looking so pretty, with their plump and rosy cheeks, she muttered to herself: "That will be a dainty mouthful!"

Then she seized Hansel with her shriveled hand, carried him into a little stable, and locked him in behind a gray door. Scream as he might, it would not help him. Then she went to Gretel, shook her till she awoke, and cried, "Get up, lazy thing, fetch some water, and cook something good for your brother. He is in the stable outside, and is to be made fat. When he is fat, I will eat him."

Gretel began to weep bitterly, but it was all in vain, for she was forced to do what the wicked witch commanded. And now, the best food was cooked for poor Hansel, but Gretel got nothing but crab shells. Every morning the woman crept to the little stable and cried, "Hansel, stretch out your finger that I may feel if you will soon be fat."

Hansel, however, stretched out a little bone to her. The old woman, who had dim eyes, could not see it, and thought it was Hansel's finger, and was astonished that there was no way of fattening him. When four weeks had gone by, and Hansel still remained thin, she was seized with impatience and would not wait any longer.

"Now, then, Gretel," she cried to the girl, "Stir yourself, and bring some water. Let Hansel be fat or lean, tomorrow I will kill him, and cook him."

Ah, how the poor little sister did lament when she had to fetch the water, and how her tears did flow down her cheeks. "Dear God, do help us," she cried. "If the wild beasts in the forest had but devoured us, we should at any rate have died together."

"Just keep your noise to yourself," said the old woman. "It won't help you at all."

Early in the morning, Gretel had to go out and hang up the cauldron with the water, and light the fire.

"We will bake first," said the old woman. "I have already heated the oven, and kneaded the dough."

She pushed poor Gretel out to the oven, from which flames of fire were already darting. "Creep in," said the witch, "and see if it properly heated so that we can put the bread in."

And once Gretel was inside, she intended to shut the oven and let her bake in it, and then she would eat her, too. But Gretel saw what she had in mind, and said, "I do not know how I am to do it. How do I get in?"

"Silly goose," said the old woman. "The door is big enough. Just look, I can get in myself," and she crept up and thrust her head into the oven.

Then Gretel gave her a push that drove her far into it, and shut the iron door, and fastened the bolt. The witch began to howl quite horribly, but Gretel ran away, and the witch was miserably burnt to death.

Gretel, however, ran like lightning to Hansel, opened his little stable, and cried, "Hansel, we are saved. The old witch is dead."

Then Hansel sprang like a bird from its cage when the door is opened. How they did rejoice and embrace each other, and dance about and kiss each other. And as they had no longer any need to fear her, they went into the witch's house, and in every corner there stood chests full of pearls and jewels.

"These are far better than pebbles," said Hansel, and thrust into his pockets whatever could be got in.

Gretel said, "I, too, will take something home with me," and filled her pinafore full.

"But now we must be off," said Hansel, "that we may get out of the witch's forest."

They walked and walked and crossed a great body of water and at some point the forest seemed to be more and more familiar to them, and at length they saw from afar their father's house. Then they began to run, rushed into the parlor, and threw themselves round their father's neck. The man had not known one happy hour since he had left the children in the forest. The woman, however, was dead. Gretel emptied her pinafore until pearls and precious stones ran about the room, and Hansel threw one handful after another out of his pocket to add to them. Then all anxiety was at an end, and they lived together in perfect happiness.[1]

The lessons for stepfamilies in this story resonate whether the mother figure is an emotionally or physically starving biological mother bereft of love or a stepmother who sees the children as a threat to what little she has. In this situation, the wish that the children were not in one's life has ceased to be the momentary fantasy which every parent may have of wishing the kids "would get lost," and has become an obsession. Stepparents who feel starved for attention and love will often hope that the biological parent will abandon his or her children, or at least see less of them. This often is not a completely conscious desire, but one that slowly grows into promoting a lifestyle where the emotional needs of the children become less and less important, and the desire of the adults to have more time with each other increases to the point that the children feel lost, evicted from the family container, as if they can't find their way home to loving and accepting parents.

In the story, the crumbs and pebbles the children left on the trail, in this tale of becoming lost, can represent memories that children hope they can hold onto and which may eventually guide them to the family in its former state. The argument between the stepmother and Hansel has many real-life variations, such as children talking about their mother's cooking or vacations when the family seemed happy enough to them; these are signs that there is still life in what they left behind, still grief work to do around the good-bye to the past. The discounting that the stepmother does, insisting that the memories are nothing but a trick of light, a distorted memory, does nothing to aid the grief process that the family is enduring.

Developing a healthy stepfamily involves both loss and grief. It is not an accident that the word "step" derives from a word meaning bereft. The new parent who is "step" is bereft. Our society places a high value on accumulating and at times hoarding objects, relationships, and self-images, but feeling loss, having fewer possessions, and ending destructive relationships is not honored with equal respect. We move through rites of passage, from single or separated to married with children, without doing the appropriate grief work. The results are poorly resolved issues and undone grief work, usurped by attempts to simply turn everything into a celebration.

We are "supposed" to grieve alone, to not need to grieve, to be "left alone," and to deny our ambivalence about any new commitment, which means new relationships are not going to develop smoothly. As children hoard the solid stones and pebbles and, finally, what few crumbs they can find, remembering the fun times in the family before its dissolution, they may continue to want to return to the sense of belonging they had, even though its structure was less than welcoming. So often, I have heard adults whose parents divorced decades ago wistfully remember the time before they stopped feeling welcome in a home with a stepparent. They have worn these memories smooth like polished pebbles, cherishing each one, and hoping the memories will lead them back to the home and feelings of safety they remember. The tears that were never shed and the grief work never done can begin at any time in life, but until it is done, the emotional poverty of unexpressed sorrow will not resolve into the ability to find the jewels and pearls of the newer situation.

Well-meaning parents may add to this impoverishment of emotional connection by being stuck in their own desire for the "divorce to not cause the children pain." Children read this as if they must experience their own sorrow silently, as if their own grief is taboo, not to be expressed, and that crying because they miss Daddy or Mommy elicits only guilt or anger from the parent listening; they quickly learn to act as if nothing is wrong. As the children Hansel and Gretel did, they may overhear their parents talking. The parents in a modern-day divorce may sometimes feel that their lives would be happier without the children. Adults have told me time and again that their parents stayed together because of the children, or the church, or the finances. When people stay together "for the sake of the kids," those children bear an enormous burden, and, like Hansel and Gretel, are terrified at what might happen if the poverty and lack of emotional food in the house is acknowledged, and the barely surviving family dissolves. In the past forty years of doing clinical psychotherapy, I have often heard these statements: "My parents stayed together for the sake of the kids; they would have never stayed married without us," teamed with "I don't believe in marriages and don't want to get married." Marriage looks like a trap in this imaging and leaves children with little sense that marriage can have a richness and depth of feeling and commitment worth experiencing.

Like Hansel and Gretel, sharing sorrows, losses, fears, as well as joys, with siblings increases a feeling of connectedness. The new accomplishments and successes increase the emotional richness too, but avoiding anything that is an unpleasant feeling dampens life energy. Avoiding negative feelings and only emphasizing positive ones may lead to a dearth of feeling that leaves families shattered and emotionally dangerous for the children and adults alike. The natural desire to feel joy and happiness is a wonderful part of human nature, but when it smothers an equally natural desire to share loss and suffering and to learn from these things, the family becomes impoverished.

When children get lost in this place of emotional poverty, they are vulnerable to anything that looks sweet and sugary. The image of the witch's cottage satisfies some kind of hunger, but clearly is not the balanced diet a good parent would recommend, although it is one that resonates for "kids" of all ages. The witch in modern culture is often drug addiction or abuse; and that meth and other drugs do devour the psyches and bodies of those trapped in a drugged enchantment is hardly debatable. The number of children from emotionally impoverished homes, both step and biological, who are seduced by mood-altering "sweets" into an addictive nightmare, caught in an oven where their brains are cooked, is pointed out endlessly in news reports, health-care statistics, police department records, and sociological works.

The witch can also appear in other forms. In the highly successful movie *Slumdog Millionaire*, the "witch" is the man who runs the orphanage and picks up children lost in the "forest" of a dump. He gives them food, shelter, and what appears to be safety in exchange for their begging skills. Initially, this looks like some wonderful heaven, but he eventually blinds and prostitutes those who serve his financial greed. This is a modern-day version of the Hansel and Gretel tale, this time with "three musketeers" rather than a sister and brother. Pedophiles and others who prey on children are another real-life, real-time danger for those whose family of origin is impoverished and in which the "secret" of not being wanted creates the child's lack of confidence and safety in the world. Emotional impoverishment creates a desperate need for connection and emotional food, which blinds a child to who is truly giving and who uses others for their own gain.

In addition, being able to bond around the rejections and losses in life is challenging at times and requires courage. In Hansel and Gretel there is a strength in the brother–sister bond that is not seen in many tales in which brothers and sisters are more often competing with each other for limited resources. In fairy tales, these resources may be portrayed as the kingdom, the gold, or the princess. The motif in this fairy tale, however, is different. Both children come through strong and able to support each other. The girl does not faint, and she does not need to be rescued while she sleeps. The two collaborate to solve the dreadful problem they face. Gretel even kills the witch to save their lives, and together Hansel and Gretel escape with the richness of shared experience and wisdom.

At the end of this fairy tale, the children find their way home by crossing a river or boundary not mentioned in their journey to the witch's home. For some children this may be a recovery program, if the witch took the form of a substance-abuse issue. For others the witch may have simply been an image that the family had of the horrors of having a stepparent. Sometimes the absent biological parent can take on the role of witch by acting like the Disneyland dad or mom, showering the child with sweets and artificial emotions in a spoken or unspoken rivalry with the new family. Effectively, this kind of spoiling sweetness entraps children in a situation in which they are stunned by unreasonable expectations about the world about them. The mother or father can keep them trapped with presents, promises, and a lack of discipline, but it leaves them unable to develop a real relationship with the other parental figures or the world. Bitter, angry, and jealous biological parents can also enact the role of the witch, wanting to devour the ability of the children to relate to the outside world, including his or her new stepfamily. The children are trapped by the parent's need for loyalty, and they bond around their hatred of the new parent. The biological parent avoids dealing with his or her own loss, and may gloat that, "My kids hate their new stepparent," but in the long run, it keeps the children stuck in the angry parent's raging oven, unable to relate meaningfully to the new parental figures in their lives. Many children learn to hand their parents fake bones to settle things down; their loyalty to the "witch" then is not questioned. One child told me that weekends with his mother went better if he started his time with her by telling her that his new stepmother burned something, lost something, or had fought with his dad, even before they got to his mother's home. He learned to make up stories of his stepmother's failings in order to get a break from his mother's endless demands for him to express his loyalty to her and "take her side" in the divorce drama.

Finally, the pearls of wisdom that can be gathered from going through the processes of loss, being disoriented from old patterns, feeling consumed by anger, and learning to make choices, are important. Mature, emotionally aware people do their best to know what is real, what is sweet but not nourishing, and when to appease an angry witch whose goal may be to kill their genuine feelings if they are open and honest, and when to safely express themselves. These are lessons worth learning, and this learning can be helped by stepparents and parents alike who recognize that a child is feeling rejected and abandoned by the losses he or she is going through during the times of transition as the stepfamily forms.

Case Illustration

A young couple sat rigidly and quietly in the office. The woman's arms were crossed across her chest with her hands holding each arm just above the elbow with a grip that could bring bruises. Her husband glared angrily at the rug and occasionally looked as if he were about to talk, and then sighed loudly while clasping his right hand into a fist, pounding on his knee as if in frustration and rage so deep it left him speechless.

The wife occasionally glanced at her husband and finally burst into tears, while saying she was sure the whole marriage was a terrible mistake. She continued to sob while telling a story of feeling intensely betrayed and abandoned, first by her family of origin, and now by her husband.

The man rolled his eyes and said, "There she goes, using the tears to get a sympathy card again! We never get anywhere; she knows I can't stand tears!" His voice rose and tightened as he stared at his sobbing wife and added, "My mother always manipulated me with her sob stories, and now my wife seems to think she can do the same thing!"

I asked the woman if she could continue to talk about what was happening that left her feeling abandoned, if I just listened, even though she was clearly crying. The idea that a conversation could continue when one member was crying was apparently a new concept to both people. Learning to accept grief and tears, without trying to immediately change the behavior to stop the tears as fast as possible, is a skill seldom experienced by many of the men and women who come to see me.

Both members of the couple described growing up with distant, emotionally cold parents. The man's father had been a very successful attorney, who spent most of his time at his office avoiding the family, while his mother drank, at first secretively, and then openly, starting her days with a martini. By the time he got home in the afternoon, his mother might be at the country club with other "work widows" or at home, often sobbing or raging. As a boy his moments of freedom and sweetness often came at other children's homes or at a summer camp where he spent each summer for two months from the time he was ten years old until he went to college. There was never any lack of money for things he wanted, but most times of emotional sweetness came from being away from the cold tension in his parent's home. He had grown up in apparent financial opulence, but emotional poverty.

The woman had grown up in an equally cold home, but with fewer financial resources. Her father was a science teacher at the local high school, and her mother was a nurse, who worked the evening shift at the local pediatric hospital. The woman said that she thought her parents were tired of the caretaking of children, because that is what they did in their careers, and perhaps saw their only child as an inconvenience. Her mother was never home after school, and her father often did not get home until after the girl had fed herself dinner. Her only memory of good times with her dad was of him sitting at the same dining room table grading papers while she did her homework. The woman stated that the only time she remembers their acting as if they were proud of her was when she got academic awards or straight "A" grades. She had excelled academically and buried herself at the library and in school projects all through her childhood. She had gone to a prestigious university paid for with an academic scholarship and her earnings from part-time jobs. She had not used any of her parents' money to get herself through college and a master's degree program.

The man had married a fellow college student after she became pregnant their senior year in college. Two children followed quickly, and a bitter divorce followed three years after his last child was born. He had met his present wife while on a vacation, and they had dated "long distance" for six months before becoming engaged. A marriage followed six months after that, because the woman did not want to quit her job without security, and refused to move to live with the man without being married. She barely knew his two children when they married, since the majority of the weekends that they spent together were when his ex-wife had weekend custody.

Both these people had grown up in emotionally impoverished families and had left crumbs to follow in their attempts to get home to a place of comfort, shelter, and warmth. Both had been betrayed, not only by the lack of emotional food in their original homes, but also by the houses of apparent sweetness in places where they had been left. For the husband the seeming sweetness of summer camp had left him with scars that he had never shared until therapy. He had been sexually abused as a ten-year-old by a camp counselor, who at first made him feel special and gave him the emotional food his parents did not have for him. However, he felt by the end of the first month that he was imprisoned by threats of exposure and devoured by feeling "bad."

The ten-year-old boy felt rescued by another camper his age, another boy who was also being abused by the counselor and had told his parents. The man stated that, at first, he was horrified that someone had broken the silence and that he was sure something awful was going to happen, but no one else seemed to know that he, too, had been harmed. By the next year, the man said he had forgotten all about it. He shrugged his shoulders as he said this, as if it no longer mattered, but he was clearly shaking as he blurted out the story, finally stating that as a child he had never felt so special and as loved as he had by that counselor, before the abuse started.

During the next session, the wife shared her own story of feeling trapped in a situation in which the praise of a professor who had the power to provide grants and scholarships had led to an inappropriate sexual relationship. The sweetness of finally being told she was worthy, and that she might have financial freedom from being a burden to her parents, had left her trapped in an apparently sweet position by an older parental figure. When she recognized that all her research work in graduate school was going to be used in a paper by her lover-professor without mention of her as the primary author and researcher, she began to hide her results and gave him fake data while she completed her work and published the results on her own.

For each of them the house in the fairy tale was the sweetness missing in their childhood homes. The husband had been raised in a family with a father who avoided coming home to his disastrous marriage and a mother whose alcoholism left her little ability to parent adequately. Being seen as special and worthy by the camp counselor had been heady stuff. For the wife, having parents who also had not spent much time with her and often talked about all the sacrifices they made for her, left her delighted with the sweetness of being bewitched by an older man's attention and seduction of her time, her body, and her creativity.

Both had entered the new marriage hoping they had found their way to a warmer home, but both were primed to repeat the fairy tale pattern; not having enough emotional food to feed the two children in their care in addition to themselves. They had created a home to meet their needs for emotional validation and feeling special, and in which, having the time to be together interfered with them viewing the needs of the two children as an enormous drain on what little resources they had. Both were horrified at the idea that they saw their children with the same cold eyes with which they remembered their own parents seeing them, and they saw that both children were at risk of being seduced or bewitched by feigned sweetness outside of the house.

They had actually started therapy after the man's oldest boy had been caught with drugs in the bathroom at the junior high school. The sweetness of the gingerbread house was already tugging his son away. Both had blamed the other for the child's misbehavior. The school counselor had stated that the stepfamily situation and their status as divorced parents put the children at risk, making both again feel as if they were not good enough. In therapy, they finally realized that although they had not come from divorced homes, the dangers of the witch's gingerbread house had been just as real for them as for their son.

Finding the road home for two people confronted by their own devouring witches, but who desperately did not want to abandon and lose the children in their own care, was not an easy or short-term endeavor. The pebbles to show them the way home were not easily visible to them, but they were the values, time, love, and energy that they had wanted from their own parents. Giving these things to themselves while creating a family in which no one starved emotionally took strength and courage, and there were some detours and wanderings, as all seemed hopeless, or lost, at times. The task was not easy, but all four people are now happier. They make time for each other, listen and pay focused attention to each other, give praise when it is deserved, share sorrow at times, and share activities. Their home is now warm with genuine nourishment.

The pebbles of the "Hansel and Gretel" story are the positive things we find along the way during even the most deprived childhoods. Hearing someone say something that is true and loving, having someone make time to listen and to take delight in hearing our voice, listening to another person wanting to talk to us, having someone carve out time in their schedule for us, enjoying playful fun and joyous laughter, working with someone, crying together or being allowed to cry with someone else, witnessing the pain, and sharing sorrows and joys are experiences that feed us emotionally. We feel nourished and wealthy beyond our imaginations if we are truly loved and have someone we truly love. When we don't experience that as children, we get lost in a forest of false promises, imprisoned and devoured by the witches of addictions, self-loathing, and fake promises.

For the couple in this case illustration, both realized that what was wrong with their marriage was something that love and attention could mend, and that in the mending they would be stronger for having done the work together as a family. Not getting stuck in the belief which the school counselor held that stepfamilies just breed addictions and troubled children was one of the first steps. Realizing that millions of others had walked this path before them, and that they were not an abnormal family was also a part of the path that led them home.

The witch in this tale can also show up in the form of a well-meaning or judgmental friend who would be more than willing to convince themselves and all who would listen that all that is wrong with the family would be solved if the stepchildren left home. For example, sending them off to boarding school or letting the ex-spouse take them full time. Sometimes this is an inner witch in any stepparent who truly believes that the marriage would be perfect without kids and ex-spouses and the perceived "mess" they bring with them. The oven of this resentment and rage continues to be fed with this fuel. Sorting out how much of the family drama is directly related to the unique issues of a stepfamily, and how much is just the usual soup with families, is more productive. This sorting needs awareness and a tolerance for hearing comments that might sound like criticism from others.

I like the fact that the fairy tale "Hansel and Gretel," because of its different versions, shape-shifts from variations in which the original impoverished family is a biological mother and father with not enough resources to a stepmother and father. The poverty, not the marital relationship, is the issue, and how to recognize temptation and devouring energy while lost, lonely, and hungry is the lesson to learn. Hansel and Gretel are wiser for their wanderings, and the maps, such as the pebbles they followed, enable us as well to find our way home more effectively, and with fewer of us stuck forever in the land of bewitchment.

Chapter 8

Cinderella and the Issue of Favoritism

*The bond that links your true family is not one of blood,
but of respect and joy in each other's life. Rarely do members
of one family grow up under the same roof.*

—RICHARD BACH, *ILLUSIONS*

What or who is your favorite? In almost all aspects of life, people are encouraged to use their powers of discrimination to examine what they prefer. People happily talk about their favorite color, season, restaurant, vacation, sport, and actor or actress. No one is embarrassed to admit having a best friend, a favorite chair, a color they like best, a favorite song, hymn, or kind of music. It is part of being human to discriminate among objects and people, and to like some things and people better than others. People are equally happy to report on things they dislike, whether they hate boiled okra, a particular kind of music, a painting, or a person. It is natural and healthy to discriminate among acquaintances and decide who you like, love, trust, enjoy, and wish to spend time with, as well as who you find annoying, rude, boring, or untrustworthy. People who cannot discriminate are often victims of abandonment, violence, rape, and con artists, and they have few friends.

The ability to discriminate, which allows humans to bond with those they see as special and separate them from others, runs smack into present cultural myths that say people should love and like all their children equally, including stepchildren. The damage to self-esteem that occurs when a child knows that another sibling is the "favorite" is significant and can affect the whole family.

Sometimes this sense of favoritism is only a perception that may have little validity. Often in working with families, two siblings are both convinced the other is their father's or mother's favorite. The parents, for whatever reason, consciously or unconsciously, have encouraged a rivalry between the siblings that damages not only the relationship between the children, but creates a perception of favoritism that poisons the rest of the family and its ability to function respectfully and lovingly.

Parents can struggle with their own sense of their preferences, and often they not only fail to hide these, but they inadvertently send a message that one or another child is preferred simply in the natural process of rewarding achievements for traits that they wish to encourage in all their children. A statement such as "Your older brother always got A's in math—why are you failing?" may reflect the parent's frustration and hope that the younger child will do better with some competitive motivation. It also clearly states that the parent prefers A's to F's, and if the child identifies with his academic achievements, then the academically successful child will be viewed as the favorite.

I have heard this theme resound in families in which, for example, athletics, appearances, academics, financial success, or spirituality are highly valued. The child who is the prettier, the more athletic, or has saved his or her money more effectively may be viewed by the siblings and others as the "favorite," even though the parent has no intention of conveying such favoritism or even feels such a preference. As one parent stated, "I love them all equally, but my youngest daughter seems to go out of her way to make her life difficult. She skips classes, pierces every body part she can find, and now I find drugs in her purse. Her older sister is a model student and will probably get a full scholarship to college. How am I supposed to act as if their achievements are equal? They are not—but I love both of them equally." She chuckled and stated at one point, "I love them both the same, but one is sure easier to like, and she likes me. I don't think the younger one likes me at all!"

This agony for so many parents can play itself out even more strongly in stepfamily relationships, sometimes with more benign outcomes and sometimes with incredibly destructive ones. I have heard innumerable parents feeling ashamed and embarrassed to admit that they love their own children more than their stepchildren; and I repeatedly hear parents who are enraged that their new partner loves their new stepchild less than their own. This natural state of emotional connection needs to be accepted and the feelings and behaviors around these preferences addressed rather than denied.

Although we may change the wording in other family relationships in terms of our preferences and favoritism, in stepfamilies as nowhere else does admitting preferences produce such strong embarrassment and guilt. Most people can say that someone is their favorite aunt, uncle, cousin, or sibling, sometimes couched in "I am closer to my brother who is two years older than I am to the one who is five years younger." Most can nod and indicate that they might feel a "real" sisterly bond with a sister-in-law that they don't feel with their own sister, without anyone else acting horrified. But to admit that one prefers one's own offspring to those of one's spouse can be seen as a personal and moral failure by those outside the family system and as something that should be kept a shameful secret by those who are in a similar stepfamily boat.

In the stories that follow the motif of the fairy tale "Cinderella," the feelings of favoritism are described with little attempt to modify or hide the reality of the power these feelings have on all members of the family. In families where the stepparent does not have children of her or his own at the onset of the marriage, the intensity of committed love and focus on a child subsequently born may startle the parent who has only been a stepparent into recognizing for the first time how much more she or he loves his or her own biological offspring. If there is a genuine affection between the stepchild and stepparent before the new baby is born, this emotional response may not create anything more than a disturbing awareness in the parent, one that does not need to be acted upon. If there is friction already, the preference may elicit anger, jealousy, guilt, shame, and attempts to diminish the stepchild's presence in the family.

Cinderella

Once there was a man who had lost his wife. He then married a proud and haughty woman. She had two girls, who were equally

vain. By his first wife, he had a beautiful young daughter named
Ella, who was a girl of unparalleled goodness and sweet temper.
The stepmother and her daughters forced the first daughter to
complete all the housework. When the girl had done her work,
she sat in the cinders of the hearth, which caused her to be called
"Cinderella." The poor girl bore it patiently, but she dared not tell
her father, who would have scolded her; his wife controlled him
entirely.

One day the prince invited all the young ladies in the land to
a ball in order to choose a wife. The two stepsisters were invited,
and they gleefully planned their wardrobes. Although Cinderella as-
sisted them and dreamed of going to the dance, they taunted her
by saying a "maid" could never attend a ball.

As the sisters swept away to the ball, Cinderella cried in despair. Her fairy godmother magically appeared and vowed to assist
in helping Cinderella attend the ball. She turned a pumpkin into
a coach, mice into horses, a rat into a coachman, and lizards into
footmen. She then turned Cinderella's rags into a beautiful gown,
complete with a delicate pair of glass slippers. The godmother told
her to enjoy the ball, but to return before midnight, as the spells
would then be broken.

At the ball, the entire court was entranced by Cinderella, especially the prince, who never left her side. Unrecognized by her sisters, Cinderella remembered to leave before midnight. Back home,
Cinderella graciously thanked her godmother by singing. She then
greeted the stepsisters, who enthusiastically talked of nothing but
the beautiful girl at the ball.

When another ball was held the next evening, Cinderella again
attended with her godmother's help. The prince became even more
entranced. However, this evening she lost track of time and left only
at the final stroke of midnight, losing one of her glass slippers on
the steps of the palace in her haste. The prince chased her, but outside the palace, the guards had seen only a simple country wench
leave. The prince pocketed the slipper and vowed to find and marry
the girl to whom it belonged. Meanwhile, Cinderella kept the other
slipper, which had not disappeared when the spell had broken.

The prince tried the slipper on all the young women in the
land. When the prince arrived at Cinderella's villa, the stepsisters

tried on the slipper in vain. When Cinderella asked if she might try, the stepsisters taunted her. Naturally the slipper fit perfectly, and Cinderella produced the other slipper for good measure. The stepsisters begged for forgiveness, and Cinderella forgave them for their cruelties.

Cinderella returned to the palace, where she married the prince and the stepsisters married two lords.[1]

If there ever was a description of a reason not to marry when both partners have children, this is about as good as it gets! One child is an only daughter and has lost her mother. Her grief work about this loss is not finished, and she is not asked to participate at all in the creation of the new family. Once the stepfamily is formed she functions as a servant, perhaps a Roman idea of 'familia,' but not acceptable by today's norms. Why the man married the woman who dominates him will forever remain a mystery, and appropriately so, enabling all who have wondered what he sees in his new wife a chance to fill in the blanks with their own version. He may have married her for money, to have someone to take care of the house, for sex, or because he was lonely. As a therapist seeing clients with similar stories, I have heard them all. However, what seems to be missing for most when this pattern is engaged is any belief that there is a good reason for the marriage. Teenage girls are especially reluctant to accept that the home from which they are trying to separate has added stepfamily members. They are at a developmental stage during which they are moving toward their peers and away from their family, and it is normal to find one's parents "annoying, impossible, boring, old fashioned, and clueless." All of which needs to be said while rolling one's eyes! This means that the family as they knew it actually disappeared before they moved out emotionally, and they now push away from a totally foreign household, not from a familiar home, even if it was a single-parent home. If a child, such as Cinderella, has not finished grieving the loss of the original home, has a passively noninvolved father as described in this fairy tale, or can't believe that out of all the women in the world, their father chose the woman he did, then the potential for conflict escalates beyond the normal adjustment that every stepfamily goes through.

Some teen stepchildren feel that just at the time when they want to leave home to go to "balls" or parties with their friends, join clubs, go to college, or whatever else they have in mind that takes them away from their first homes, the sudden involvement of another woman and her children into their father's life threatens the sense that there is any real home to go to, or to leave. This pattern can emerge even when all family members involved have been out of the house for years and even when the children from the first marriage have children of their own. Holiday patterns, financial arrangements, relationships with grandchildren may all seem torn asunder, and all that is left is ashes and the need to clean up the mess that the intruders into the family have made. These children often feel as if they are doing all the work to maintain some sense of the old order and structure that existed before the "invasion," and they are truly living in the ashes of the hearth, the central place of warmth, nourishment, safety, and love, which hearths have symbolized for thousands of years.

The longing to go to the ball, to be part of the dance of life that moves young people out of their homes of origin and into their own lives, where they can marry their own princes and rule their own households, is a part of every teenage girl's dreams. Boys, too, find themselves in this pattern, wanting to make their way in the world and start their own families, but now feeling as if their developmental need to leave the safety of the first home is being rudely restricted by the demands of a stepparent who dominates the child's biological parent.

Case Illustration

A young man stated that his father and mother had promised him that they had a savings account for his college education, and that he would be able to go to the same Ivy League school his parents had attended. However, the parents divorced when he was in the tenth grade, and it was not until he began applying for colleges, after his dad had remarried and the young man had two stepsiblings, that the fact that the family savings had been consumed by the divorce expenses and the down payment for the new home they all lived in was revealed. Instead of his dream of going to college, join-ing a fraternity, and spending summers traveling, he was only able to afford to go to a state college, while living at home and working at a part-time job. He came into therapy when his tendency to fanta-size that somehow he would magically get his college dream back by gambling began to harm his academic successes and led only to increasing debt.

A woman told her own Cinderella story of being sent to board-ing school in the ninth grade when her parent's marriage began to deteriorate. She loved the boarding school and was finding the academics and sports challenging, the new friends warm and fun. Coming home while her parents were still married was "no picnic," but she was totally unprepared upon returning home for the sum-mer between her junior and senior years to find that not only were her parents divorcing, but her father had moved out to live with his mistress of many years and her two children by an earlier marriage. The young woman's mother was hurt, angry, and humiliated by the years of betrayal, and was planning to sell the family home and move to Seattle, where she felt she could resume her career in the airline industry that she had interrupted to raise a family.

The woman spent one Thanksgiving vacation with her mother in her tiny efficiency apartment in Seattle, listening to her mother's rage toward her ex-husband and complaints about the men she had been dating. The woman realized that with no social circle of her own in Seattle, she really did not feel at home at all with her mother. She also felt like Cinderella with her father and his new family. The young woman looked like her mother and strongly iden-tified with her mother's feeling that her father had been lying and playing a pretend game of trying to make the family work. It took very little more for the new stepmother to find herself hostile to her new stepdaughter and defensive of her own son and daughter, who were much happier in the new, big home with the man who had been a part-time dad for so many years. For them the new home was wonderful; for this young stepdaughter it was a cold, unwelcoming place. She tried hard to be pleasant and cooperative, but it felt like work and as if she were constantly cleaning up her father's mess, keeping some sense of family alive. She at one point looked up at me and said, "They are all having a ball, and I feel like

every day is just a grind of pretending it isn't work just to be nice
to these people."

So where does one find a fairy godmother that can make the
shape-shifting that is needed to have the tale come out well at the
end? For many young people in this situation, the fairy godmother
is the light side of the stepparent structure—another parental figure, not biologically related, who may be able to help the child
shape-shift, turning the dark attitudes and beliefs of their lives into
something magical and golden.

> Once the man began treatment for his gambling addiction, he
> met another recovering gambler at a meeting who seemed to see
> something special in the young man and helped him apply for schol-
> arships and grants, which allowed him to go to a top-notch school
> and live in an apartment just off campus. The young student never
> fulfilled his dream of joining a fraternity, but later wondered if that
> was a blessing. He was proud of his work history during college
> and was given a job and money for graduate school by a firm he
> interned with during his summer between his junior and senior
> years. He joked that if it hadn't been for the divorce and his own
> poor behavior, he might have become one of those drunken party
> boys who were still without direction or a job. Instead, he found a
> series of mentors who got him on the fast track for a Ph.D. in engi-
> neering and employed doing something lucrative that he loves. He
> hardly saw himself as unlucky. He stated that he loved this dance of
> life, and was wearing shoes he never would have dreamed of, prior
> to his parent's divorce, but he ruefully acknowledged it was not
> always easy and all family members involved behaved badly for a
> while. He wondered if, in fact, he would have happily gone to the Ivy
> League school of his parent's dreams, partied, and studied enough
> to get through, but not enough to do much other than go to work
> in his father's business, something which he saw as deadly. Both his
> parents seem happier in their new lives, and he actually liked his
> stepsiblings, who saw him as some kind of role model with his new
> job and were already calling him "Doctor."
>
> The woman, too, found her fairy godmother in an unexpected
> place. She found a part-time job through one of her friends with

a family from South America who needed a nanny and tutor for their young children. Although her Spanish was not much more than what high school and college kids learn in order to pass a required class, she found while working for the family that she was actually good at languages and loved the family stories of traveling to other countries for the work that the father did. The mother was also educated and had found jobs when her husband was assigned to new countries. The two women bonded over their love for the children and the young woman's new fascination with the rest of the world. She changed her career goals entirely and now is working toward a degree in international business, spending her summers doing internships in a variety of places that her mentor's contacts provided. She talked about the journey to where she is now as being difficult and, at times, painful, but was also convinced that she was having a "ball" and studying for a career she didn't know existed, but which became her "soul's work."

People who have experienced something that resembles this Cinderella-like pattern of psychological growth often talk of "having a ball," or not "being asked to dance," of wishing they could go some place or have experiences to which they feel they should have been invited or to which they are entitled, and now resent having to work to achieve them. They talk about shoes they were supposed to fill, a relationship that doesn't fit but pinches or restricts them in some way, unconsciously using the metaphors in the Cinderella story. Sometimes they are Cinderella; sometimes they are the sisters who don't want to work.

Shoes have universally been a symbol of what we do in the world, our status, and how mobile we are. To be shoeless for most people throughout history meant impoverishment or at least limitations in how far they could travel or in what they could do for a living. If you look at someone's shoes, you can tell a lot about what they are planning to do or have done recently. People do not wear high heels to go jogging or sneakers to go skiing. Flip-flops make a statement, as do cowboy boots. Cinderella's glass slipper for the tiny foot is a red velvet slipper in some cultures and other colored footwear in other languages. Cinderella has small, dainty feet, and she can wear glass slippers; despite her role as servant, she is meant to have a better life. Someone with large, calloused feet was more likely to be a day laborer or even a slave or field hand in the days when only the wealthy and privileged wore shoes. The historic custom of binding feet in China so that the upper-class woman had tiny, relatively useless feet was more extreme than the cultural norms for dainty feet in Europe, but it seems to be universal to think that a foot that is petite and callous free implies a standing in the social structure that bare, calloused, bigger feet do not have. The slippers can also imply grace and an ability to walk lightly in the world. Glass is transparent and only a recent addition to the fairy tale. The story itself is probably older than the word glass, and some other material, such as gold, may have preceded it. But glass was a symbol of wealth and was a barrier or boundary that still allowed one to see through it without feeling the rain, wind, heat, or cold. Glass was special because of its transparency: it hid nothing about Cinderella's true feet or standing in the world.

The goal for Cinderella is to find her unique place in the world that honors her special and royal qualities, and the average person rarely sets this type of goal. Many people will not take the risks in order to find their way to the ball uninvited or invited. They will not seek their own special place, and will settle for the images given to them by the culture, or well-meaning parents, or stepparents who cannot see or admit to their special qualities. As young people, they may continue to think that their only jobs are to serve their parental homes, rather than find their unique ways in the world, to dance with their own destinies. The fact that Cinderella is a stepchild offers her a unique possibility to do this task, which so many people, because they feel valued and are comfortable in their assigned roles, do not attempt.

Cinderella-like patterns are innumerable. Stepfamilies often unconsciously resonate with jealousy and competition between children and stepparents. They seem to be living a mythological script, enchanted by the universal, or archetypal, energy that is deeply embedded in our very nature, giving us an awareness of who is related to us by blood and who is not. Those bereft of that biological connection may be aware on many levels, some barely conscious, of the number of conditions on the steprelationships in which they are engaged when compared to those biological bonds, which seem to make so many fewer demands. Babies seem able to recognize their mother's heartbeat, and this may account for the perplexing sense of abandonment that some adopted children experience when given to an adoptive mother even immediately after birth.

One of the first signs of development is the child's fear of strange faces and relief at the sight of his or her own mother. Children left with a new babysitter may scream in despair as their mother disappears. It is instinctive to be wary of strangers. *Strange* is originally from a Latin word meaning *external*, and for many children the sudden arrival of a stepparent is a violation of their perceived safety, because the person who is external, or strange, is being brought into the center of their place of safety. All biological and childhood conditioning about not speaking to or including strangers is being violated, and no one is talking about this danger except perhaps the stepchild who feels threatened.

A lesson to be learned from the Cinderella story is to allow the old pattern to be grieved. The loss of the first family structure deserves respect, and time should be honored for tears, anger, bargaining, denial, and all the other stages of grief. Parents who feel so guilty that they cause their children pain because they, on levels subtle and not so subtle, insist that the children "are just fine," that "everyone will be happier," or that the parents "can give you (the child) something to cry about," do not allow this process to move forward. There is nothing wrong with suffering when a loss occurs. In fact, it is unhealthy when no pain, sorrow, or grief is expressed when parents separate and divorce. Some children do act almost numb, especially if there has been strife and tension before the decision to end the marriage; others act out, hoping that the parents will bond around their mutual displeasure with the "black sheep" of the family. Some regress to earlier stages of development, such as in wetting a bed or choosing toys and games they have long outgrown. All of these are ways of expressing the fear of change, the real pain of loss, and the feeling that no matter how much better things may be in the future, now life is not so hot.

A gradual introduction of the new person into the lives of the children who are about to earn the title "step" is imperative if the transition is to be even vaguely pleasant, and even that will not guarantee anything akin to a "smooth ride" for the first two or three years. The parent who is marrying or planning to live with a new partner is choosing this person for his or own needs and longings for romance and companionship. She or he may suddenly feel as though the new partner is the person they are closest to on earth. To the children this person is a total stranger, uninvited and unwished for by the rest of the family, but this is often overlooked by the parents as the first surge of in-love hormones wash through the couple's system. The hormones are like physical, archetypal patterns that can make one feel one has met one's soul mate, even though one knows nothing about the other, and may even give one a druglike high, of feeling that one is unconditionally loved. The rest of the family is certainly not feeling this surge of connectedness, and often while Dad may feel like he sees his soul in the eyes of his beloved, the children more often see a wicked stepmother ready to devour or destroy all that is precious to them. This person may be seen as the final destroyer of any possibility that their parents would get back together. At the very least, they see a stranger, someone external to their lives, and they have been trained not to trust strangers.

When stepparents avoid the fact that the new member is for others a stranger, refusing to discuss the natural animosity, the threats to security, and grief the children may be feeling, they can create a spoiling resentment bubbling just below the surface, a distrust that is hard to dissolve, and even a bitter competition between stepparent and biological parent, which has its own cost. Some stepmothers are so immobilized by the fear of showing their prejudices or feeling any jealousy from their stepchildren that they become powerless and fearful of applying discipline or restrictions, and thus become the spoiling "Disneyland" parent. Children are often aware of this competition between father and stepfather, or mother and stepmother, or between the parents themselves, and the poison of the competition can create an atmosphere that is stifling for everyone. Children will manipulate it at times, and find that if one parent says, "No!" another one may say, "Yes!" This splitting behavior is not healthy for anyone. I have heard as many versions of rationalizations, real and imagined, for the dissolution of a stepfamily that revolve around kids with no restrictions, as I have heard of jealousy and overt competition. The ground between tyrannizing children and letting them tyrannize adults is wide open, and neither pole serves anyone well.

Biological fathers and mothers often increase the power of this setup for divorce by refusing to allow the new marriage partner any rights to discipline, set limits, or provide structure for children. Stepparents who do not feel they have the right to demand the same respect and decent social interactions that a teacher or coach or clerk in a store can insist upon are headed for a land mine of problems. Those that conversely do little to restrain their feelings of jealousy and fuel the competition between stepsiblings, stepparents, and children produce an age-old pattern of bad outcomes for the family. Yet the ability of the psyche to overcome all odds and be stronger for travails is repeated time and again in these tales. How to achieve the good outcome for the individuals involved while maintaining a viable, loving family structure is a task that demands personal growth and maturity. Stepparenting is not for the faint of heart or for those who do not see the opportunities in the difficulties. As in so many of the myths and fairy tales, the problem lies not in the feelings, but in the behaviors associated with them, and in the inability of those experiencing the feelings to self-soothe, self-regulate their emotions and make ethical behavior choices while accepting that their emotions are real.

The difficulties in designing a structure or pattern that makes step- and biologically related family members feel at home takes time and thought. The personalities, strengths, and weaknesses of the members and of the family itself need to be honored. Birth order is often important. Children who are used to being the oldest of a set of siblings who suddenly find themselves one of the younger ones often experience that loss of status as challenging emotionally. Allowing the older new stepsiblings time to adapt to the idea of having an older brother or sister in a way that is bonding for all takes some appreciation of the fact that these children may feel drafted; they did not volunteer for the job. Sometimes children find it easier to project their resentment of loss of status, loss of family image, loss of space, and loss of time with their parent onto other children rather than tackle the adults in the family. However, most children want friends, they want to belong to a group or pack, and using this energy can enable them to feel they have just found new, permanent friends. Making sure that each child is aware of some of the advantages of having more siblings is something that parents can provide consciously and lovingly to the point where the new family image becomes inviting instead of "strange." Introducing each new member of the proposed family to each other gradually, as one would introduce any new set of friends, helps this process go more smoothly.

The feeling that someone is external to one's family is transformed into inclusiveness by trust building. Meaningful trust comes with predictability over time. To trust someone unknown immediately is a symptom of deeper psychological problems. People need to be able to trust close relationships and to be able to count on people to be predictable in ways that are important, but this trust comes slowly through experience. Most people mistrust those around them in specific areas where there is unpredictability. It is healthy to know when not to trust. One may trust one friend to be on time, but not to pay back loans in a timely manner. One may trust one person's opinions about the stock market, but not about vacation spots. To expect children to trust a total stranger without some history of enjoyable and healthy interchanges and time together is asking the child to go against all the other training parents and adults have given the child about getting to know someone before they open up to them or trust them.

The father in the Cinderella tale does not take her feelings or longings into account in bringing home a stepmother and two stepsisters. It appears that the two new stepsisters are also not consulted about their feelings of including Ella. The absence of the father in this process is repeated in daily present-day life with parents who date people their children don't know or ever meet until the parents have decided that this person will be a committed partner. This role modeling is fraught with potential problems, as it is often the children of these kinds of relationships who follow in the parental pattern and date people their parents know nothing about. The lack of intimacy and sharing is repeated. Cinderella, at the end of the fairy tale, marries the prince without so much as a conversation with her father, who has virtually abandoned her. The patterns created by the parent continue.

Children do not have total veto power over their parent's dating life, any more than they will tolerate easily a veto from their parents when they date in college or after they leave the family home. The rules for how to include family in one's dating life in a way that is respectful of everyone concerned are often passed down from one generation to another. There is a middle ground that is not rigid, but respectful. Dates can be introduced as friends, and stories about why the parent is enjoying the friendship can be told in a way that is appropriate to the age of the child. Just as most parents want to know who their children's friends are, and ask for appropriate information about why their child considers his or her friends more than acquaintances, children want and need this information about their parents' close friends, romantic or otherwise.

Acknowledging jealousy, envy, fear of change, and the grief and pain that goes with this kind of transition leaves room to experience the joy and pleasure that new friendships can bring. There is nothing more special to a future stepparent, who has developed a friendship of his or her own with a future stepchild, than having the child ask if he or she can call that person Mom or Dad. The joyful expressions I see on my client's and friends' faces when they have patiently done the work of befriending a future stepchild, who is now also inviting them into the new family structure, is worth all the patience and delay of a marriage or premature move.

This in no way implies there won't be rough times when both stepparent and stepchild wish the other one would "drop dead." But that can be true of all friendships, and even sometimes between biological parents and children, although admittedly much less often and with a more fleeting flash across the brain.

The tale of Cinderella warns all of us to take the multiple layers of relationships into account in starting a stepfamily. It warns us of sibling rivalries, of the preferences that biological parents have for their own children, and of the dangers of not involving everyone in the complex business of creating a family unit with so many members. It also assures us that those who play the role of Cinderella can find mentors, or "fairy godmothers," outside of the home who will allow them to find love and opportunities they might not have found if all went more smoothly at home in the first place. The mentors are usually older, more experienced people who seem to know what a younger person needs to grow through the challenges of life, and not be overwhelmed by them. They do not spoil them with more than they need to become independent. They can be a boss, a teacher, counselor, pastor, older relative, or friend, but they often appear when things seem the darkest. It is in the struggle to adapt to difficult situations that people often experience the most personal growth and develop their own wisdom. "No pain, no gain" may be a motto for physical exercise, but it is often only too true for psychological growth as well.

Chapter 9

The Problem of Power Without Love: Snow White and the Perfect Stepparent

"Don't let what you can't do stop you from doing what you can do."

—JOHN WOODEN

The use and abuse of power in any family, whether step or not, is the subject of endless stories, research studies, and debates and is seldom discussed without high emotion by all participating in the conversations. Parents have immense power over their children in terms of lifestyle, values, family goals, financial resources, rules, and norms, as well as the rewards and punishments attending such that reinforce appropriate behaviors in the system and attempt to extinguish inappropriate behaviors.

The fairy tales are quite clear that power used without respect or concern for the child results in bad outcomes for one or more of the fairy tale characters, and it is usually the stepmother or stepfather figure who loses, dies, or is banished. In contrast, mutual respect between the child and stepparent figure almost always has a "happily ever after" fairy tale ending. The endless history of oral tradition, in which storytellers handed down fairy tales to future generations for centuries, addresses a question that is fraught with emotion today. How does one discipline children? The complications around discipline increase with stepchildren, who often see the stepparent as a stranger and intruder into their world and whose permanency in their lives depends totally on the relationship with the biological parent. What fairy tales clearly state over and over again is that even the youngest child can tell the difference between loving guidance and power games that serve the control needs of the parent rather than the growth of the child. Within stepfamilies, this differentiation is even more starkly outlined.

The most recent wisdom among researchers in this area is that children are not that different from adults. Positive reinforcement produces the most long-lasting behavioral changes, and punishment produces the least. Punishment, when it is humiliating, terrifying, shaming, or violent, produces temporary cooperation from a person of any age, but in both life and in fairy tales the reliability of what is said by the fearful person is minimal. For example, in the language of fairy tales, deceiving the bully or adult who is cruel is considered a positive survival skill. In the world of myth, lying to save one's self is a skill learned from living with abusive people. Today's research in this regard validates thousands of years of mythological wisdom: Children who are spanked are more skilled at lying, at figuring out what the power figure wants to hear.[1] The truth is less important to all of us who fear physical harm if the truth is not what the potentially violent person wants to hear.

I have often been baffled by the high emotional charge and defensive, distorted thinking that accompanies any discussion of corporal punishment. Most of those with whom I interact, both professionally and personally, who were born prior to 1950, find the idea of raising children without spanking them novel. However, some adamantly disagree with any policy of not spanking, even though the evidence is overwhelming that the outcomes are better for all concerned without corporal punishment.[2]

In all fairness, the mythological stories are sometimes brutal, and most mothers and fathers do not see themselves becoming the large monster climbing down the beanstalk or the witch asking to feel the fat on a child's finger. But heroes and heroines in myths and fairy tales and in our present-day stories and movies of heroic people often believe in their ability to lie for the "right reasons." What is clear is that power wielded abusively and lack of respect result in the victim of such treatment using deception to deceive the abuser and to protect the innocent. Whether in movies like *Defiance* or *The Terminator*, the numerous James Bond movies, or the fairy tale–like story in *Slumdog Millionaire*, deception in the face of evil or physical danger is considered good and virtuous to us. As a child who was taught the "rule" that lying was a bad thing and who was proud of my belief that "I was not a liar," I remember reading *The Diary of a Young Girl* by Anne Frank and then listening to stories told with pride of my great-great-grandparents' involvement with the Underground Railroad and moving slaves to Canada. The ethics of lying suddenly became very complex.

All children at some point do realize that the virtue of not telling a lie comes smack up against the natural human tendency to lie to protect yourself. In one recent movie, *Goya's Ghosts*, a young heroine who is being tortured finally breaks and screams: "What is the truth?" To stop the torture she is willing to say anything her abductors want to hear. On a much less dramatic level, even the most mildly bullied person searches to say what the bully wants to hear to prevent an attack, whether it is a verbal, emotional, or physical attack. All children develop this skill to varying degrees. The more severe and repeated the corporal punishment or the verbal or emotional assaults from a powerful parent, the more effectively children develop a vigilance that focuses more on "What does the parent want to hear?" than on "What is the truth?" Children who are repeatedly caught lying at early ages have experienced parenting with threats and punishments, often by parents who are doing what was done to them without any awareness of other methods of discipline that work more effectively. Stepchildren, particularly, are less ambivalent about seeing the abusive side of the stepparent than biological children; they often see the hostility and rage of a stepparent without the longing to be loved and accepted that biological children have. The emotional connection of a lifetime of dependency, need, and desire for love may result in a biological child feeling conflicting loyalties to their own safety and to the harsh parent. Stepchildren who do not have the emotional bond of longing, love, and a need for a biological parent may feel that the stepparent's violence is further justification for the child to assault the marriage ties, and they recognize quickly when an adult's behavior toward children would be illegal outside of the home. As one stepchild said with painful puzzlement, "My dad was arrested when he punched my mom, and we couldn't see him for a long time. When my stepfather hits me, he should be arrested, too."

Respect and the feelings of being safe and admired are earned. Respect as a stepparent always needs to be earned, not automatically given because of the title. Many well-meaning parents have started down a very hostile path by insisting that they deserve respect (meaning obedience and deferential treatment) because they have suddenly assumed the title of wife or husband. Statements such as, "You will do what you are told because I am your parent," or "You will do what I said because I said so," or "You will act with respect because I am in charge," serve little purpose in developing a close relationship with anyone, let alone a child who is unsure about their feelings toward the person married to their parent. Statements such as this imply a threat, which distances and shuts down intimacy. They seldom serve any relationship very well, but they are worse than useless in steprelationships.

The truth is that adults are no different from children in attempting to protect themselves through deception. If their perception is that they will be punished, embarrassed, rejected, or threatened, they will also weigh the appropriateness of telling the truth or telling the person in charge of their anticipated bad outcome whatever that person wants to hear. Society has endless laws protecting adults from being slapped, stripped, spanked, belted, or punched. There are also laws about slander, improper firings, imprisonment, sexual harassment, and other crimes that for some reason are generally not seen as illegal or even improper when done to small children by their parents. If what is being done to a child by an adult does not result in charges for felony assault when that would happen if the same things were done to another adult, then something is dreadfully wrong. Families in which punishment includes physical pain inflicted by the bigger person have a tendency to guard the truth, sharing such only when it is clearly safe to do so, whether they are stepfamilies or not. This guardedness is done for self-protection from a perceived unpleasant result. In the name of family loyalty, dark secrets are kept out of fear. Some of this deception is healthy and normal in casual social interaction, often referred to as "white lies," and these are skills all people learn, but it is not the language of intimacy and mutual respect. It is the language of fear and power.

"Snow White and the Seven Dwarfs" is a fairy tale that emphasizes the need to lie and the dangers of being naive around a person with the power to harm you if you tell the truth. The value of hiding and doing your own internal work is another theme in the tale. The fact that Snow White ended up in a coma because of her naive innocence and honesty, and for her inability to lie or determine when she was being lied to, is not lost on some level of every child's consciousness. Children are humans learning how to become successful, happy adults. Living in a world where power rather than love dominates is not intimacy, but it is normal in many human interchanges. Adults, for the most part, can chose to leave, divorce, quit, or cease friendships that become dominated by the needs of another who wields the power. Children, who must wait until they can leave, can, as in the fairy tale, go to "sleep," developing attachment and dissociative states in order to avoid the intolerable pain.

All of us want control in some area of our lives, and certainly, children can sometimes challenge any adult's sense of control. There will always be times when we resent those who disrupt our peace and routine, and when we feel jealousy and rage toward those who make us look bad, foolish, or out of control. Such feelings can occur when relating to children, as they do in other social relationships throughout our lives. As adults, we can choose our behaviors, and those behaviors determine our effectiveness in changing an unpleasant situation, resolving a problem, or teaching a child something he or she needs to know. When parents tell me, in my role as a therapist, "I lost it!" they are usually referring to having an intense feeling of being powerless, embarrassed, belittled, or interrupted. Actually, the feelings were not what they "lost." What was lost was control over their behavior. They may temporarily feel better spanking a child and reexerting their sense of mastery over a difficult situation and their power over the child. Parents can get behavioral compliance, but the loss of trust and honesty increases with each time "losing it" occurs.

You can see the outcome of this kind of parenting decades later in adults who are more worried about saying the right thing, or discovering what someone wants to hear, rather than caring what the truth is. Healthy adults weigh both what is true and what is appropriate to share. However, when a child is abused, he or she can develop a hypersensitive psychological antennae and will often focus on the needs of others out of fear for themselves if they fail to give others what they want or need, while having no idea what they need themselves. They can, if the punishments are constant and harsh, be very good at people pleasing, placating, and truly have no sense of their own identity except in those roles. Likewise, children who were punished often carry an exaggerated fear of what others think, or whether who they are will result in rejection, humiliation, or some other equally unpleasant outcome.

Children who are guided respectfully and given positive reinforcement for desired behaviors, and whose feelings, no matter how unpleasant, are mirrored without judgment, tend to be more open with their parents. The first person they consult on any important issue is often their parents, throughout their lifetimes. Adults who were punished more than praised by their parents, however, may have much more guarded relationships with others, sharing little. One of the gifts of the human spirit is that love can override much of the tendency to feel fearful in intimate situations; therefore, up to a point, we can all forgive the times when loved ones "lose it" and say things they later regret or "didn't mean." Asking forgiveness goes a long way toward normalizing our lives and regaining broken trust.

The problem continues when the abuse of power over a child is never addressed, and the child and adult remain in some state of tension, with the child still fearful that they could be humiliated, judged harshly, or harmed physically or emotionally when some "truth" is revealed. The number of people I have worked with and known who do not share information with their parents due to fear of rejection is immense. Even as older adults, telling a parent of a job loss, a financial difficulty, a pending divorce, or even a change in church membership can become "truths" not shared.

Parents need to use and model age-appropriate discipline. Discipline is a word related to the same root that produced the word "disciple." Disciples are not made by spanking, hitting, washing a mouth out with soap, or scaring someone else. Discipline does not mean ignoring bad behavior, and it implies work, dedication, and commitment. A better method for creating disciples of a disciplined life is to reward good behaviors and validate unpleasant feelings because although punishment produces compliance with its often temporary relief, it seldom transfers to other situations and doesn't produce open, trusting, problem-solving children who feel they can rely on their parents to help them with the complex problems of daily life.

Family dynamic theories, fairy tales, and myths are clear that the greater the danger to self-esteem experienced in a person's living situation, no matter what age, the greater the number of secrets for protection there will be, and the harder it will be for the person to trust him or herself and those he or she loves. The bullied child can grow into a generous, open adult with some heroic psychological effort, but in both fairy tales and families, the parents and stepparents of a child having experienced such a childhood are rejected. In terms of real relationships, the young adult finds other places to establish his or her own kingdom, psychologically and physically.

Strong, trusting relationships at home create a safe place to experience ourselves and practice relating, so we can move into the adult world with confidence. Safety involves a sense that you are respected as a person and member of a family and community. In our culture and language, we often use words such as "respect," "love," and "honor" as if they are interchangeable. Power is a shadow twin to all of them, and often this twin is never mentioned openly. Respect without fear or respect with love and admiration are very different feelings from respecting the power of another person without love. Loving respect based on trust and admiration elicits different behaviors and loyalty than respect driven by fear. Parents and bosses, teachers and spouses often get this dynamic confused and enmeshed, as do people in fairy tales.

To be honored and obeyed without question is not respectful of most human interactions, unless the person doing the obeying knows exactly what the parameters of the obedience are. Usually that kind of obedience is time or task limited. Respect is often given the same way. A person may respect someone's skill, knowledge, or ethics without respecting other aspects of his or her behaviors or attitudes. Families, especially stepfamilies, push our limits in learning to honor and respect another human being who lives in the same space and same social constellation, but is sometimes not a person of our choice. However, behaving and acting in a respectful manner toward other human beings is a social skill vitally necessary, one of the disciplines of being a successful member of society. Whatever doubts a person may have about their feelings toward another, acting disrespectfully is seldom an appropriate response to those feelings. That said, it is often daunting to a stepparent and a stepchild to act respectfully toward a human being they initially don't like or see as a threat. To accomplish this task is a gift that seems to be exceptionally well developed in many stepchildren. It is learned in their homes in a way that most children in homes with only biological parents do not experience.

Honoring and respecting the rights, the developmental process, and the needs and hopes of a group of people with little choice in being part of the group is immensely difficult under the best of circumstances, and is even more challenging in stepfamilies. But it is a skill all adults experience in classrooms and careers. As adults, we can limit the time we spend with someone—quit a job, leave a church, or end a friendship when we find it hard to respect or like a person or a group. Children have no such choices, although a few have "fired" their parents when in their teens and courts do support their emancipation. This is not a goal of a successful family. Children naturally long to be loved and to be guided positively in the process of becoming happy, successful adults. They want and need to be successful disciples of successful, mature adults, but often find themselves in a land of emotional starvation and extreme danger in the process of growing up. Fairy tales and myths clearly describe the emotional and behavioral traps that can make life difficult for stepchildren and parents. Cinderella suffers verbal abuse, threats, and abandonment; Snow White suffers abuse and attempted murder at the hands of her jealous stepmother. The Greek gods, as children, were often hidden in the homes of foster families from raging stepparents and parents alike. The list goes on; the warning is often clear of the lack of family bonding and of adult stepchildren at some point finding their own vengeance in an ongoing cycle of violence.

Further study of the Stockholm response, in which people attach emotionally to their kidnappers or abusers who hold them prisoner, shows how similar it can be for children in homes where their physical safety is not guaranteed and their physical-body boundaries are violated. The relationship between this syndrome and the loyalty and sometimes desperate attachment that battered women and children who have been treated with violence have toward the captor, abusive spouse, or abusive parent is probably the same type of psychological response. The gratitude that naturally occurs when there is a cessation of pain, and the desire to have the person in power stop causing pain, can lead toward behaviors that mock love and respect. Acting like the omega wolf or dog in a pack that grovels in submission in order to be allowed to survive by the alpha animal seems to be a mammalian response, designed to assure survival in dangerous situations. Modeling a parenting style on this type of power structure is unadvisable. In my forty years as a therapist, I have never worked with a battered woman who was not spanked and slapped as a child. Convincing a woman whose life is in danger that violence is not part and parcel of loving relationships is difficult. People who cut themselves, hit themselves, and scar themselves seem to share this same history to varying degrees. I have not worked with as many men or women who perpetrate violence on their spouses and others, but the ones I have worked with were treated violently as children, and the longing to be in the power position and in control in a relationship continues to create an endless stream of angry and hurt children and adults.

The learning process these situations create can lead to disaster or to a set of unique skills and a depth of understanding of complex systems in which people who are not necessarily together by choice or common ground survive and thrive. Diplomacy skills can be learned much more thoroughly than in a group in which all share a common history and biology. As humans, we find it much easier to get along with those with whom we share common values, history, ancestry, and biases, than with those with whom we don't. In fairy tales and in real life, the challenge to ego strength is to enjoy someone who has different values, history, and biases. For a stepparent to accept a child who says, "My dad is cooler than you are!" and love him or her for his or her loyalty to the birth parent is much harder than to hear that child say, "You are the coolest dad in the world!"

We are entering the world of narcissism, with its gifts and its injuries.

Snow White and the Seven Dwarfs

Once upon a time, as a queen sits sewing at her window, she pricks her finger on her needle and a drop of blood falls on the snow that had fallen on her ebony window frame. As she looks at the blood on the snow, she says to herself, "Oh, how I wish that I had a daughter who had skin white as snow, lips red as blood, and hair black as ebony." Soon after that, the queen gives birth to a baby girl who has skin white as snow, lips red as blood, and hair black as ebony. They name her Princess Snow White. As soon as the child is born, the queen dies.

Soon after, the new king takes a new wife, who is beautiful but very vain. The queen possesses a magical mirror that answers any question, to which she often asks, "Mirror, mirror on the wall, who in the land is fairest of all?" to which the mirror always replies, "You, my queen, are fairest of all." But when Snow White reaches the age of seven, she becomes as beautiful as a spring day, and when the queen asks her mirror, it responds, "Queen, you are full fair, 'tis true, but Snow White is fairer than you." In another version of this story, the mirror simply replies, "Snow White is the fairest of them all."

The queen becomes jealous, and orders a huntsman to take Snow White into the woods to be killed. She demands that the huntsman return with Snow White's heart as proof of his killing. The huntsman takes Snow White into the forest, but after raising his knife to stab her, he finds himself unable to kill her. Instead, he lets her go, telling her to flee and hide, and brings the queen the heart of a young deer, which is then prepared by the cook and eaten by the queen.

In the forest, Snow White discovers a tiny cottage belonging to seven dwarfs, where she rests. There, the dwarfs take pity on her, saying, "If you will keep house for us, and cook, make beds, wash, sew, and knit, and keep everything clean and orderly, then you can stay with us, and you shall have everything that you want." They warn her to take care and let no one in when they are away delving in the mountains. Meanwhile, the queen asks her mirror once again, "Who's the fairest of them all?" and is horrified to learn that Snow White is not only alive and well and living with the dwarfs, but is still the fairest of them all.

Three times the queen disguises herself and visits the dwarfs' cottage while they are away during the day, trying to kill Snow White. First, disguised as a peddler, the queen offers colorful stay-laces, and laces Snow White up so tight that she faints, causing the queen to leave her for dead. Snow White is revived by the dwarfs, however, when they loosen the laces. Next, the queen dresses as a different old woman and brushes Snow White's hair with a poisoned comb. Snow White again collapses, but again is saved by the dwarfs. Finally, the queen makes a poisoned apple, and in the disguise of a farmer's wife, offers it to Snow White. When she is hesitant to accept it, the queen cuts the apple in half, eats the white part and gives the poisoned red part to Snow White. She eats the apple eagerly and immediately falls into a deep stupor. When the dwarfs find her, they cannot revive her, and they place her in a glass coffin, assuming that she is dead.

Time passes, and a prince traveling through the land sees Snow White. He strides to her coffin. The prince is enchanted by her beauty and instantly falls in love with her. He begs the dwarfs to let him have the coffin. The prince's servants carry the coffin away. While doing so, they stumble on some bushes, and the movement causes the piece of poisoned apple to dislodge from Snow White's throat, awakening her. The prince then declares his love for her, and soon a wedding is planned.

The vain queen, still believing that Snow White is dead, once again asks her mirror who is the fairest in the land, and yet again the mirror disappoints her by responding that "You, my queen, are fair; it is true. But the young queen is a thousand times fairer than you."

Not knowing that this new queen is indeed her stepdaughter, the queen arrives at the wedding, and her heart fills with the deepest of dread when she realizes the truth.

As punishment for her wicked ways, a pair of heated iron shoes are brought forth with tongs and placed before the queen. She is then forced to step into the iron shoes and dance until she falls down dead.[2]

The narcissistic need to be seen as the best is clearly illustrated in this fairy tale. Narcissism in its healthiest form is an ability to see and care for oneself, with self-awareness but without negating the place of others in one's life, and accepting oneself and others without constant, unnecessary competition. Narcissistically impaired people lean on others for self-esteem and value in ways that drain and exhaust others. When a person is in the land of magical mirrors which tell him or her that he or she is the best or the smartest or that their ideas and attitudes or religious practices are not only the best, but of more value than those of others, which then also carries a response of rage at any threat to the above, then he or she is in the land of pathological narcissism. A need for validation and admiration, at its most extreme, turns into blind, killing rage with a desire to devour the life of any person who threatens the fragile sense of self. Narcissists often are described as having "big egos," which are displayed along with an apparent sense of entitlement. Actually, their egos, in Jungian terms, are weak and need constant reassurance. They have a fragile sense of self, which may appear as a grandiosely inflated concept of themselves in an effort to protect the limited sense of self-worth they do have.

The pathologically narcissistic stepmother or stepfather (as the fairy tale can apply to both parents) needs constant reassurance of specialness, and any threat or perceived insult from the child elicits an attack by the stepparent. This slight can be simply that the other parent wants to spend one-on-one time with his or her child or that the child disagrees with something the stepparent says. The issue is seldom physical beauty, although it can be a simple statement by another that the child is more beautiful, talented, or special in a way that results in the narcissist thinking she or he has placed second. This is not tolerated, and the severity of the narcissism is directly related to the intensity of the rage.

There are four ways the stepmother in this tale tries to remove the threat of the child's sense of self. The first is to attempt to rid herself of the child altogether, to have her killed by a huntsman and then to eat the child's heart. Children often feel as if they are in danger of being consumed by the needs of the parent figure, so that their love of life is gone. Feeling as if the stepparent is always hunting for things to attack, many children flee into the relative safety of homework, friends, drugs, or in worst cases flee from home to live on the streets. Protective biological parents often intervene at this stage and another divorce ensues, or in many cases, the other half of the divorced couple becomes the source of refuge. Many children feel as if the new stepparent killed their ability to have a warm relationship with their own father or mother, who is now focused on keeping peace in the house and is endlessly answering the question put to the magic mirror. For either partner to be stuck in an endless ritual of, "Yes, dear," "Whatever you say, dear," "Of course you are right, you know best, that is just perfect," is to be trapped in a heartless job or mirroring what the stepparent wants to hear. Stepfamilies are not the only families to play out this ritual, but the mirroring ritual can be more dramatic in stepfamilies. Biological loyalties and a sense of enmeshment with a child more often occur in families of origin.

The three final attempts by the queen to destroy the threat to her sense of power parallel almost all narcissistic family relationships. The first motif is the corset that is too tight. The person being fooled by the disguised queen often feels as though he or she can't breathe or as if they are walking on eggshells. Restricted emotions, no sense of power, and the inability to breathe deeply are all common feelings for them. Clients will tell me that the air was so tense that they were glad to get away and get some breathing room, or that they didn't dare breathe, or that they held their breath waiting for the next thing to happen. All of these statements are quotes from people who have encountered a narcissist person at their seemingly sweetest, acting innocent and harmless, but all the while only making room only for his or her opinions, attitudes, and ideas.

The second motif is the poisoned comb, and hair, like thought, is what comes out of our heads. The way that the old woman straightens out or rearranges the child's thinking function is poisonous. When people try to arrange their thoughts to please such a person, they begin to make statements such as, "I am going crazy. I remember what happened so differently, but she or he keeps telling me I am wrong," or "I didn't mean what she says I did," or "I don't dare tell her or him what I think," or "Maybe I am wrong about what happened." There is a poisonous cloud of self-doubt that pervades the thoughts of the young person. Those resigned to the situation often only respond, "Whatever," which is one of the most common statements given in response to the narcissistic person who can't tolerate differences in thought. Why bother looking for true thoughts or feelings? The child gives up and stops thinking for him- or herself, at least until the parent is out of sight. The child is then revived by inner thoughts—the dwarfs who have been mining all day (such as in the unconsciousness), looking for gold, or that which is eternal and solid and valuable. Therefore, burying oneself in school, hobbies, music, and all too often drugs while looking for feelings of self-worth, as children often do, can be as dangerous, but seemingly as rewarding, as any mining for gold done by the dwarfs.

The final motif is the apple that is poisonous for the child and yet healthy for the queen. Here is the final difficulty of getting out of a narcissistic mirror. What is good for the ego or sense of self-worth for the stepparent may be a death of sorts for the child. Children may feel and believe that the family would be better off without them. What nourishes the parent is hard for the child to swallow, and children will say things such as, "She makes me gag," or "I wanted to throw up." And if the messages, which can be poisonously cruel, sink in and are consumed as nourishment, then the child's sense of self is harmed. The awareness of individuality will sink into a symbolic coma, and learning that he or she is lovable after all is the only way to wake up the soundly sleeping, barely breathing sense of self.

Case Illustration

An eight-year-old boy sat staring at the toys in front of him in the toy box, but touched none of them. His face was rigid and motionless, but his feet squirmed under the table. His mother admonished him to sit still and behave, at which point the boy sat up straight, folded his hands in his lap, and sat with his legs firmly pressed together in almost military attention. The mother began to tell in detail why her son and she were sitting in my office, although I knew she had been referred to me by the school counselors after the boy was repeatedly suspended from school for being inappropriate and violent with other classmates. At this point, he was not to return to school without counseling; one of the school counselors had recommended family counseling, but the mother was not willing to involve her new, second husband in this "dreadful situation." The child's biological father lived in another state, and blamed the divorce and new stepfather for all the child's woes. The school counselor also implied that the boy's behavior was probably due to the fact that he was a stepchild.

My breathing became more shallow, and I realized I was wondering what constraints I would need to use in talking with this defensive, angry woman, whose sense of self was clearly involved in how this child made her look to others. I suggested that the boy play in the waiting room for a few minutes so I could get a clearer history of what had happened to cause a child so small to be expelled from an elementary school. The child glanced at his mother's hands and waited for her consent. Her quick and harsh, "You heard the lady. Go to the waiting room," was accompanied by his slow march out of the room. Before he could even turn the knob to open the door, another harsh, "Don't slam the door," came from his mother.

The mother then began emphatically to tell me the story of her son's "issues." She blamed her first husband, a man she described as a con artist, liar, and a drunken womanizer with no redeeming value, for most of the child's problems with his temper. When I asked if this man had any relationship with his son, she stated, "No, I have told my son what his father is like, and he understands why he must never see him. My boy has had to be a little man in this family since he was small, but he is like his mother, made of tougher stuff than most." There was evident pride in this statement, but also a demand in tone and expression that I agree with her.

We were in the land of Snow White, and I needed to tread carefully. The mother had grown up in a similar situation. She was her mother's mirror and had learned to agree with the woman without thought. She ran away in college and got pregnant, assuming that her boyfriend would do the right thing and marry her. He did, but the romance and all its feelings of being special ended at the altar as a resentful young father felt he was trapped. The marriage had been short-lived. The woman remembered endless fights; some of the detailed and pertinent descriptions of their fights included him calling her a "witch" and "old bag" and accusing her of "ripping my heart out." The young mother had finally fled with their son, and was working in an office when she met her present husband.

The woman's description of her life was very black and white, with lots of sprinklings of the word "perfect." She stated she had tried so hard to be a perfect wife and mother for her first husband, and that he simply had been too immature to understand what he had and what he had lost. Her attempts now again to be the perfect wife and mother were being shattered by suddenly being seen as the mother of the school bully. Both mother and son had a history of panic attacks, and the child seemed to have episodic asthma attacks. The mother blamed the school, the other kids, and her ex-husband for all the problems she so desperately wished would go away. She had even threatened to send her son back to his father if the boy's behavior at school did not improve. Recently she had decided to induce her new husband into acting like a "real father," and now told him all of the child's misdeeds at the end of the day so that the new stepfather could punish him.

After several sessions, I was able to get the new stepfather to come in and join the family. He was a quiet man who described himself as only wanting calm and order. One of his initial attractions to his new wife and her son had been that the boy had initially appeared so well behaved. He finally acknowledged that meant that the child accepted his mother's orders and acted as he had as a child, being "seen and not heard." He now felt overwhelmed and ill equipped to deal with the needs of his new family, and was intensely resentful of the boy's constant lying and reputation in the neighborhood as a bully and a tattletale. He actually stated he was glad to be the disciplinarian, as his own father "had beaten some sense into him" as a kid, and he felt that by meting out the punishment he could do something to improve the situation.

This small family and child were truly in trouble, and the rage bubbling beneath the surface could have easily destroyed the marriage and the child. Mining for gold in this situation was going to be a long-term process. Fortunately, the couple was very motivated to keep the family together, and the pressure from the school and neighborhood where the boy was viewed as a bully, tattletale, and liar, resulting in a lack of friends, kept the pressure for change on everyone.

The boy responded to all the attention as if he, like Snow White, had awakened. His mother and stepfather attended parenting classes, initiated by the stepfather, who truly wanted to be a better father and invited his wife along to help him. He assured her at first that it was only to help him. She was less defensive with it framed that way and she learned a lot; she even had several painful soul-growing moments when she realized that her son was mimicking her behavior in the way he related to others. She began her own individual therapy and joined a dialectical behavior therapy (DBT) group. The boy began to play more openly in therapy, and his need to reconnect with his father was supported by his new stepfather. Two years later this family had accomplished a lot of personal growth, including the child stating that he wanted to take both his fathers to a baseball game for Father's Day. It was not the most comfortable time initially, but the boy's joy in being heard, having his own feelings accepted, and having his suggestion honored went a long way to making the day a pleasure for all. The mother was initially convinced the whole thing was a dreadful idea, but with help she was able to admit she was most fearful that the men would talk about her behind her back in a cruel way (repeating an experience from her own childhood drama and something she had done to others) and was able to give the three others the gift of a day at the ballpark. She bought the tickets for them, and feeling genuinely generous, went off for a girls' day with a friend.

The boy woke up in many ways. The poisonous nurturing of his existence to make his mother and others look good was gone. The days of being unable to breathe easily, of not knowing what was true about himself or his fathers, or of how to express feelings and know which behaviors are appropriate for friendship building and which aren't faded into a more age-appropriate set of normal childhood experiences. He still, at times, feels fearful and makes up stories to gain attention that he hopes will be positive, but both parents are now working at being more accepting and curious as to why he makes up sometimes inappropriate, but relatively harmless, fabrications.

This is a transformed stepfamily in which everyone is growing and working together. As pointed out in other chapters, the fact that it was identified as a stepfamily was not a helpful diagnosis of the child's problematic behavior and had little to do with the final problem solving. That diagnosis is all too often a poisonous apple to the stepfamily, while making professionals feel healthy and happy.

The tale of Snow White and the Seven Dwarfs teaches that the power to allow loving, creative people to grow, the power to control your own behaviors, and the ability to understand yourself and others are inherent to being part of any family. The power to abuse and control is still there, but wielding such power is ineffective and damaging to growth, trust, and intimacy. When those involved in abuse and narcissistic power games finally realize these behaviors have been ineffective and that such self-serving power games do not result in effective discipline or anything vaguely resembling a child whose attitude is that of a disciple looking to the adult for guidance, other more productive methods can be introduced. Power games serve us best by dancing away in their iron shoes, leaving the family behind.

Chapter 10

The Pleasure of Forgiveness: Premature? Taking too Long? Just Right!

"I am not what has happened to me, I am what I choose to become."

—CARL JUNG

If there is anything that being in a steprelationship has the capacity to teach, it is forgiveness. In the adjustment process of making a new stepfamily, there are almost always unpleasant and hurtful things said and done. Spouses may feel every insecure bone in their psychological bodies, and often find themselves competing in a bizarrely embarrassing way with children seeking the attention of their biological parent. In the new marriage, children often feel left out of decisions they may have participated in before, whether it be what they do on weekends, eat for dinner, watch on TV, or do as a family on vacations and holidays. For the adults and children, feelings may be elicited from being forced to compromise and from giving up their old power dynamic. Emotions triggered by these losses need to be acknowledged, for without discussion and awareness regarding the choices available, people in this situation will say and do things that range from annoying and rude to cruel and, more destructively, violent. Adults and children need to learn to self-soothe and self-regulate their feelings, acknowledging them while not minimizing them, so that titanic levels of emotion or pain, rage, envy, and loss don't overwhelm and sink the family into a place of no return.

There seems to be a division in the field of psychology as to whether people allow others to hurt their feelings or make them mad, or whether emotions are more spontaneous and outside of control. The truth is undoubtedly a combination of choice and spontaneity. However, behaviors are chosen, even while acknowledging emotional responses and sorting out thoughts and beliefs without harming others in a manner considerate of self and others. Marriage and families are human growing machines, and they stretch human limits in terms of compassion, flexibility, and strength. In human development and growth of personality, mistakes in behavior choices are made, and the examination of the choices made and the beliefs that govern such may show them to be inappropriate. Statements later regretted occur, and sometimes what is said is misheard or misinterpreted. Over time the recognition comes that hastily acting out impulses and blurting thoughts may leave people with negative consequences: minimally embarrassment, and at the other extreme some behaviors can get someone killed. Learning to forgive one's self for one's poor choices is as important as learning to forgive those who have inflicted their poorly controlled outbursts on the family. Showing compassion for those in pain who attack and demean other family members is a strength that deserves respect and is needed more often in stepfamilies than in biological ones. Humans tend to tolerate inappropriate behavior from relatives they have known all their lives than from those who appear uninvited and unrelated.

Tristan in the following myth is pushed to grow as a person in several directions. His naiveté about the hostile projections of his stepmother not only lose him a brother, but send him far from the safety of home to grow as a person. The naiveté of Tristan's father and his resistance to looking more closely at what is happening in his family set the stage for behaviors that all regret in the long run. Forgiveness heals many wounds, and although it can't bring the dead back to life, it can and does restore some sense of family and loving relationships.

The Story of Tristan as a Stepchild

King Meliadus, who lost his first wife, Lady Elizabeth, when she died giving birth to Tristan, grieved for seven years and took little pleasure in life, even less in the son whose birth had ended his wife's life.

He was eventually encouraged to take a second wife, as the security of the kingdom depended on the family of the king having other children, and not leaving the fate of the kingdom dependent on the only son from the king's first marriage.

The king knew that he would not love another as he had loved Lady Elizabeth, but he took another queen, who had been married to an earl of Britain, and who had a son the same age as Tristan. The two children got along well and became fast friends. The queen, however, was exceedingly jealous of Tristan and began to hate him, as she knew her son could not inherit the kingdom as long as the older Tristan lived. She began to meditate on how she might do away with Tristan so that her own son could inherit the crown.

At the time, Tristan was about thirteen years old, of very large and robust form, with extraordinary strength of body and beauty. The more noble and beautiful was Tristan, the more the queen hated him. So one day she called upon a very cunning chemist and said, "Make me a draught that anyone who drinks of it will certainly die." And the chemist did as requested and gave it to her in a cup, the liquid golden of color.

Tristan and his stepbrother enjoyed playing ball together in the heat of the day. The queen knew that they would be thirsty at the end of their play, and she was sure that Tristan, being the bigger and stronger one, would insist on the first drink. So she filled a chalice with water and the poison and placed it where the two young men were playing ball.

The two boys played fiercely and were both exceedingly hot and presently extremely thirsty. Tristan said, "I would we had something to drink." His stepbrother saw the chalice and pointed to it saying, "Go have a drink and I will drink some after you." But Tristan said, "No, you saw the chalice and are just as thirsty. You drink first." They argued a bit, and then the stepbrother drank from the chalice with the poison his mother had prepared for Tristan. The stepbrother fell down writhing in pain, and cried out as he died. Tristan cried out for help, but it was too late.

The queen was in great torment because she had destroyed her son in her attempt to destroy his competitor for the kingdom, and she hated Tristan even more passionately than before.

She brooded on ways to destroy Tristan, and finally told one of the pages to take a chalice that she had prepared of both wine and poison to Tristan as a peace offering. Tristan, having nothing but loving thoughts toward the queen, the only mother figure he had ever known, had no suspicions about the wine goblet or its contents. He reached for the wine goblet just as the king, his father, came into the room. The king was exceedingly thirsty and took the goblet from Tristan, who offered it to him immediately.

The queen cried out and stated, "Do not drink from that chalice!" The king and Tristan were both startled by her vehemence, and the king asked for an explanation. The queen ran sobbing to the king and confessed her crimes. The king drew his great sword and was about to slay the queen, who cried out, "Do not kill me with your own hand. It will stain your honor!" She then asked that the lords of the country should judge her, as she knew the law and that she was guilty and would be put to death. When the day came for her to be killed, Tristan asked a boon of his father, and when the king granted such, he asked that the queen's life be spared, even if she be banished from the kingdom.

The king agreed to the banishment rather than following the law as he was sworn to do, and banished them both, his heir for not following the law, and the queen for the attempt on Tristan's life.

Tristan then left the country too, and did not return for many years, during which time he grew into young manhood and explored many other countries. He found favor among many other kings and lords for his nobility and honor. But he became homesick eventually, and in disguise with a friend he returned to his father's kingdom. There he played the harp so beautifully that the king offered him a gift, if he would only name it. Tristan asked only for forgiveness, and it was granted.[1]

The story begins with a man marrying before completing the grief process from a previous relationship, which usually prevents a person from focusing on the development of a new and happy family. This motif frequently occurs in myths and fairy tales as well as in real life. In the past, men often married in order to provide a secure life for their children and home. Now it is easier for both men and women to raise their children without a partner than it was even a hundred years ago. However, avoiding the grief work or staying in pain, anger, or depression for any length of time leaves a person in a place in which hope for future growth is stifled. This scenario, of an arrangement between two people with children who need each other to make their families or kingdom happy, but clearly do not find much joy in each other, is a setup for the tragedy that ensues. Today, similar reasons for people in this situation to marry include loneliness, career demands, help with raising children, increasing one's financial resources and social position, not wanting to mourn their loss, and wanting someone they can really love.

The experience of a wife dying in childbirth is less common than it was when childbirth was the leading cause of death for women, but there are other ways in which this myth still holds true with its images. Some men and women find that having a child is a death to their freedom, career, or sense of self, and may no longer feel connected with their marriage. Abandoning a child and spouse because of these figurative deaths is more common today than dying in childbirth, but it has the same impact. There is no longer a mother or father figure in the picture, and often the remaining parent feels trapped and may neglect, ignore, or even abuse the child left behind. Remarriage may seem to ease the burden of being a single parent with a child with whom one is not fully connected or engaged. This reason alone for forming a stepfamily is a setting for a disaster as potentially damaging to children as being in a single-parent family with a mother or father who has ambivalent feelings about the child. The worst stories about stepfamily violence often occur with a stepfather figure who is not bonded with the child, who is being abused while the mother remains indifferent, or is willing to sacrifice the well-being of the child in order to keep her romantic or financial relationship with the abuser.

Children who have been totally abandoned by their parent, or by both parents, have an additional set of issues to cope with. When one parent has totally abdicated all parental rights and a stepfamily is formed, the stepchild may adore or resent the stepparent, but there is less feeling of needing to prove loyalty to the biological parent who is clearly out of the picture than when the biological parent is still present and needing spoken or unspoken reassurances. On the other hand, adopted children often feel the insecurity of having been abandoned and rejected. "Why was I not good enough?" resounds through their psyches and needs to be acknowledged, discussed, and the wound allowed to start healing.

The joy that the two boys in the myth find in each other is not unusual, and when neither feels as if he is losing a battle for attention from one parent or the other, this joy can nourish the family if it is allowed to be expressed. There are many examples in history and mythology, from David and Jonathan, to one of the oldest myths of Gilgamesh and his wild brother, in which the connection of stepbrothers not related biologically becomes stronger than most siblings ever experience. But as in real life, the shadow often appears. In this story, the shadow of the boys' love for each other is the reality that Tristan's stepmother naturally loves her own son more than she loves Tristan, and wishes that her son could receive the best of the inheritance. Her poisonous jealousy will fatally ruin the friendship. For this kind of parental dilemma to occur does not take a stepparent relationship, as the story of Esau and Jacob in the Bible so vividly shows. Only one child will inherit the birthright, and the mother or stepmother who can't communicate her wishes, fears, and concerns or make a cooperative plan with her husband becomes bitter and vengeful. This scenario may sound antiquated, but the feelings and inheritance difficulties continue today. Mothers today sit in my office talking of their resentment of the fact that their husband's children will inherit more financial or emotional support than their own children will. They experience a poisoning bitterness about that "inequality," leaving no doubt that these patterns still exist.

The desire to poison the image or life of the biological child who stands to inherit more is alive and well. As in this story of Tristan, it often backfires, killing the connections between siblings and between stepparent and stepchild. It can be lethal to the marriage as well. Poisoning often takes the form of words in conversation or gossip rather than in drinks of poison in the modern world. Ruining relationships with caustic talk, innuendos, and bitter anger can result in families dissolving, banishing all members from the home, sometimes forever. Sometimes one or another of the relationships within the stepfamily survives, but poisonous talk usually comes back to injure the person who started it, and in stepfamilies already smoldering, it can be explosive.

This myth carries a strong warning to all men and women who truly can't find it in their hearts to enjoy, or even like, their stepchildren. Their poisonous feeling may cause a temporary sense that one has gained some power or distance from the disliked stepchild, and that one's own child is the better son or daughter, but it will seldom last. Usually, if people truly don't like their future stepchildren, it is better not to marry, unless they can find a way to connect respectfully with the children. The love that new spouses have for each other will not survive attempts to convince them that their own child is as good as the stepchild.

Case Illustration

A man sat grimly in my office, staring at the floor, fists clenched. He finally grabbed a pillow from the couch and slammed it into the floor. "How could I have made two such miserable marriages?" he shouted. "I loved both women so much and tried to be a good husband. I worked long hours, and at times two jobs, so they could have what the family needed. I was willing to put my stepson through college, which his no-account father would not do. But that wasn't good enough. I think my wife wanted me to hate my own kids."

He had been married to his second wife for only two years, and the marriage was in shambles. The man's first marriage to the mother of his children had lasted for twelve years, the last five of which both had acknowledged that they were staying together for the sake of the kids, but had little to do with each other as spouses. They were already rotating weekends with their son and daughter. Both had started dating and finally found the charade of a marriage impossible to endure, especially after it became clear that the man's daughter knew of his girlfriend and was terribly upset about the game that was going on.

The first wife's parents were wealthy enough to have college trust funds put away for both of their grandchildren, and they had bought their daughter her own home, after the divorce, larger than the one she had shared with her former husband. When the first wife's parents died within three years of each other shortly after the divorce, she inherited enough money to be comfortable without working.

The divorced man was delighted to then meet his new wife after his youngest left for college, and was thrilled that her young boy and his older son seemed to get along. The man's older boy had dropped out of school after his sophomore year, and spent most of his time skiing in the Rockies in the winter and working for an Alaskan cruise line in the summer. This son had been arrested twice for drinking and driving, and repeatedly stated that he was not ready to go back to school. He seemed to take a certain delight in his self-described "immaturity." His father, on some level, envied his son's light-hearted freedom, which he had never experienced in his youth. At this point his younger daughter had decided to explore the possibility of being an actress, and was living with several other young people in a small apartment in New York, waiting tables, taking classes, and as her father put it, "getting handouts from her mother."

The couple's courtship had been a whirlwind romance fueled by sexual attraction, a love of theater, and fine dining. From the start, the man enjoyed his new girlfriend's son, but had not realized until they were engaged that her first husband was chronically unemployed and seldom made child-support payments. The man felt it was acceptable to him to take on the financial support of his new stepson, since his own children seemed to have been given enough to get them through college and had the "time to find themselves." He sent both of his children money each month, as he had willingly agreed to do until they were twenty-one, and he felt he made enough that no one would suffer while he supported his new family and contributed to the well-being of his children by his first marriage. Their mother's financial situation now allowed her to take the kids and her new boyfriend on an expensive vacation to Europe once a year, an extravagance that the newly remarried man did not feel he could offer his children or his new family.

The man stated that after his children came back from the first European cruise, the trouble began. His new wife felt her son was being shortchanged and did not have the advantages her husband's older children had. The man felt that this was true, but it was neither his fault nor his problem. The fighting grew increasingly intense as the new wife lobbied to prove her son was more responsible, got better grades, and was more respectful than her stepchildren. The husband began to feel that she was hostile toward his children, and she wanted to poison his relationship with them. In fact, his visits with his children did become increasingly strained as his new wife's feeling of her son being treated unjustly increased. Then the new wife insisted that Bill leave her son a larger share of his estate in his will than he intended to leave his own children, "since they have their mother's family money, and my child does not." The man walked out of the lawyer's office and refused to go further on any will. He felt that his new wife expected that her child and she should have the same financial security and standard of living that his first wife and children experienced.

For the man, the love was gone. His embarrassment at having made "such a huge mistake" kept him from asking for a divorce for a year, hoping that his feelings for his newer family would return and that his wife would give up being so venomous about his children. Neither happened, and he was now filing for his second divorce, angry, bitter, and hurt. Both his children had refused to come home for Christmas that year, preferring that he visit them elsewhere without their stepmother. He felt he had betrayed them, as they no longer felt welcome in his home.

This man, unlike the king in the Tristan story, had done his grief work about the loss of his first marriage before remarrying. He walked into his second marriage thinking it would be better than his first, if for no other reason than it was more romantic and sexual, and because he was older and less anxious about his career. But rushing into a marriage with little understanding of the larger financial situation or the feeling of competition his own children would elicit had put the family in a poisonous atmosphere, which the man did not help by complying as much as he could to avoid an explosion, which then left him seething with resentment.

His children felt banished, and were mistrustful of him for a long time after he separated from their stepmother and had banished both her and her son from his life. His feeling of being conned and duped for his money was a simplistic explanation for the anger and bitterness he felt, and it will probably be a long time before he can heal and forgive himself for what happened. Hopefully, as with Tristan's tale, his children will forgive him long before that. But as was true in the Tristan myth, the mother and her son lost everything: their home and the financial security the man could have offered.

The issue of inheritances is tricky for most stepfamilies. Things are not as easily made "equal" when ex-spouses may have more or fewer financial resources. Some inheritances are intellectual and emotional, others are skills—not always in dollars and cents. Recognizing and accepting this before the marriage can be difficult, and many relationships end up on the rocky shores of premarital agreements, which all too often bring to light the irreconcilable dreams of both parties. Who is paying for what in terms of the needs of the children for health care, education, vacations, etc., can cause endless, often painful, discussions and impasses. If stepchildren have a biological parent who never remarries or does not have other children, they could inherit 100 percent of what the biological parent leaves, while half or stepsiblings divide what the stepfamily has to offer. Life is not fair, and how each couple decides to level that playing field is up to them. Unfortunately, when it is not discussed until after the marriage or until there is a crisis of some sort, the agony is greater, and the possibility of a shipwreck such as the one described above is greatly increased.

The interesting twist in the Tristan story is the banishment for breaking the law that Tristan experiences for his gracious act of forgiving his stepmother for trying to poison him, killing her own child, and almost killing her husband. Tristan is both naïve and innocent in his affection for his stepbrother and in his need to immediately forgive his stepmother. Premature forgiveness takes its own toll on families and individuals. When the stepmother confesses and acknowledges her guilt and sorrow, the appropriateness of this behavior goes a long way toward her forgiveness, but by breaking the rules of the kingdom, Tristan causes his father to lose trust in his son's ability to rule.

The conflict between family members about what is forgivable and what is not, and the need to distance yourself from those who want forgiveness for behavior that one can't be sure won't occur again, is age old and real. Has Tristan gained enough wisdom not to so naive again? Would he allow another person to attempt to poison him, not seeing the poisonous level of the envy and jealousy that went unexpressed and unresolved? In the case study described earlier in this chapter, the man hopefully will not allow his own inner Tristan loose on the world again or trust his ability to commit to another woman until he is sure of her intentions, and will go more slowly into a loving relationship, testing along the way. These are positive outcomes, just as the banishment in the story results in Tristan having more life experience and less certainty of his teenage immortality. Learning that relationships, even between a father and son, can end in hard lessons is valuable.

The story also teaches lessons about forgiveness. Asking for forgiveness requires several things in order to be meaningful. Being specific about acknowledging the infraction of trust is first. Then, recognizing what needs to be done to prevent the same thing from happening again is second. Asking for and giving forgiveness for vague things or when there is no reassurance that the injury will diminish in frequency or intensity any time soon is premature forgiveness, and it cheapens and makes forgiveness relatively meaningless. Forgiving someone for something that will recur is also naïve, at its most benign, and enabling at its worst. Bullying behaviors often accompany demands for forgiveness that are simply exercises in compliance with the bully's wishes, and may even be attempts to negate the impact of ongoing abuse or poor behavior. Therefore, statements like, "Please forgive me; it is just my lousy temper," really mean, "Please accept me as I am. No changes anticipated." Tristan's stepmother admitted her guilt before asking forgiveness, and with no other children, she is unlikely to commit the same offense again. She also did not blame anyone else for her actions. If she had made up excuses or refused to accept the guilt, one hopefully would not have found Tristan begging for forgiveness for her.

These issues of forgiveness and acceptance, when a person is bullied into a victim stance, abound in stepfamilies. In these families, the opportunity to learn and develop skills in compassion and in setting firm boundaries that don't tolerate the unacceptable, but do accept some errors in judgment, occurs frequently. This constant expansion of assessment and compassion skills can lead to a calm, assessing wisdom and a "wait and see" attitude for its members, which leaves fewer people running headlong into repeated situations that will cause harm.

> As the man from the above case illustration so ruefully stated, "Every time my second wife knew she had gone too far in her sales pitch about what losers my kids were and how her kid deserved better, she would cry and apologize, and I would forgive her. Then it would happen again and again. In the end, it pushed my kids away. I would promise them that their new stepmother would be the fun-loving woman I thought she was, and a few hours into a visit, she would begin the nasty, cold comments about whatever it was she thought proved they didn't deserve any of my admiration, respect, or money. My kids no longer trust my assessment of my relationships or me, and I don't blame them. I have forgiven her a hundred times, and nothing changes. It just gets worse."

Many people think forgiveness is a spiritual virtue, and it is hard to argue with this ideal. But while holding grudges is emotionally draining and is seldom held as a spiritual goal, forgiveness of ongoing poor behaviors that never seem to change is premature, unearned, enabling, and often dangerous. In family systems as in life, learning from mistakes needs to be part of the forgiving dialogue. When it is clear that nothing is going to change, detachment without vengeance might be a more spiritual response and a different kind of forgiveness. If the person can't change, then get out of the way. Set a safe boundary, protect those you can, and learn to accept the things you can't change without obsessing about it. Genuine forgiveness that maintains relationships is more likely to encourage attachment and strengthen depth of commitment with a trust that changes have occurred.

In the case above the man actually felt very connected to his stepson and was sad that the relationship with him could not go on as it had. On some level, the stepson's mother's insistence that he have it all had left the boy with nothing, and his only way of going to college was to get loans and scholarships, and to work part time. The man considered helping, planning to put aside some savings in the hope that he can help the boy pay off some or all of his student loans after college, when he hopes that time and detachment have been a stabilizing factor for all involved.

The wisdom and patience stepparents need in order to determine when to forgive, when to let go and accept things that may not change soon, and when to insist on permanent change, can bind and connect partners in a way seldom experienced in other kinds of partnerships. Making strides toward this connection is a monumental task, but a very important one. To learn when the statement, "I am sorry, please forgive me," means only that the person is sorry that he or she got caught this time, but nothing will change, is an important life lesson.

1 Adapted from the story in *Champions of the Round Table*, Written and Illustrated by Howard Pyle, Dover Fairy Tale Books, 101–104

Chapter 11

Stepmother as Fairy Godmother: Does It Get Any Better Than This? Well, Yes.

Yesterday is a history. Tomorrow is a mystery. And today?
Today is a gift. That is why we call it
the present.

—B. Olantunji

The image of an immortal mother figure, a presence who bestows blessings and riches on the suffering innocent, is universal. The longing for a fairy godmother, a goddess, a saint, some ancestral spirit, the Virgin Mary, or a divine animal guide are all expressions of this pattern of hope. They are most often described as intervening after someone's prayer, hard work, sacrifice, ritual, or when someone is at the depths of despair. The images that go with this universal pattern exist in every culture.

For Cinderella, the fairy godmother appears when she has obeyed her stepmother and has toiled and given up everything but a tiny ray of hope. In other myths, the need to honor the deity or entity with ritual or sacrifice is expressed in a variety of forms. This honoring, prayer, or ritual is ignored at the peril of those who are involved with her. It seems there is always a catch when blessings come.

Sleeping Beauty

A king and queen had long awaited the birth of a child, and when a princess was finally born, the fairies of the land were invited as godmothers. There were thirteen fairies, but as the castle only had twelve place settings of gold, only twelve were invited. Those offered gifts, such as beauty, wit, and musical talent. However, the resentful fairy who had not been invited arrived as the next to last gift was given by the others, and this thirteenth fairy placed the princess under an enchantment as her gift, saying that, on reaching adulthood, she would prick her finger on a spindle and die. A twelfth good fairy, though unable to completely reverse the spell, said that the princess would instead sleep for a hundred years, until awakened by the kiss of a prince, and true love's first kiss.

The king and queen banned spinning on distaff or spindle, or the possession of one, upon pain of death, throughout the kingdom, but all in vain. When the princess was fifteen or sixteen she chanced to come upon an old woman in a tower of the castle, who was spinning. The princess asked to try the unfamiliar task and the inevitable happened. The uninvited fairy's curse was fulfilled. The good fairy returned and put everyone in the castle to sleep. A forest of briars sprang up around the castle, shielding it from the outside world; no one could try to penetrate it without facing certain death in the thorns.

After a hundred years had passed, a prince, who had heard the story of the enchantment, braved the wood, which parted at his approach, and entered the castle. He trembled upon seeing the princess's beauty and fell on his knees before her. He kissed her, then she woke up, then everyone in the castle woke to continue where they had left off ... and, in modern versions, starting with this version, they all lived happily ever after.

The neglected thirteenth fairy godmother in "Sleeping Beauty" curses the child because she was not invited to the celebration of Sleeping Beauty's birth. The other twelve fairies were invited and gave wonderful blessings. Not paying attention to some aspect of life to one's own detriment in the end is a common pattern in human life. The fairy godmother in "Cinderella" casts spells that have an expiration time that is seriously exact, with dire consequences if not honored.

Even new age medical practitioners can get caught in this belief pattern. If people develop cancer or some other illness, they may no longer blame a neglected and vengeful goddess, but new age medicine sometimes puts the blame on neglected spiritual obligations or a failure to honor the body and its alleged demands. This places the blame for the illness on the shoulders of the patient, as if there is some thirteenth fairy he or she forgot to invite.

Blaming the patient for the illness, or blaming the parents for not inviting all the fairies, or blaming the biblical Job for his bad fortune, is as old as humanity's ability to tell stories. People try to explain life in terms that give them more control over destiny than is probably realistic. It is also healthy to sort out what is our responsibility, what is random chaos, and what is truly caused by someone else. Although fairy tales may seem childish, they are metaphors for the complex, ethical questions which resound wherever there are humans, no matter how technically skilled those humans may be. When does the gift of nuclear energy, which powers homes, hospitals, and businesses, turn into a toxic waste? When does Agent Orange, used to save the lives of U.S. troops in Vietnam, become the killer of more veterans than the entire war did? When does the joy of battle and winning a war turn into posttraumatic stress disorder (PTSD), which destroys families and lives? In other words, when does the coach that at first seemed so wonderful turn into a smashed pumpkin or a neglected fairy cursing us in an otherwise joyful time?

These images resound in stepfamilies, and often the people involved are so entranced with the wonderful ball they are attending, the joy of new life, the new homes, and the new relationships that the cost of the blessing is ignored or denied, until eventually, the cost is revealed and paid for. The blessings of the fairy godmothers eventually end, or are removed by the daily demands of a full human life, and often the cost feels overwhelming.

Case Illustration

A woman had become pregnant her junior year in college and dropped out of school just before her son was born. She had planned to put the baby up for adoption, but decided not to, and with sizable financial help from an aunt, she began to raise the boy, as a single, working mom. She began attending night school when her son was two, and after several years of working full time and going to school at night, she was able to finish college and find a job that paid well enough for her to move out of her parent's home and into her own condo, again with help from her aunt, who gave her the down payment money as a graduation gift.

Her social life had been somewhat limited by the demands of school, work, and parenting, and her belief that living with her parents and her son made anything more than a casual date impossible. Once she had finished school and moved into her condominium, she found she had the time and opportunity to start seriously dating, and she hoped for a husband and family. She stated that she had been dating for about three years, repeatedly broken hearted after falling in love with men she called "players." She stated that most of the men she dated were wonderful, romantic, and perfect sexual partners for a few months, and then they would end the relationship suddenly by disappearing or breaking the relationship off, making up an excuse that it was no longer fun for them. One man had left her when he began dating a friend of hers. That romance ended suddenly too, but she felt she not only lost a boyfriend in an ugly way, but lost her best friend as well. Then she met a man who seemed different from the others, and thought she had finally found her prince. He, too, had a son from a first marriage, and the two boys got along famously. The couple had met picking up their children from an after-school program and fell in love quickly, marrying when they had known each other for about eleven months.

The woman came into therapy anxious, depressed, and convinced that every gift in her life had been cursed. She literally described her aunt as the fairy godmother who had rescued her repeatedly from the ashes of her life. "She allowed me to keep my son, finish school, and buy a home, all when I needed it the most. I worked hard, but she always showed up when I really needed more money."

The woman had not consulted anyone when marrying "her prince." She had no idea that her aunt was no longer as financially well off as she had been, nor that her aunt had a very rigid idea that her role as the fairy godmother stopped once her niece married. The gold coach became a pumpkin at this point. The aunt had told her repeatedly that she would always help her until she found a guy to take care of her, but the woman had dismissed this warning as old-fashioned silliness. She realized that she thought her aunt and her magic money wand would never disappear. At this time, her stepson's mother suddenly appeared and wanted to sue for custody of her son. The financial and emotional drain on the couple was something neither was prepared for, and the fairy tale prince was now working two jobs and in a terrible mood a good deal of the time. The woman felt her life was cursed, both by her aunt's apparent withdrawal from the scene and by the arrival of the ex-wife—an ex-wife who was playing well the role of the thirteenth uninvited fairy and her curse.

The couple had been fighting "continuously" since they received the legal bill for the custody evaluations needed for the court case. The woman felt that her husband was a "stranger," and just like all the other "players" who had populated her life before him. "He never was totally honest with me, just played me to get what he wanted." At this time, she interpreted her husband's story that the "mother of his son was just like the father of her boy, not interested in being involved in their children's lives," as a sales job. She considered her new husband just another man with a line to get his own way.

The story the ex-wife's lack of interest was, indeed, turning out to be false. The man had married his son's mother, who was eighteen at the time, because she was pregnant, and they had divorced shortly after their son was born. At that time, she had been more involved in "growing up and going to college," and according to the man, "partying when she was not studying," as long as her position as the only mother was not threatened. She had stayed out of the picture the whole time that the new couple were dating, spending a year studying in Europe while getting her master's, an opportunity she had not wanted to give up and which had caused many fights before she left. The man had met his new wife shortly after his first wife's departure, and in his rage had ceased all communication with her. If the traveling mother got messages about her son, it was through his grandparents, not him. Therefore, the ex-wife had not been told that her son's father was getting married until she returned. She had planned to spend a month with her son getting reacquainted, and also catching up on the back child support she owed, which the father had never pursued. Both women were furious with the man for his "half truths," and he was, at this point, unable to feel anything other than victimization because he felt that his intentions had been good.

He felt that he had honestly interpreted his first wife's absences as being a permanent loss of interest, and after seeing the same scenario of the noninvolved parent who never appeared in his new wife's life, he felt reinforced in his rather naive assumption about how his future family life would look with an uninterested, absent ex-wife.

All three adults had a lot of work to do on themselves and their relationships if this stepfamily was to succeed in providing a place for children to grow into healthy adults and for the adults to succeed in becoming wiser, happier people with richer lives. Once the legal threats and custody evaluations calmed down, the three were able to empathize with each other's positions, largely because the custody evaluator and judge were so clear that the three people were in danger of harming the children with their enraged positions of entitlement. All three wanted the boys to be happy. The first wife's guilt at leaving her son when she had been "too young, too irresponsible, and too resentful of motherhood demands," needed to be processed. She needed forgiveness to allow that guilt to heal. She had been shocked and frightened to suddenly find that her son had a new mother. The competition for the boy's loyalties, which his biological mother was sure she had lost, needed to end, and the man owed everyone, including his son, apologies for being so hopeful that his mother was gone for good that he denied to everyone her presence in the family picture.

The struggle to find a way for everyone to work through this difficult situation involved prayers and pleas to all manner of mortal and immortal beings. The two women actually found common ground with each other in their experiences of having been pregnant when they had not wanted to be and being glad their sons were alive and well. Both had gone through agonies about abortion as an option and rejected it, and they shared a history of ambivalence about the pregnancies, being too young by most standards today and not being in love with the fathers of their babies. They stretched their empathy and compassion skills as they formed an odd friendship, at times nurtured by some darker bonding about how annoying men could be, especially "lying manipulators who only say things to get what they want!"

The new stepmother realized that because of the gifting her fairy godmother of an aunt had done, she had never understood finances, and she was stunned and scared by the struggle to make ends meet that her husband and she were facing, with legal bills suddenly overwhelming the budget. Her own spending habits had never been restricted, and although they were not extravagant, she had never worried about being comfortable before.

The husband realized that he had a lifelong pattern of not asking any questions and hoping that what he wanted to be real would turn out to be true. He laughed and stated, "I even assumed that a modern girl like my first wife was doing something about birth control and never asked. Then when she left the country, I assumed that she would not be coming back into my life. But I never asked."

In the end, the newly formed couple was able to get a no-interest loan from her aunt after talking to her about the struggle that meeting the legal bills was causing. The aunt was initially not interested in paying for the problems of "that man and his son," who were no relation to her, but realizing that her own great-nephew was suffering from the loss of parental time and from all the emotional tension, she felt comfortable with a formal loan. When the ex-wife realized that her panic and guilt had triggered her running to lawyers before assessing the reality of the intentions of the couple, she actually paid off half of the bills when she got her first bonus. The new wife realized that she was tempted to accept the woman's offer to pay all of it, but also realized it would just be her old pattern of getting herself out of jams with someone else's money.

Now, the stepfamily is doing well, and the couple has actually talked about the possibility that her boy's father may someday reappear or that the boy may want to find him. They are both determined to keep their heads out of the sand for that potential change in their lives. The ex-wife is now dating a man who has two children from his first marriage, and she is determined to be wiser about approaching the role of stepmother if the relationship grows into something more serious. She stated that she planned to meet the ex-spouse and get to know her. Her own reaction to the surprise and shock that her son had another mother is not something she would wish on anyone else.

Their lives will not be perfect, and they will all struggle to deal with calendars and holidays. Whomever the ex-wife marries will add another dimension to the complexity, but the boys are thriving, and are known as the mediators in their school, even though they are still young.

Everything that is real has a shadow when light is thrown on it. The blessings of the fairy godmothers in our lives are real and not to be ignored, but taken seriously. There is, however, always a cost involved somewhere. Those who receive these gifts or blessings from others will live life more calmly and adapt to the changes life brings more successfully if they are aware that gifts come with shadows. The gifts are often ones we will find enriching and help us to grow, but they are not free and they don't last forever. They only last until midnight, or until the piece of our life we forgot to include shows up demanding attention.

In stepfamilies, the role of the fairy godmother and the role of the spoiling energy of the thirteenth fairy can be played back and forth between mother and stepmother. Children, too, know how to be "players," and they often play the role of poor Cinderella in the ashes with one parent to get special treatment or get something from one parent that the other denied them. Being uninformed about decisions or plans in your children's lives can trigger the raging thirteenth fairy, who resents not being included in the planning or consulted about something that seriously impacts her child or her life. In the fairy tale, the thirteenth fairy was excluded from the invitation list due to a perceived shortage of places at the table.

In real-life stepfamilies, the reasons that one couple may exclude another parent from decisions or making plans are endless, such as not enough time, unresolved issues from the prior marriage, the inability to discuss even minor issues with calm objectivity, and financial fears.

The need to be included in plans that impact your children, finances, and life is normal and healthy, and the raging of the "wicked" fairy, who seems to be reacting mostly to being excluded, can be experienced by anyone. Avoiding these kinds of situations in stepfamilies is never totally successful, and dealing with your own rage at being excluded is part and parcel of stepfamily life. It also provides growth opportunities. To assume the role of the beloved fairy godmother is also normal, and is much more fun than that of the spoiling stepmother or biological mother who has to say no.

My office often echoes with anger and resentment because one parent has either said no to a child or wanted the child to earn something, and then finds that that the other parent or stepparent is providing the item for the child. As one mother in tears stated, "I told my daughter she could get a new computer when she brought her grades up to a 3.0, and then her stepmother bought it for her when she made the cheerleading squad, which I didn't think she should be allowed to do unless her grades were better." The reward can be new toys, later hours, vacations, hobbies, being allowed to date someone that one set of parents thinks is acceptable while the other does not, etc. These all elicit the battle between the child having to earn something or being allowed to have it at all. The fairy godmother showing up with a magic wand and providing wondrous things simply because the child thinks they will be bereft and in the cinders without them stresses many stepfamily relationships, financially and emotionally.

The need to communicate with three or four parental figures, or even more if grandparents and aunts and uncles get involved in "helping," can be immensely challenging. One young man complained bitterly that his mother had insisted, "I ruin my life doing chores around the house" in order to get a new iPod. His stepmother bought one for him during the weeklong vacation he went on each summer with his father and her, whom he saw only a few times a year. When his mother discovered the iPod, she smashed it and took away his keys to the car. That was totally unfair to the young man, who now found his social life, which had revolved around his car, sharply curtailed. Many of these scenes happen even with good communication, but anticipating them and talking them through would be more productive for all concerned.

Just as the fairy godmother can cause problems, the thirteenth fairy can appear at almost any turn when decisions are made that the whole group has not agreed on, and even when consensus is reached, disagreement may leave the rage and spoiling energy simmering.

Case Illustration

One young man lived with his mother and stepfather for most of his life, and saw his father and stepmother every other weekend until his teen years. Then he felt that the biweekly trips to a county one hundred miles from his friends were boring and refused to go more than once a month. The discrepancies between the income levels of the two families was significant, and as college approached, the decision-making process around where the young man was going to go was forefront in the minds of the parents.

The boy's stepfather had attended an Ivy League school and wanted his stepson to have the same opportunity. The boy's father had gone to a large university in the state in which they now lived, had wonderful memories of being on the university's football team, and had hoped his son would share the same alma mater and love of sports. The father had contributed money to the alumni fund, had taken his son to many of the football games over the years, and longed for the day when he would watch his son play on the field as he had done years before.

The summer before his senior year, the young man came to visit his father and stepmother and told them that his stepfather, mother, and he had all just returned from a weeklong trip to the East Coast to look at colleges, and that he was very excited about going to Brown or Yale. This was the first time that his father or stepmother had heard of any other plans besides the state university, and they were outraged that no one had talked to them about them. Their dreams of spending weekends, getting closer to the young man while they all went to football games or other activities, were shattering around them. The aspiring college student was stunned at how enraged his father was, and with his father's threats of refusing to help fund such an outrageously unnecessary expense ringing in his ears, he called his mother and stepfather in tears.

The divorce from decades earlier decreed that child support by the father be provided until the boy was eighteen (or twenty-one if he went to college), with both parents sharing the cost of college if the young man decided to continue his education that way. The cost of an Ivy League school was beyond the imagining of the father, and with the young man's grades being decent but not Ivy League–scholarship material, the idea of him attending such an expensive school had never crossed his the father's mind. The step-father was prepared to pay the added burden, but also loudly made it clear who was the better provider for the young man's education and future.

The families had never learned to make joint decisions, and this was only one of the many incidents that the young man now saw clearly were caused by the lack of consultation on the planning around his life. Whether it was summer camp, buying a car, college, etc., the plans had been made by both sets of parents separately, often leaving him in the middle wishing he could go to sleep and wake up when the uproar was over. He wished he could be in two places at once. Although the dream of going to his father's alma mater was fun, he liked the lifestyle his stepfather provided and felt he had a much better chance of making more money by attending an Ivy League school than by going to the school of his dad's dreams.

The young man realized that his parents were still civil to each other for his sake, but that the competition between them and their refusal to include each other in anything other than decisions about holidays was leaving him feeling torn in two. He was left taking sides rather than having a supportive parental team who could help him make decisions that were in his best interests and not part of some cold war his parents had been engaging in all his life.

As Christmas approached, he had applied to both the local university and to three East Coast Ivy League colleges, and was seriously thinking of dropping all of it to spend a year in Europe just "hitchhiking around" before making up his mind about college. He even considered joining the Marines and then being able to pay his own way without either father being involved. Neither was a decision that he was making due to his sense of what was best for him, and both were ideas that allowed him to get himself out of the family drama in which neither set of parents would invite the other set to any planning sessions about their son.

Everyone longs to sometimes have things given to us without our having to work. Also, the longing to be included is universal and needs to be honored. When stepfamilies acknowledge these human desires and needs and honor them in communicating about what needs to be earned and what needs to be given to children, including each other in discussions that are important to everyone, children and adults develop skills that emphasize cooperation. They become thoughtful of the needs of others and are fairly quick to apologize if they have forgotten to include someone important in the decisions of the family. These are important qualities in any human life, but are particularly important in stepfamilies.

Chapter 12

The Stepfather as Mentor: Where Is Merlin When We Need Him?

In dwelling, live close to the ground.
In thinking, keep to the simple.
In conflict, be fair and generous.
In governing, don't try to control.
In work, do what you enjoy.
In family life, be completely present.

—Tao Te Ching

The tale of King Arthur and Merlin has enchanted generations of young men and women for at least one thousand years. The versions of this tale of the wise old wizard who guides and protects the young hero, while also demanding and challenging him, are probably older than writing itself. The images in the painted caves throughout Europe reflect times when this mentor role and tribal elder probably guided young men into rituals that allowed them to accept adult responsibilities.

In the stories, none of these rites of passage, which are guided by Merlin-like figures, are performed by a biological father, probably for good reason. Luke Skywalker in *Star Wars* is raised by stepparents, an uncle and aunt, after his mother dies and his father vanishes. He then suffers another loss when these parental figures, whose guidance he is destined to outgrow, die. Merlin comes to him in the form of Obi-Wan Kenobi, a Jedi master who appears when needed and disappears when it is time for Luke to act on his own. Later, he is guided by the next wizard and mentor, Yoda.

For King Arthur, this wizard mentorship starts at birth. King Arthur's father tricks Arthur's mother into sleeping with him, and he impregnates her. Merlin appears to orchestrate the seduction and midwife the birth, providing the boy with a foster family much like Luke Skywalker's aunt and uncle. Likewise, Gandalf the Grey in *The Lord of the Rings* plays this role, knowing somehow when he is needed and knowing when to vanish, allowing the young hobbits to face their own challenges.

Stepparents, uncles and aunts, grandparents, and even some temporary romantic partners of their parents can play this role for children. They seem to show up when the situation demands change and a new attitude toward life. These figures are needed in the lives of young people facing the fears associated with change, and they bring with them a demand that the young people face their fears and develop the courage and strength needed for independence. They do not hang around the way parents do to make sure the child succeeds. Instead, they test, prod, and sometimes even insult, humiliate, and embarrass the child as part of their function as guides through rites of passage to adulthood or at the next level of maturity, which would not be achieved without them. Coaches, professors, and the military all serve this function as children move into young adulthood. Without them, humans seldom test their limits, and the kind of strength and courage that only comes with facing fear and the unknown is never developed fully. After all, courage does not exist when there is nothing to fear. Perhaps this is why this wizard role is not filled by father figures in mythology. Fathers provide safety, rather than leading children into increasingly terrifying places far from the comfortable safety of home. Wizards are scary and have power to harm and to help, to demand the best that we can give, and to push us beyond our known limits.

Case Illustration

The despondent-looking woman sat calmly in the office while tears filled her eyes. She stated she just needed to have someone hear her story and tell her she wasn't crazy. Her son was about to leave for college, and for the first time she was crying over a love affair that happened eight years before. She had been divorced for seven years and had two children, a boy and a girl, when she met a man who she thought was bigger than life, her soul mate, and the future stepfather for her boy and girl. "He was bigger than life, and swept me off my feet the way no other man ever had. He seemed to be so happy to be with us and focused on each of us with such intensity it was at times scary." She went on to describe being in love with an intensity she found terrifying and exciting at the same time. She had met this prince at a local coffee house where he was playing guitar with a small band. His dark, tousled good looks and worldly sophistication were new and mesmerizing qualities for her.

The woman had grown up in a small Midwestern town and had known most of the boys she had dated in high school since they were in elementary school together. She had married her high school sweetheart and assumed her life with him would follow the same path her mother's and grandmother's had taken. Raising kids, supporting the family through her homemaking skills, growing a garden in the backyard, and going to community picnics at church were her life goals. She worked to help put her new husband through college, where his initial plan had been to get a teacher's license and return to the town they grew up in to teach high school mathematics.

The woman stated she had known her husband all her life and always felt safe with him. "It was so comfortable and I felt so fulfilled being his wife, doing things I had been taught to do. I thought I was being the perfect wife." At some point, she realized that her husband was spending more time at school than at home, but he said it was studying and the demands of the college that kept him out late. She stated that in retrospect she should have seen signs that things were not what they seemed to be. Their sexual life had practically disappeared, lovemaking only occurring rarely and only when he came home from school late and smelling of beer. She got pregnant with twins in the spring of the husband's senior year, after one of these rare connections, and his rage at her pregnancy was the first time she had felt fear in their marriage. During the angry fight that ensued, she felt as if she didn't know him at all. This stranger wanted her to have an abortion or to get rid of the kids somehow. She also found out that he had changed majors from education to accounting without telling her, and was planning to go to graduate school to get a master's degree in economics, hoping to be accepted at a school in Europe she had never heard of. The plan to return to their hometown had apparently been placed in some trash bin without her being told. This strange man who looked like her husband told her that he wanted to escape the "dreary prison of a life" she had expected for him. The stunned and terrified young wife fled to her parent's home in despair.

The twins were born six months after their father graduated from college. She believed that her husband would come home after graduation and was shocked when a mutual friend told her that he had moved to London. She made futile attempts to communicate with him, and to pursue child support at the very least. He sent brief messages stating he was a student, had no income, and was fine if she gave the kids up for adoption. The young wife's sense of self and her trust in her own perceptions about people were crushed.

By the time her twins were in kindergarten, she stated ruefully that at times she could see their absent father's point of view. She felt imprisoned by her life in the small town and finally got brave enough to move to "the city." She initially shared an apartment with her children and a friend from high school, but it was crowded. Eventually she divorced, found a good job, and moved into her own small, but comfortable, home with some help from her ex-husband's parents. They were furious with their son and didn't want to lose their only grandchildren.

She dated men off and on, but found most were interested in her until they saw the twins, for whom she was the sole provider at this time. She stated, "I am a single mom with two kids, no college education, and I don't make much money. That is a lot of baggage for most men. I understood why they never stuck around very long." However, this wild new love seemed different. He stated he admired her commitment to the kids, thought they were wonderful children, and was awed by her ability to work a full-time job and raise such great kids. He started talking of marriage almost immediately, and the romance was, in her words, "light-years from anything

I had ever experienced." The man was ten years older than she and seemed so open in talking about his life, accepting of its ups and downs, honest about his self-doubts, his struggles, and dreams of making it big as a musician. The intimacy, both sexual and emotional, was new and powerful for her. However, her lover's talk of marriage and adopting her children, which initially was mentioned almost daily, began to disappear, but his involvement with the children and her life was immensely helpful to her. Since he worked nights as a musician, he was able to take the children to and from school, and he began to teach the boy to play guitar. The man took the whole family fishing and camping, things the woman had never dared do by herself. She said, "It felt like the happiest time of my life! We were a family that loved and laughed. The fact that he had stopped talking about marriage didn't bother me. We seemed to be so happy that it didn't matter."

The man continued to enjoy spending most of his free time with the family, and she stated that her son seemed to delight in having a man with whom he could identify. The boy, at one point, looked adoringly at the older man and said, "Finally, there are just as many men as girls in this home." Looking back, the woman said she knew something was wrong because her lover didn't say anything, but just smiled and looked uncomfortable. No one mentioned the son's observation again. Future plans began to be vague and were never discussed. The man had never moved in fully; he said he didn't want to wake the family when his musical gigs ended so late in the early morning. Then his nights with the family began to be fewer each week, and one morning he announced that his band had signed a contract for a tour and he would be away for a while. The woman stated, "At this point I knew he was more relieved than regretful, but no one said anything, and he left. He left my son a guitar that he still has, and a new fishing pole, but no good-bye. He just vanished."

The family felt the hole left by this father figure but moved on, seldom mentioning his name. The woman married a man she met at a church outing, and finally settled into a home to be the housewife she had always wanted to be. Her new husband had two grown daughters, with whom she struggled as they adjusted to being demoted from center stage in their father's life, but by the time she came into therapy those relationships were warm, and the woman was astonished to realize she was turning thirty-eight and about to become a step-grandmother.

However, she still missed what she had with the vanished musician and said she tried for a while to follow his musical career, but it was too painful. Now, with her son leaving for college, the boy had showed her a check and letter he had received from the musician's lawyer. The mother stated she was once again shocked at how little she knew the men in her life. Her son had been accepted at a music conservancy on the East Coast and had told her he would work his way through, get loans, and do whatever he had to do in order to attend. She had contacted the boy's father for the first time in eighteen years, and after threats of lawsuits for back child support, the man had begrudgingly promised to help the son he had never met and about whom his new wife and family knew next to nothing. Now her son had a lawyer's letter stating that the man she had loved so dearly had died and left a life insurance fund for her son to pursue his love of music. The son did not want to share her old flame's letter to him with his mother yet, but he assured her that the man had loved all three of them and wished he could have become a family man, but said he didn't have it in him. The son still had the guitar the man had given him eight years before, and still loved to hike, fish, and camp, things he had learned from this man who had been such a wonderful mentor to him.

Both mother and son talked for the first time about what this vanished man had meant to them. He had appeared out of nowhere, turned their life upside down, and then disappeared. The young son had been terrified of men, of being onstage, and of the "out of doors" until that time. Now he was off to start the education for a formal career in performing music, and found his soul and creative time best nourished during camping and fishing trips by himself. The mentoring that he had received from the older man had pushed him into a life he would never have considered, and then left him the financial ability to become the professional musician his mentor had only dreamed of becoming. The young man stated that when he auditioned for the conservancy he was to attend, he was sure he had seen his beloved mentor in the back of the auditorium. "I knew I could do it with him watching," he stated, and his fear had not stopped him from giving the best performance of his life in front of the most critical audience he had ever faced. Whether it was really his mentor, or only the young man's imagination, the presence of this wizard figure had empowered him to do his best.

The woman realized she needed to talk to someone other than her son about her memories of a man she had loved deeply and to whom she had never been able to say good-bye. She told me "He woke me up to being a woman and gave me confidence in myself I never had. My marriage is nothing like what my relationship was with him. I am safer, my husband does what he says, and I can count on him in ways I never could trust my former love, who was mercurial, unpredictable, and I am not sure I have any idea about who he really was, where he came from, or who his family was. But he gave us all a gift, and my life is different and better for his having appeared and disappeared. He acted the role of stepfather only for six months, but it impacted my son's whole life." She was silent and then said, "I think it was my memory of him that gave me the courage to demand that my first husband help his son. I was so terrified of my first husband's attitude about the twins that it would never have occurred to me to ask him for anything if I had never met my musician love."

The woman may not have felt blessed in the weeks and months after her lover so abruptly disappeared, but he was more than the shallow "player" she thought he was in those sad months. He gave what he could with all that he had and left when what was needed was something he could not provide. Those six months transformed the family into a group of people who could move on to the next stage of their lives. The woman stated she just needed someone to talk to about it and was not sure this was a story that her husband, whom she loved deeply, should hear because of the way that she needed to talk about her gratitude and love for the man she had known only so briefly. There was pain in her voice and tears in her eyes, but joy and courage, too.

These Merlin figures in life seem to be unable to stay for very long, and seldom make lifelong commitments to anything except their own independence. Some men and women find they play that role once or twice in their lives, and then find themselves needing such a figure to challenge themselves for some next stage in their own personal growth.

The Merlin, Gandalf, and Yoda figures in our psyches live on the fringes, face death calmly, and often serve in the role of trickster, helping us see life from a new perspective, with a vision we could not have achieved with the tools and awareness consciously achieved. The movie *Bridges of Madison County* is one of the many movies about this kind of energy in human form, without the bells of whistles of George Lucas's "Industrial Light & Magic" effects or the fairy tale creatures that can wave wands and possess out-of-this-world means of transportation. Owls and coyotes play this role in many tribal myths. They appear suddenly and uninvited, vanish without good-byes or explanations, are seldom forgotten, and leave us with a self-perspective that can be larger and richer than it was before these tricksters appeared.

The saddest part of the Merlin mythology in our culture is how resistant we are to these temporary relationships. Most of society would label the relationships like those described in the case illustration above as failures; but in that case, the woman's greatest achievements came because of them. Because of them, she found the courage to keep her children and experience meaningful love. She is stronger because of the men she loved and appreciates her present husband far more seriously than she might have without the pain of losing the others. She giggled at one point and said, "I now enjoy life a lot, and I just thought how that man gave my heart a real workout. "No pain, no gain," is the runner's motto, but the charley horse knot my heart had after he left I would not wish on anyone. I still miss him, but I would not go with him and leave my present life if he suddenly appeared and asked me to do that. I am where I belong."

No one calls going to college and leaving after graduation a failure, and careers often are stronger after a change in jobs. No one sees the fact that someone who retires from a job that is different from the one he or she had at age eighteen or thirty as a failure. Likewise, sometimes relationships, marriages, and affairs can be learning experiences, as are schools where people graduate from and move on to something better matched for their present needs and maturity. However, this is not an excuse for people to treat relationships lightly and leave them at the drop of a hat. Likewise, the ability to harm and hurt should never be taken for granted, as if doing so is justified because "everyone needs to learn."

Being in the role of trickster is dangerous. It can ruin lives, just as effectively as it can improve them. Not everyone is up to the task of taking on Luke Skywalker's challenges in the mythic story, and not everyone is as courageous as the woman in this case illustration. Perhaps that is why "coyotes," wizards, and people, who come and go so quickly in and out of our lives, causing such confusion and demanding steep learning curves, can both scare and attract us. They are a force of nature for both good and ill. Things with the power to transform also have the power to destroy. People who are caretakers of children and want to take care of themselves should approach these tricksters with caution, but should also be receptive to the positive transformations these guides can inspire us to experience.

Chapter 13

Stepsibling Rivalry as a Rite of Passage: What Joseph Learned on His Way to Egypt

*"If you are going through
hell, keep going."*

—WINSTON CHURCHILL

All families, whether stepfamilies or biological, have to deal with the need to adapt to life successfully in relationships with others and to dance between the need for both control and change. A certain amount of predictability in life is needed to feel secure and trusting; a certain amount of change is needed or people sink into boredom and depression. The right balance is hard to find, especially since for different people what is just right is not always the same for others, and it isn't even the same for the same person at a different time in his or her life. However, it is safe to say that for those planning a stepfamily, the abilities of adapting to change creatively and being willing to look at new and surprising scenarios will serve the new family better than being fearful of change or having a strong need for control, or both. A certain level of tolerance for chaos helps tremendously, combined with a strong ability to control your behavior even in the face of a perceived threat or an infuriating situation. People who tend to be cautious about change, who have obsessive-compulsive tendencies, and who strongly need predictable rituals in their lives may find stepfamily situations intolerable. Conversely, an acceptance of chaotic family situations in which boundaries and rules are never honored is destructive to all.

Stories of siblings, stepsiblings, and half siblings growing up with the need to adapt to a larger definition of family than most youths experience are numerous in the Bible and in Greek mythology, as well as in fairy tales and other mythologies. Many tales describe a family's need for a balance between control and change in adapting successfully and the need to learn to compete and cooperate with others. These attributes are often learned by children from each other and their peers rather than from their parents. These stories serve as a warning of the perils of being out of balance in structuring a stepfamily.

The Old Testament is filled with stories of siblings, their rivalries, and their competition for land, wealth, and success. Competition, loyalty, love, jealousy, bonding, and murder fill these stories with emotional intensity and bonds of hatred or love, which are stronger with siblings than in most friendships. Biblical stories, Greek myths, and Celtic and most European myths and fairy tales tell of the bonding of siblings and the depths they will go to in order to protect and support each other. Yet, other stories talk of attempts by siblings to kill each other. Clearly, sibling relationships can be either life giving or murderous in their extremes. The danger of extreme competition, the favoritism of a parent shown for a child, and the murderous rage these conditions can elicit are presented in stark terms. In both the Cain and Abel story and the story of Jacob and Esau, the brothers are not stepsiblings, but their longing to be equally accepted by God or their own father sets off chains of events with dreadful consequences. These patterns continue today. Blood is often thicker than water, with family loyalties exceeding all other attachments. Murder statistics show that a person is more likely to be killed by a family member or someone well known than by a stranger.[1]

There are few of us who have not heard "I could kill him," muttered under someone's breath, and few of us consider that statement as being more than a verbal exaggeration of annoyance or disgust. But the metaphors and stories hold psychological truths. Jacob, his mother's favorite son, must flee for his life after deceitfully getting his father's blessing, which was meant for Esau, his older brother. After that life lesson, it would seem that Jacob should have learned not to play favorites, but he didn't learn from his childhood, and Jacob's favorite son, Joseph, suffered similar consequences. Whether it is a person who triggers jealousy, or a home, job, position, or some other sign of power, the dark side of this favoritism can become murderous jealousy (this is not envy as there is not endless parental attention or gifts) by those less fortunate. For Joseph, his father's favoritism led to plots by his half siblings, first to murder him and then to sell him as a slave to be sold again in Egypt.

At the same time, stories of deep male bonding between unrelated men put them in a role similar to that of brothers. There are also stepbrothers who care deeply about each other, men for whom the sibling rivalry of biological and other stepbrothers has transformed instead into a bond in which cooperation and support for each other is the dominant force. What energy makes the difference between males bonded by biology having death wishes and acting out violently or having bonds of loyalty, affection, and respect, which we normally associate with blood brothers? Many ancient tales deal with this question, and describe the competition and cooperation among siblings as that of family members adjusting to life changes and needing to responsibly control those changes while flexibly adapting to them. These stories and life experiences show that competition can be helpful because it pushes some people to be their best, but it can also be one of the most destructive energies that can trigger murder and betrayal. Likewise, cooperation is a skill that increases cohesiveness and allows for larger and larger groups to succeed, but it is not the only energy pattern that produces the best leaders and innovators. The biblical story of Leah and Rachel, sisters who share a husband, describes a relationship poisoned because their husband clearly favors one over the other. Subtexts of the danger of playing favorites abound, since favoritism seldom produces loving relationships, but it can push children out of the home to survive in a new way. The complexities of striving for some constructive interplay between cooperation and competition, so that both are honored, are delineated in these tales. Stepfamilies deal constantly with these issues between full, half, or stepsiblings.

Competitive and cooperative energies affect both men and women. People need to learn when which energy is important and how to use it effectively in their families and in society. Many times competition with others or within oneself is both healthy and constructive, and makes everyone better at the tasks, skills, and behaviors around which competition occurs. Learning cooperation is equally valuable, and the larger the group of people, the more important it is to engage the support of the group. However, both energies can be misused or used in the wrong place and at the wrong time when the other would be more effective with fewer disastrous results. Most families seem to have a preference for either competition or cooperation in their functioning, and will often label themselves to clearly state this preference, praising their cooperation or bragging about how competitive they are. Both are needed if a family is to reach its full potential. All energies that produce positive results have to be engaged, though one may be dominant in one area of life and another in some other area.

Like families, children seem to come naturally into this world with varying preferences for relating competitively or cooperatively. Children often divide themselves into groups with various degrees of competitive and cooperative behaviors with varying degrees of popular success, especially during their teen years. Children who can't compete or cooperate successfully within their peer groups are sometimes impaired by some physical or mental disadvantages that leave them limited in the competition for social and economic success in which the rest of society participates. Siblings naturally compete with each other, with cooperation being a more advanced skill, which can be nurtured and developed in a healthy family. Children will naturally decide who is the best athlete, student, artist, communicator to adults, and know who is the strongest, fastest, prettiest, tallest, shortest, etc. This recognition of how people rank among others starts as soon as children begin to have peer relationships. The first tears that come when a child realizes that someone else is "better than me" provide the opportunity to work internally on self-acceptance and the ability to self-soothe and improve our skills for further competition. Fairy tale after fairy tale, and case after case, describe the disastrous consequences of refusing to compete when it is necessary, but also how equally dangerous it is not to know how to cooperate with others.

It is important for families to realize that some competition is unavoidable and springs naturally without any encouragement or coaching from adults. Sisters who decide one is the prettiest, but the other has the brains, do this differentiation together, even if their parents discourage this form of competition and labeling. In any family group, people seem to decide spontaneously that someone is the family clown, mediator, jock, nerd, drama queen, or any other label that identifies the winner of some competition for a position in the family. The family "black sheep" usually knows who she or he is, and without question may accept the family medal for that position. Just as often everyone else claims to have taken his or her turn as the black sheep, or other role identity, depending on the current conditions of his or her life. These familial competitions may extend as a group when family members describe their system to others. Statements such as, "The people in my family are all competitors," and "We are all team players," make assertions about what the family values are and which family members are at the risk of being "the one who doesn't fit in." Every family has one of those, the odd member of the family who actually serves to help define the family system more clearly by showing what it is not. One family's black sheep may be another's crown prince. For example, in one family of politically active liberals, the lone conservative may feel out of place and be labeled the "greedy one, who cares about nothing but himself," while in another family of conservatives the lone liberal may be seen as the "bleeding-heart commie." This tendency of groups to elicit cooperation by stressing common values and excluding those who do not share them is normal until it results in violent rejection and creates lone wolves. Those who don't fit into the family mold often feel attacked and left out, and may go off and find another pack, another family system in which they feel more at home, or they may become loners, perhaps a lone academic in a family of blue-collar workers.

Although competition may come spontaneously and seems part and parcel for siblings in the human population as well as in the animal kingdom, as with people the focus on cooperation is more typical of animals that travel in herds and packs. The competition for food and position that goes on from infancy among herd and pack species results in a pecking order in which cooperative skills develop in order to hunt or protect the group from other hunters. Animal species characterized as loners, as well as people with that trait, have less developed cooperative skills. However, unlike animals, people have more choices in which of these energies they allow to dominate when facilitating development in their families and in their own personalities.

Children in any home explore where they fit in groups, what makes them unique, and what makes them feel like they are part of a system of relationships, and this exploration is particularly important when the child has to reexplore his or her position when a family is re-formed. Since one of the primary functions of a family is to help children learn how to relate in groups, how to fit in, and how to be a successful member of a group, new families need to provide that assistance for children who may have new positions. Also, families help children learn how to choose the group they want to belong to and determine when to abandon a group whose goals are out of line with theirs. These are complex tasks, and the endless skill sets and knowledge of self and other that it takes to succeed at them are learned at home and in school by most people. Siblings are also both teachers and antagonists in this process; this system polishes relational and competitive skills with an intensity no other system does. Later in life, people usually have the choice to quit or change jobs, leave clubs and teams, and divorce, but in childhood situations, it is much more difficult to totally reject a sibling without destroying the family unit.

When two sibling systems begin to form another system that includes both of them, the original identity is seldom lost. The biological siblings usually form a subset of the original set. Attempting to break this pattern or deny it is seldom useful, but it can become beneficial or destructive. Just as parents can't forget which child is biologically theirs and which is not, siblings are aware through shared history, shared relatives, and perhaps by last name that they are different from the step- and half siblings who have a different history, parents, grandparents, and who sometimes come to the new family with a different set of family myths. If combining families seems hard for parents, remember it can also be hard for children who did not choose any of these new relatives, and who may or may not want more siblings with whom they must vie for the adults' attention, time, and resources.

In stepfamilies, loyalty and betrayal, forming bonds that can't be broken, and murderous rage are enacted repeatedly. When constructing a stepfamily, close attention to siblings may allow these patterns to develop into lifelong, vital relationships that can tolerate rivalry at a level that is constructive and can support bonds that will last a lifetime. It doesn't matter whether sibling robins are looking to grab the biggest piece of the worm brought by the parent bird or whether two children are looking at adults for their emotional, psychological, and physical needs, because for bird and human alike, existence depends on the ability to compete well enough with others to sustain life. For humans this competition also enables them to meet the emotional need for self-esteem. At the same time, there is a need for humans to learn to cooperate with each other to succeed. Humans are a pack species; we cannot survive without others to help us with everything from finding food to securing clothing and shelter. Therefore, the skills of gathering a support group, developing relationship ties with peers who will support us in our ventures, or being unable to learn these things in a poisonous family system either creates relational people or people who fall to the fringes of society, isolated on the streets, or in homeless shelters, psychiatric units, or prisons. Humans need each other and have ever since they first walked upright and realized that the predators around them had better solo hunting skills and survival attributes than any humanoid possessed, and that their human offspring required a longer period of protection and feeding than any other mammal species.

Humanity also has the ability to form the largest cooperative groups known on this planet. Because of modern transportation and communication, these groups can span the globe, and a thought or plan in one city, on one continent, can start a wave of communication signals that change behaviors over thousands and thousands of miles for people of other cultures and languages. People learn the skills necessary to make this possible as siblings and classmates and in their family and peer groups if sibling relationships are not available. How successful a person can make friends, gain loyalty from others, or participate in a group depends to some extent on sibling relationships.

Joseph and His Half Siblings

Joseph's father Jacob favored him and gave Joseph a coat as a gift; as a result he was envied by his brothers, who saw the special coat as indicating that Joseph, as Jacob's favorite, would assume family leadership. His brothers' suspicions grew when Joseph told them of his two dreams (Genesis 37:11), in which all the brothers bowed down to him. The narrative tells that his brothers plotted against him one day when he was seventeen, and would have killed him had not the eldest brother, Reuben, interposed. He persuaded them instead to throw Joseph into a pit, and secretly planned to rescue him later. However, when Reuben was absent, the others planned to sell Joseph to a company of Ishmaelite merchants. When the passing Midianites arrived, the brothers dragged Joseph up and sold him to the merchants for twenty pieces of silver. The brothers then dipped Joseph's coat in goat blood and showed it to their father, saying that Joseph had been torn apart by wild beasts.

The envy of Joseph's brothers may have also stemmed from the fact that he was the oldest of the two sons of Rachel, Jacob's first love. The other ten were the sons of Rachel's older sister, Leah, and the sons of the handmaidens, who were given to Jacob during a time when Rachel could not conceive. There was a battle between Leah and Rachel to compete for Jacob's attention, and although Leah was more productive, Rachel was clearly his favorite.

Jacob had told Joseph, when he was seventeen years old, to go check on his brothers. Joseph would report back to his father of their misbehavior. In addition to lack of sibling loyalty, when Joseph shared one of his dreams with them, their anger towards him only increased.

Joseph's story is important for stepfamilies because of the hero's ability to use what he learned as a child to place himself in a favored position once he arrives in Egypt, without learning the lesson of how dangerous being the favorite is because it triggers jealousy.

Once more, he ends up imprisoned. There is never any question that Joseph is special, and he knows it. He has gifts of dream interpretation and the ability to charm and gain the loyalty of superiors, but neither of these gifts helps him with peer relationships. Yet the Bible and many other stories and myths seem to accept that heroic people are loners and not always the most skilled at cooperative management. For example, in the story of Moses leading the tribes of Israel out of Egypt, God calls his brother, Aaron, to accompany him because Aaron communicates better than Moses does. Cooperation and communication are very important to stepfamilies, because in families with step- and half siblings, the possibility of personal clashes and differences increases due to the number of children as compared to the number of adults involved. This may be why in many tribal groups, competitions with a clear winner and loser are discouraged and punished, whereas in less bonded groups competition is encouraged and supported. Whatever the usual roles of competition and cooperation are in the family system before adding step- and half siblings, they will probably become exaggerated when steprelationships are added.

In the Bible story, Joseph and his siblings clearly were a family in which the resource of the father's affection was a scarce commodity. The subsets of children related to Leah and those related to Rachel were clearly in place, and Joseph's inability to cooperate with his half siblings left him vulnerable to being the unwelcome outsider, part of Leah's family structure unwanted and unwelcome by her sons. This kind of subset loyalty is common and even more extreme when the children belong to two stepsibling sets, and avoiding the kind of ostracism displayed in the Old Testament is certainly the goal of most families. However, over the last forty years as a therapist I have seen the pattern of a rejected man or woman, sometimes a younger child and sometimes an older child who was rejected by the stepfamily, go on to make a new and highly successful life with very little family support or even contact. These people often feel like the ugly duckling in the fairy tale, who, beaten and abused, flees the family of origin in search of a place where they belong. Like Joseph, they seldom go home, and often after becoming successful, they find the original family may suddenly appear, wanting to share the wealth or power even though the only contribution these members made to the success of the rejected sibling was in making him or her so miserable that a heroic and often frightening journey to another culture was achieved.

When two adults with children combine, the level of competition will increase if that is the dominant energy in either of the families. However, if cooperation is the strongest value in both families, the children will attempt to cooperate with each other and with new siblings in ways that may bring peace, but also may or may not result in personal sacrifice that may or may not serve them well. Accepting the differences in personality and development and accommodating each may sound daunting, but the reward can be increased communication in a family that is strong, yet flexible enough to adapt to new experiences.

Case Illustration

The thirty-four-year-old man stated that his mother had married his father, a college professor, when she was in graduate school. His father had been involved with her while he was married to his first wife, with whom he had five children. The first wife came from a wealthy family, and the divorce had been bitter, with the wife and five children moving out of state to live with her parents. The young man's father seldom saw his older children initially, but eventually set up a once-a-month weekend visit. None of the boys felt close to their father, who spent most of his time at his lab and office at the university. The father seemed uncomfortable with children, especially his older set, who were hostile to the new family, disrespectful of the new wife, and often bullied their young half brother, who was more like his father than the other children, loving books rather than sports. All the children longed for their father's approval, but this absent-minded, cerebral professor did not seem to understand the needs of young children. His graduate students were his favorite children. His youngest son by his new, younger wife adored his father, and although starved for attention, too, received much more of it than his other siblings received by attempting to share in the older man's love of intellectual pursuits. That this youngest son was the favorite was unspoken, but obvious. The man's mother had attracted the attention of the professor because she, too, was happier in a library or lab doing research than anywhere else. However, the man had a lonely childhood, punctuated by feeling overwhelmed by angry, rowdy half siblings who visited once a month, a weekend he always dreaded.

The friction between the man and his half siblings during their visits became intolerable to all. As the youngest boy, he was endlessly mocked by the more athletic, older brothers, and often ran in tears to their father, who at times raged at his older sons for bullying the younger child. However, this parenting style did little to change the dynamics. The man finally left home at sixteen after an older stepsibling had come home drunk and severely beaten him. The others, also drunk, had laughed and threatened that the adolescent would get another beating if he told his father about the incident. He had run out of the house, and after walking and bleeding for hours, had sought medical help at a local emergency room, where he told the staff he had been in a car accident. Shortly before being released, a nurse had told him that his story had been overheard by a policeman, who was in the waiting room, and that the office wanted to talk to him about a hit-and-run accident about which the sixteen-year-old knew nothing. He fled and hitchhiked out of town. He had kept in touch with a favorite teacher who had moved to another state, and he sought her help.

In the immediate years after he left home, the young man struggled with depression and abuse of illegal recreational drugs, but the emotional support of his teacher and her family helped him to recover while he worked through college and then medical school. His life was not easy; his fear that he was in danger of going to jail because of the traumatic night of the beating and the curiosity of the policeman dominated his late teens. Although he can laugh at it now, it was not an easy time, and his anger and bitterness drove him to succeed in ways that left him exhausted. He still battles depression and trust issues in relating to groups of men. When he graduated from college, he reconnected with his parents, hoping they would come to his graduation. Both were upset and relieved to hear from him, but wanted more explanations than he was prepared to give, and most of the discussion was about the pain his disappearance had caused them. They never attended the graduation, but communication had begun. No one questioned why he left or what his life had been like.

Communication with his parents continues to be sporadic, and the man, now an M.D., spends most holidays with his "adopted" family. When his stepbrothers were told he had graduated from medical school, one of them wrote and asked for a loan. The new doctor is able to see the humor of this at this time, and has found that talking about his childhood and its similarities and differences from the life pattern of Joseph has been helpful. He began to see how closed off his parents were to discussing the conflicts between the children, and how naïve his hope was that if he let his half siblings know how much their father loved him, it would reduce rather increase the hostility. He also knows that the requests for money may surface again, but he doubts that he will follow in Joseph's steps and reunite with his family, as his father is now dead and his mother has remarried. He has no wish ever to see his half siblings.

With most conscious parents, the above tragedy could have been avoided, but if the children and parents had been more effective at healing the tension and hostility, the man might not have chosen to become a successful medical doctor. Children, like adults, want to feel appreciated and needed. Finding a place in the family system and adapting to changes usually occur over time, and introducing future siblings to each other takes some discussion and planning ahead of time. When a secret affair and unplanned pregnancy begin the life of a stepfamily, the transition is usually rapid and fraught with anger and bitter feelings. Therefore, more attention needs to be paid to the needs of the children, not less.

Birth order and personality typology all need to be considered in creating a stepfamily. Some children who are the oldest in the original family system may find themselves a middle child, or an only child may find herself or himself the youngest of four. Making sure there is a plus side to this position loss is immensely important. If all that the children perceive is that their new family means they have less love, less space, and less freedom, the story of Joseph may repeat itself, producing fractured families ruled by jealousy instead of connection or affection. In all families, parenting styles and values evolve as the parents and children age and the need for guidance and supervision evolves. It is important to allow a family time to adapt gradually to sets of children of different ages and experiences, especially when the children have experienced radically different parental styles before the new stepfamily formed. Rushing or avoiding this process only delays and intensifies any problems.

The values that stepparents bring to the new family need to include an awareness of their priorities in helping siblings feel that they are valued, and need to minimize hostile competition between people who may feel they have nothing in common with their new rivals for parental affection and time. As highly as a culture values what Joseph brought to history, there are few parents who wish such a drama to occur in their modern homes.

The following lists can be used to discuss parenting styles, goals, and values. Partners can discuss how they see themselves with their children and their ex-spouses, and what they want to value in the newly forming system. There is no right or wrong in these pairings, but some may be more effective in certain situations than in others, and some people are more comfortable with certain skills than other people may be. What the parents' own childhoods were like, how they were treated as children, what they appreciated about the way they were treated as kids, and what they wish never to repeat are also important considerations.

Parenting Attitudes and Behavior
Discussion Checklist

- Is the objective control or change?
- Is giving orders or teaching or facilitating more appropriate?
- Should we focus on family hierarchy or connections between members?
- Is it more important to know all the answers or to ask the right questions?
- Is taking orders or asking questions more valued?
- Is discipline more valued than creativity?
- What does respect mean? Can respect include challenging the parents or asking them questions?

- When and why is rewarding good behavior preferred to punishment?
- What is punishment? Are time-outs, restrictions of privileges, or verbal expressions of anger appropriate?
- How can children be motivated?
- When do you tell children what to do and when do you want them to solve problems, even though they might make mistakes?
- How much time is devoted to each child by each parent? For what? When?
- What does "family time" mean? How do subsets get time alone with each other and with the parents?
- Which is more important: being a good role model or demanding obedience?
- What kind of home environment will nourish growth of individuals and family?
- What are age-appropriate secrets? What should not be secrets in a family?
- What are family rules? How flexible are they? How are they changed?
- In the family vision, how do parents serve children and their growth? How do children serve their parents? Is the vision hierarchical or a network?
- What power is within the parent's control? What are the children's responsibilities?

Though some of these items may sound vague, discussions of them can be dynamic and enlightening, and may prevent unnecessary conflicts. There will be plenty of conflicts, so being proactive to prevent as many as possible is very important.

The more concrete issue of including everyone in a stepfamily that is being formed, to reassure everyone that balance and fairness in the treatment of family members will be honored, is also more complicated. Discussions can be lively, and although painful at times, can increase trust and open communication. The issues will differ with each child since children at different ages have different concerns. A five-year-old boy may not want to share his toys, but a new clubhouse where he and his new stepbrother can get away may seem to him a fine way to share. Some children of certain ages love the idea of a roommate, and others resent that intensely and view sharing a room, after having had one of their own, as a demotion. In my practice, one teenage girl was totally distraught, sure that her new stepbrother was a "total nerd" who would be a complete embarrassment to her. His feeling about having a "ditzy Barbie doll bimbo" in the family who would never let him in the bathroom was equally negative. With therapy, support, and parental guidance, the "ditz" took a few months to appreciate her new "geek" brother, who was helping improve her grades and was making homework more fun. When her friends also sought out his help and suggested they do a makeover on his hair and wardrobe, they began to have fun with each other. The "ditz" is now more of a scholar, and the "geek" now looks much more polished. They enjoy each other's social network with less fear and hostility, and they sound like siblings as they call each other "Ditzy" and "Geek Squad," names to which neither objects.

Even if children are grown and out of the house, a new stepparent can be traumatic to the original family system, and relationships with grandchildren can be harmed unless adjustments are made and grandparents' relationships with the children acknowledged. Inheritances can be jeopardized. Some feuding may occur anyway, but destructive and expensive lawsuits and fractured relationships are all too often the outcome if no attempt is made to minimize the financial losses and emotional upsets that adult children may experience when a new stepparent appears. Even if there are no large sums of money or property involved, there may be mementos and items that adult children thought would eventually be theirs. These desires to save memories need to be respected and acknowledged, if at all possible, especially if the items have sentimental rather than monetary value, and the new members of the family don't share the sentiment.

One woman of fifty expressed rage at her seventy-five-year-old father who remarried two years after his first wife died. The new stepmother had helped her dad move into a new home in a lovely retirement community, bringing all her own furniture, which was considerably more expensive and newer than anything the woman's dad owned. In the process, a lot of old and worn family furniture, dishes, and pictures had been donated to Goodwill or trashed. Many of the lost items were of no monetary value, but the woman felt that her mother, her entire childhood, and many cherished pictures had been destroyed and lost to her.

Acknowledging adult children when a new family is formed is essential. There is no point at which children with anything close to a good relationship with parents stop feeling as if their parents are family. As much as a parent may love his or her new partner, that partner will be a stranger until there is some reassurance that the love between the adult child and their parent will not be harmed or lessened in any significant way. Rituals with grandchildren every year at Granddad's may feel like a substantial loss if Granddad marries a woman with her own children and grandchildren with a different set of customs for holidays and no longer honors those of his first family.

The family, as an institution, exists in every culture and has survived thousands of years without a better format for raising children and supporting adults. Stepfamily formation is never simple. Marriages without children are not simple either, but the greater the number of children involved, the more complex the problems become. The joy is in the potential of the larger family of interesting, loving people who can learn, support, and share in this ancient system of people connected by bonds of love, biology, and by experiences shared. A large family can have a complex richness in its provision of support, and builds nurturing as it flexes and bends and grows. Stepfamilies have always been a significant proportion of those large families, and friendship and loyalty between stepsiblings can exist just as easily as hostility and dislike. There are always choices.

Chapter 14

Dancing with the Ages and Honoring Stepfamilies

Courage is resistance to fear,
mastery of fear—not absence of fear.

—MARK TWAIN

People perceive their experiences of life based on a combination of external events that impact them and the internalization of these events after they have been put through a variety of filters. How people experience stepfamily life is driven by a multitude of complex factors. First, experiences of stepfamilies are filtered through the five senses: hearing, seeing, tasting, smelling, and touching. For many people, the first time they heard "stepfamily," stepmother," or "stepfather," the words were associated with a nightmarish fairy tale or were spoken with some derision in an adult conversation. Our personal history and how we remember and interpret such begins to form our concept of stepfamily relationships. Which of multiple inputs from the external world people focus on through their senses depends on their biology (how well they hear or see) and their personal and collective history (how their brains choose to focus attention). Then what is processed goes through individual and cultural filters that sift the information, leaving what is important and discarding that which does not fit into the belief or value system. The information about stepfamilies has been processed through a cultural "complex," a set of emotional biases and beliefs that, unfortunately, often has filtered out any positive meanings and has exaggerated negative ones. This filtering process results in shaming and guilt, leaving people imprisoned in a dark attitude toward a family structure that has actually often functioned quite well throughout human history.

How people emotionally react to any event is determined by what they select to perceive; the ongoing imprisonment in a negative attitude toward stepfamilies that is not constructive or helpful needs to be faced with courage, with its biases challenged. Hopefully the fear and negativity around the idea of having to develop a stepfamily can change over time. The difficulty in broadening society's perspective on stepfamilies is further compounded by the differences in perception of the same data from research, as well as the personal experiences of those who lived in difficult stepfamilies. Since many who have been grateful for their stepfamily upbringing are less vocal than those who see harm, the media pays little attention to the millions of families with steprelationships that have produced happy, competent, and relational people. The multitude of choices in behavior and response to any given situation is complex, and stepfamilies often provide a complexity of role models and adult examples children can observe and learn from. Since the skill of diplomacy, and working with people of varying backgrounds, is an increasingly important ability in this diverse world, stepfamilies can be a wonderful, loving training ground for such if honored for this.

The warnings in myths and fairy tales about the dangers of family life, with or without stepfamilies, resonate with all people. Whether the stepmother in the tale, who pushes the child to increased consciousness with her tasks and demands, is an actual stepmother or a biological mother who sometimes acts differently from the all-loving mother they trust, every child has the experience of seeing a "stepmother" making demands on them. This drama is enacted for some children with actual stepparents; for others, it is experienced with biological parents, but the imagery holds up because of its resonance on many layers of experience in the psychological makeup of human beings.

This imagery is reflected on a collective level, too. The culture in which a person lives is multilayered; it may include Western culture, English culture, American culture, regional culture, class and economic cultures, as well as ethnic, religious, and family cultures. All of these cultures, individually and collectively, impact our belief systems. It is through these lenses that we process our life experiences. It is important to realize that many of the subcultures in Western society have been placed in the stepchild role, as members of those groups often experience the dominant cultures of gender, sexual orientation, or religion as treating them like unwanted stepchildren, making them feel less loved, less cared for, less valued, and assigning them the role of cleaning up the ashes of the dominant culture and sometimes even performing the jobs no one else wants for less pay. These step subcultures are undervalued at the expense of society as a whole.

It can be very hard to imagine what it is like to walk a mile in someone else's shoes when the shoes look so different from the ones a person has worn all of his or her life. People can become prisoners in their own lives due to rigidly held beliefs, thoughts, and rote responses to experiences. Although many beliefs and attitudes can provide enough structure and meaning needed for social systems to work and for allowing personal satisfaction and creativity within this safety net to be maximized, some rigid structures and beliefs hinder the quality of life for everyone. One of these unnecessary prisons is the negativity that the mention of the word "stepfamily" elicits in so many people in our culture. This belief and attitude puts misplaced blame on stepparents, causes shame for children and adults alike, and results in the frequent successes of those living and growing in such structures being labeled as anomalies rather than normal outcomes of stepfamily life.

Collective perceptions that stepfamilies are a recent phenomenon, almost always harmful to children, and a sign that modern families are weaker or less moral than families in the past have imprisoned many people into guilt- and shame-based behavior patterns, which affect decisions and attitudes and cause a loss of self-esteem. Freeing society from this negative perception about stepfamilies, and allowing society to see these families as having the full potential to enhance the growth and life of their members, not just harm them, is essential for families to be able to do the important job of raising successful children. Stepfamilies are not easy or simple family systems, but much in life that is the most rewarding is neither simple nor easy.

There are unique gifts that every family brings to its members, including difficulties that cause suffering and can lead as well to tremendous personal growth. Just as intact biological families have some unique gifts that a stepfamily might not have, stepfamilies have unique characteristics that can enhance positive personality characteristics more readily than the original biological parent family. From the patriarchs of the Bible to modern-day presidents, the successful experiences of people who grew up in stepfamilies and those who created such families for their own children do not indicate that the outcomes are as gloomy as mythology would have us believe. Being imprisoned in this fearful perspective does not aid anyone in making informed, empathic, and caring decisions about life. It is as if we have a collective complex about "step." Individuals certainly have complexes, which heighten emotion and distort thinking, making anything close to objective observation impossible, and groups and families can share a common complex, too.

The following is a way of describing complexes, which can be used to look at how we react with the world on any emotional issues:

Complexes

The Jungian term "complexes" refers to highly charged emotional states accompanied by distortions in thought that are triggered by events, internal or external, that are related to an emotionally charged set of memories or expectations. In therapy, most of the complexes that are examined are negative, and the therapy process is an endeavor to make them less highly reactive and damaging to the client's relationships with him- or herself and others.

Complexes can be pleasant psychological states, such as infatuation, but due to their enjoyable nature, they seldom bring people into therapy until they cause difficulties in someone's life. Falling head over heels in love with someone barely known is certainly a complex, but few complain to anyone about such a state until disappointment or disillusionment occurs.

To others observing a person in a complex, the heightened emotionality may seem exaggerated, and in hindsight, even the person who was overwhelmed by the complex may feel they *were beside themselves*. Statements such as, "I was not myself," "You know I didn't mean that," "I couldn't have said that," or "You know I was exaggerating," often follow the experience of being in a complex, which can feel as if a subpersonality has taken over the person expressing the heightened emotions and distorted thoughts. Statements with loaded phrases that may include: *You always* or *you never*, or *you should*, or mind reading such as *I know what you are thinking*, are clues to complexes being engaged. They are defensive positions, as if some part of the person was engaged in protecting an aspect of the psyche that feels vulnerable.

Couples and families often find themselves engaged in arguments with several complexes raging at each other, no one hearing the other accurately and with little resolved in the fight.

There are many forms of illogical thinking that occur when one is in a complex. They are generally characterized by the following:

1. **GENERALIZING AND LABELING:** Generalizing a few personality traits into a negative or positive judgment. Generalizing can also mean coming to a conclusion based on only one or two pieces of evidence, and ignoring, dismissing, or minimizing other information or evidence. For example, you have been late to work three days this week, so you are "always late" or an "irresponsible human being" and "never on time."

2. **NEED TO BE RIGHT**: Where one acts as if one is on trial, needs to prove him or herself right and other ideas and opinions are wrong. For example, refusing to admit any responsibility for a bad outcome, because being right is more important than relationships or anything else. This can be characterized by an inability to apologize genuinely or at all.

3. **CONTROL ISSUES**: This can be characterized as feeling either controlled by others who are victimizing you, or thinking you have to be in total control to avoid such. It can also lead to

self-blaming inappropriately, feeling responsible for the suffering or joy of others.

4. **DEMAND FOR CHANGE**: The belief that others will change their minds or behavior if you do a good enough sales job on them, pressure, cajole, plead, or make them feel guilty because you can only be happy, or they can only be happy if they comply.

5. **MIND READING**: Belief that you know how others feel or think without them saying anything. You know why they act the way they do, and you know how others feel about you without checking your assumptions or guesses. The word "exactly" often appears in sentences when this kind of thinking occurs: "I know exactly what you are thinking!" or "I know exactly what he is up to now."

6. **FILTERING AND SIFTING**: This form of distorted thinking occurs in most of the other complexes. One magnifies details that support the complex and minimizes or dismisses all details that contradict the complex's position.

7. **POLARIZED IDEAS**: There are no gradations of gray or color in this thinking. Things are good or bad, right or wrong. Perfection images are acceptable, or everything is a failure. Nothing is in the middle.

8. **IT ISN'T FAIR**: You think you know what is fair, and that such should be the dominate value for all around you. Intense resentment can occur when either others are not concerned with your idea of fairness, or they disagree with it.

9. **SHOULDS AND BLAME**: One has a list of rules about how humans ought to behave and think and feel. Anger and blaming often follow the image of another who does not abide by these rules. Any pain or reversal of fortune is someone else's responsibility, and they are to blame, probably because they broke one or some or the rules you live by.

10. **EMOTIONS, THOUGHTS, AND BEHAVIOR ENMESHED**: If you feel unloved, then you are unlovable and your actions are justified. Feelings and the thoughts that sometimes accompany them are not examined as independent experiences, and the endless choices in behavioral responses are not examined.

11. **CATASTROPHIZING:** Constantly hypervigilant for a disaster to happen. Problems are seen as always having the worst outcome possible. Endless questions of "What if ..." seem to characterize this kind of thinking.
12. **TAKING EVERYTHING PERSONALLY:** Thinking that everything people do or say or how they look is in some kind of reaction to you; believing that everyone in a room has the same thoughts about you. Refusal to believe it may have nothing to do with you. Spouses often do this with questions like, "Are you mad at me?" when the other spouse is grumpy and may be mad about work or something else that has nothing to do with the marriage.
13. **COMPETITION:** Constantly comparing oneself to others on some imaginary scale as to who is prettier, smarter, more successful, etc.
14. **I DESERVE BETTER:** Belief that one will be rewarded for doing things for others without their asking. Feeling that self-sacrifice is a payment on some benefit that you have come to expect.

Using the above as a reference guide for our perspective culturally on stepfamilies, may help aid the discussion of their value, gifts, and dangers, with more clarity.

Carl Jung and Joseph Campbell wrote extensively on "the hero's journey," a narrative structure that both men described as an inner process towards individuation, and living one's adult life to its fullest, with the heroic sense of self having to separate from its unconscious matrix.[1] All the myths related to this process include a second or unusual birth, an ability to give birth to a new attitude or adaptation to life as an adult. The venture is fraught with dangers, and the hero is often orphaned. Suffering, facing fear, and the resulting courage are themes that are needed if the hero is to reach an aware and conscious life as an adult.

Stepfamilies have a unique ability to partially replicate this mythic journey without the hero ever leaving home! The second birth into a different life or family is a process that children growing up in stepfamilies all experience in a very real way. The flexibility and openness to new perspectives, seeing others more empathetically, and putting oneself in very different shoes are all traits that, though all healthy families may strive to develop, may be developed more readily and more quickly in stepfamilies.

Another positive for stepfamily life is that the brain has a window of opportunity at young ages, during which learning a second language is easier than if one is an adult. In fact, the earlier you learn the second language, the better chance you have of not only becoming and remaining bilingual, but of adding more languages later in life. As children move between family units, often ones that are different from their original family and societal cultures, their ability to accept differences of perspective and appreciate these differences can be enhanced.

In my practice, adults who find it hard to believe that another human being could see the world from a completely different perspective are more likely to come from unbroken homes. Adults who almost unconsciously assume that others will have a different way of perceiving the same situation, and see different responses and different behaviors as fascinating, rather than threatening, are more likely to have a steprelationship in their background. During ten years of teaching graduate-level psychology courses at Naropa University, I observed that some students seemed to accept my grading system, which I described at the beginning of the class, and others seemed to feel my demand for the timely delivery of papers was "unfair" because my policies for late papers and attendance were not the same as other teachers'. Those who easily understood the varying policies by different professors more often talked of being in stepfamily relationships. Those who thought all teachers should have the same requirements were more likely to come from a family without steprelationships. The ability to move between systems that have somewhat different rules and standards enhances personal and professional lives. For example, in my work as a therapist I see that those who come from stepfamilies find developing relationships with in-laws easier and less stressful than those who have never, before their marriage, needed to relate to a parent figure who was not biological kin. This is a valuable personal skill.

There are many research questions that might be investigated if the assumption were accepted that good outcomes could be a possibility for people growing up in stepfamilies. After all, marriages with stepchildren in them have a better survival rate than first marriages, if they survive the first three years.[2] Also, in biblical history, we will never know if Moses would have had the skills needed to impress the pharaoh, or even get an audience with the pharaoh, if he had stayed with his Hebrew birth family. His ability to understand and communicate with the Egyptians, and his willingness to move to different lands are hallmarks of many people who were raised in stepfamilies. The legendary King Arthur became who he was because he had been raised as a stepchild in a less-than-royal family. His Round Table, with its implicit images of equal time for diverse needs and opinions, was a new system of ruling and not one likely to have been created by someone who had grown up in an intact royal household.

An example of a society mimicking a stepfamily situation in order to develop personalities occurred during the Middle Ages, when upper-class children, sometimes as young as seven, were sent to another home to be fostered. Some of this may have been a successful attempt to bind the loyalty of the child to a larger clan or grouping of people, to get to know others beyond the family. Many tribal people also acknowledge this need for a second set of parents, or elders, who can bring the young person into a larger society with its varied ways of perceiving the world.

Those innovative leaders who embraced changes, and often took the group culture, as well as their individual lives, into territories where no one had gone before, are heavily populated with stepchildren. George Washington and Abraham Lincoln were mentioned earlier, and they consistently are mentioned as presidents who embraced change. I do not think it is an accident that Barack Obama, who uses the word "change" as his rallying cry, is a stepchild. His autobiography echoes with the search for meaning and collaboration among varying, and sometimes conflicting, groups and subcultures in this country.[3] He tries to communicate with all of them and hopes that all feel heard. Children who have been terrorized by change, whether in a stepfamily or original family, do not find this skill natural or easy.

This skill of seeing the world through new eyes, and embracing change due to stepfamily relationships comes with suffering, as it did for John Lennon, Ringo Starr, and Paul McCartney of The

Beatles, and for Eleanor Roosevelt, through the death of a parent or hostile divorces, or with less hostility, as it did for Nelson Mandela, Bill Clinton, and Mahatma Gandhi. The list of successful people who pushed the known limits of society and culture could fill pages if you add people such as James Madison, Benjamin Franklin, and Ronald Reagan, who were stepparents with functional families, whose members successfully contributed to the social systems that were important to them.

If our culture could concern itself with what the difference is between those stepfamilies that produce outstanding people and those that produce troubled and destructive people, my sense is that the wisdom to know the difference is written already in myth, fairy tale, and legend. But the research will not be objective as long as our gloomy image of "step" continues to distort with our assumptions that dictators such as Saddam Hussein and Adolf Hitler were who they were because of their stepchild status, and that people such as Abraham Lincoln are successful in spite of having had a stepmother, not because of it. Narcissism and self-absorbed, thoughtless attitudes do not stand much of a chance in the complex relatedness of stepfamilies. Sharing, flexibility, and change are all larger-than-average issues for these families, and successfully negotiating them at an early age certainly has its advantages.

The journey is not easy, and making a stepfamily that works well for all concerned takes energy, compassion, and awareness, both of self and others. It is a path I would not recommend for the faint of heart or self-absorbed. As with the development of the body's muscles, stretching and strengthening emotional muscles is painful and needs to be undertaken with the right pace and timing, but the outcome can be gloriously worth all of the moments of self-doubt, irritation, and pain. The self-knowledge, connection to others, and joyful times within the stepfamily are well worth the effort.

Appendix I

Stockholm Syndrome

Stockholm syndrome is named such as it was first defined and observed during a hostage situation that occurred in Stockholm, Sweden, beginning on August 23, 1973. Two men armed with machine guns entered a bank and took four people hostage for one hundred thirty-one hours. The people being held hostage were bound and locked in a vault tied to dynamite. They were rescued five days after the incident began, and the victims seemed to have bonded pathologically with their kidnappers, expressing fear of the police who rescued them, and loyalty towards those who had terrorized them.

It has been observed in other kidnapping and hostage situations, such as the more recent Patty Hurst kidnapping, as well as fitting the description of symptoms and behaviors of battered women and children who have been abused by their parents.

Researchers such as Murray A. Straus, in *Beating the Devil out of Them*, describe the consequences of corporal punishment on children and the adults they become. The loyalty of children toward abusing parents resembles this syndrome, and even so-called discipline that has been termed "normal" corporal punishment can result in behaviors and attitudes described as Stockholm Syndrome.

It is characterized by the following:

- "Positive feelings by the victim toward the abuser/controller
- Negative feelings by the victim toward family, friends, or authorities trying to rescue/support them or win their release

- Support of the abuser's reasons and behaviors
- Positive feelings by the abuser toward the victim
- Supportive behaviors by the victim, at times helping the abuser
- Inability to engage in behaviors that may assist in their release or detachment
- The presence of a perceived threat to one's physical or psychological survival, and the belief that the abuser would carry out the threat
- The presence of a perceived small kindness from the abuser to the victim
- Isolation from perspectives other than those of the abuser
- The perceived inability to escape the situation"

Dr. James Carver, http://www.mental-health-matters.com February 3, 2009

Appendix II

Vocabulary of Feelings

Happy	Caring	Inadequate	Fearful	Hurt	Angry	Lonely	Guilty	Sad
Thrilled	Tenderness toward	worthless	terrified	crushed	rage	isolated	sick at heart	down
Ecstatic	affection for	good for nothing	frightened	destroyed	furious	abandoned	unforgivable	
Overjoyed	attached to	desolate	intimidated	ruined	seething	all alone	humiliated	depressed
Excited	romantic	confused	horrified	degraded	outraged	forsaken	disgraced	flat
Elated	devoted	dejected	desperate	pain(ed)	burned up	cut off	degraded	bored
Sensational	loving	hopeless	panicky	wounded	nauseated		horrible	no interest
Exhilarated	infatuated	powerless	terror stricken	devastated	violent	alienated	mortified	lost
Fantastic	enamored	helpless	dread	disgraced	hate	remote	exposed	bitter
Terrific	cherish	impotent	vulnerable	humiliated	indignant	alone	crummy	unloved
Turned on	idolize	crippled	paralyzed	anguished	bitter	estranged	remorseful	tearful
Euphoric	worshipful	inferior	self-conscious	at the mercy of	galled	aloof		morose
Enthusiastic	caring	useless	afraid	unappreciated	vengeful	apart from	to blame	blue
Delighted	fond of	finished	scared	tortured	hateful	others	lost face	down
Marvelous	regard	whipped	fearful	cast off	vicious	insulated	demeaned	crummy
Great	respectful	defeated	apprehensive	forsaken	resentful	from others	regretful	dysphoric
Cheerful	admiration	incompetent	jumpy	rejected	irritated	left out	wrong	dejected
Lighthearted	concerned	inept	shaky	discarded	hostile	excluded	embarrassed	
Happy	trust	overwhelmed	threatened	belittled	annoyed	distant	at fault	
Serene	close	ineffective	distrustful	overlooked	upset with	lonesome	in error	
Wonderful	warm	lacking	risky	abused	agitated		responsible for	
Up	friendly	deficient	alarmed	depreciated	mad		blew it	
Aglow	like	incapable	awkward	criticized	aggravated		goofed	
In high	positive	small	defensive	defamed	offended			

Happy	Caring	Inadequate	Fearful	Hurt	Angry
spirits	toward	insignificant	hesitant	discredited	antagonistic
Elevated	prized	unfit	discredited	disparaged	belligerent
Neat	lust	unimportant	shy	maligned	exasperated
Glad	romantic	melancholy	worried	censured	mean
Good	delighted in	incomplete	uneasy	laughed at	vexed
Contented	attracted to	uncertain	bashful	mistreated	spiteful
Satisfied	longing for	weak	embarrassed	devalued	vindictive
Gratified		inefficient	ill at ease	ridiculed	uptight
Pleasant		blah	doubtful	used	bugged
Pleased		sad	jittery	exploited	disgusted
Fine			on edge	debased	turned off
Giddy			uncomfortable	slandered	put out
Silly				let down	grumpy
				cheapened	critical
				minimized	impatient
				put down	miffed
				neglected	irked
					teed off
					chagrined
					cross
					dismayed
					impatient
					critical

Adapted from a Workshop presented by Claudia Black, PhD

Notes

Chapter 1

1. http://www.divorcereform.org/rates.html#anchor168283
2. http://www.adopting.org/adoptions/stepfamily-research-and-statistics.html
3. Barack Obama, *Dreams from My Father* (New York, New York: Three Rivers Press: 1995, 2005

Chapter 3

1. Claudia Black, *It will Never Happen to Me*, (Mass Market Paperback, 1987).

Chapter 5

1. Adapted from: Lily Owens, ed., *The Complete Hans Christian Andersen Fairy Tales* (New York: Avenal Books, 1984), p. 438.

Chapter 7

1. Jacob Grimm and Wilhelm Grimm, *Grimm's Complete Fairy Tales* (Garden City, N.Y.: Nelson Doubleday, Inc.), p. 101.

Chapter 8

1. Jacob Grimm and Wilhelm Grimm, *Grimm's Complete Fairy Tales* (Garden City, N.Y.: Nelson Doubleday, Inc.), p. 80.

Chapter 9

1. Murray A. Straus, *Beating the Devil Out of Them: Corporal Punishment in American Children* (Brunswick, N.J.: Transaction Publishers, 2001).
2. Jacob Grimm and Wilhelm Grimm, *Grimm's Complete Fairy Tales* (Garden City, N.Y.: Nelson Doubleday, Inc.), p. 330.

Chapter 10

1. Howard Pyle, *The Story of the Champions of the Round Table* (New York: Dover Publications, 1968).

Chapter 11

1. Jacob Grimm and Wilhelm Grimm, *Grimm's Complete Fairy Tales* (Garden City, N.Y.: Nelson Doubleday, Inc.), p. 96.

Chapter 13

1. http://www.cdc.gov/mmwr/preview/mmwrhtml/00001189.htmhttp://www.cdc.gov/mmwr/preview/mmwrhtml/00001376.htm

Chapter 14

1. Joseph Campbell, *Transformations of Myth Through Time* (New York: Harper and Row, Publishers, Inc., 1990).
2. Wednesday Martin, Stepmonster: *A New Look at Why Real Stepmothers Think, Feel, and Act the Way We Do* (Boston: Houghton Mifflin Harcourt, 2009), p. 30.
3. Barack Obama, *Dreams from My Father* (New York, New York: Three Rivers Press: 1995, 2005).

References and Resources

Black, Claudia. *It Will Never Happen to Me*, (Mass Market Press, 1996).

Bureau of Justice Statistics

Dieckmann, Hans. *Twice-Told Tales: The Psychological Use of Fairy Tales*. Wilmette, Ill.: Chiron Publications, 1986.

Booth, Alan and Judy Dunn. *Stepfamilies: Who Benefits? Who Does Not?* Hillsdale, N.J.: Lawrence Erlbaum Associates, 1994.

Bullfinch, Thomas. *Bullfinch's Mythology*. New York: Dell Publishing, 1959.

Campbell, Joseph. *Transformations of Myth Through Time*. New York: Harper and Row, Publishers, Inc., 1990.

Carver, Joseph M. "Love and the Stockholm Syndrome: The Mystery of Loving an Abuser." www.mental-health-matters.com, February 3, 2009. Retrieved on January 13, 2010, from www.mental-health-matters.com/index.php?option=com_content&view+article&id+167.

Chetwynd, Tom. *A Dictionary of Sacred Myth*. London: Unwin Paperbacks, 1986.

Cooper, J. C. *An Illustrated Encyclopedia of Traditional Symbols*. London: Thames and Hudson, 1978.

Downing, Christine. *The Goddess: Mythological Images of the Feminine*. New York: Crossroad Publishing Company, 1984.

Goodrich, Norma Lorre. *Ancient Myths: Vivid Re-creations of the Oldest Stories in the World from Ancient Sumer to Imperial Rome*. New York: Meridian Publications, 1994.

Grimm, Jacob and Wilhelm Grimm. *Grimm's Complete Fairy Tales*. Garden City, N.Y.: Nelson Doubleday, Inc., XXXX.

Hamilton, Edith. *Mythology*. New York: New American Library, 1976.

King James Version of Bible

Lofas, Jeannette. *Family Rules: Helping Stepfamilies and Single Parents Build Happy Homes*. New York: Kensington Publishing Corp., 1998.

Martin, Wednesday. *Stepmonster: A New Look at Why Real Stepmothers Think, Feel, and Act the Way We Do*. Boston: Houghton Mifflin Harcourt, 2009.

Meade, Michael. *Men and the Water of Life: Initiation and the Tempering of Men*. San Francisco: HarperSanFrancisco, Inc., 1993.

Mental Health Matters Web site. http://www.mental-health-matters.com.

Moir, Anne, and David Jessel. *Brain Sex: The Real Difference Between Men and Women*. New York: Laurel Trade Paperbacks, 1989.

National Stepfamily Resource Center Web site. http://www.stepfamilies.info.

Newton, Lara. *Brothers and Sisters: Discovering the Psychology of Companionship*. New Orleans: Spring Journal Books, 2007.

Norwood, Perdita Kirkness and Teri Wingender. *The Enlightened Stepmother: Revolutionizing the Role*. New York: HarperCollins, 1999.

Obama, Barack. *Dreams from My Father*. New York: Three Rivers Press, 1996.

Owens, Lily, ed. *The Complete Hans Christian Andersen Fairy Tales*. New York: Avenal Books, 1984.

Pinkola Estés, Clarissa. *Women Who Run With the Wolves*. New York: Ballantine Books, 1992.

Pyle, Howard. *The Story of the Champions of the Round Table*. New York: Dover Publications, 1968.

Samuels, Andrew, Bani Shorter and Fred Plant. *A Critical Dictionary of Jungian Analysis*. London: Routledge & Kegan Paul Ltd, 1986.

Schectman, Jacqueline. *The Stepmother in Fairy Tales: Bereavement and the Feminine Shadow*. Boston: Sego Press, 1993.

Shinoda, Jean. *Goddesses in Everywoman*. New York: Harper & Row, Publishers, Inc., 1985.

Shinoda, Jean. *Gods in Everyman*. New York: Harper & Row, Publishers, Inc., 1989.

Solomon, Marion F. *Narcissism and Intimacy: Love and Marriage in an Age of Confusion*. New York: W. W. Norton, 1992.

The Stepfamily Foundation Web site. http://www.stepfamily.org and http://www.stepfamily.org/statistics.html.

Stepping Stones Counseling Center Web site. http://www.step-families.com.

StepWisdom Web site. http://www.stepwisdom.com.

Stevens, Anthony. *Evolutionary Psychiatry*. New York: Routledge Press, 1996.

Straus, Murray A. *Beating the Devil Out of Them: Corporal Punishment in American Children*. Brunswick, N.J.: Transaction Publishers, 2001.

Straus, Murray A. "Children Should Never, Ever, Be Spanked No Matter What the Circumstances." *Current Controversies about Family Violence*, 2nd ed. D. R. Loseke, R. J. Gelles and M. M. Cavanaugh, eds. Thousand Oaks, CA: Sage, 2005. 137–157.

U.S. Census Bureau

Verrier, Nancy Newton. *The Primal Wound: Understanding the Adopted Child*. Baltimore: Gateway Press, 1996.

Von Franz, Marie Louise. *Shadow and Evil in Fairy Tales*. Irving, Texas: Spring Publications, 1987.

Von Franz, Marie Louise. *The Feminine in Fairy Tales*. Irving, Texas: Spring Publications, 1987.

Wisdom, Susan and Jennifer Green. *Stepcoupling: Creating and Sustaining a Strong Marriage in Today's Blended Family*. New York: Three Rivers Press, 2002.

Zweig, Connie and Steve Wolf. *Romancing the Shadow: A Guide to Soul Work for a Vital, Authentic Life*. New York: Wellspring Books, 1997.

Acknowledgements

There is no way to express my gratitude adequately to all of the families, friends, and clients who have taught me so much about the resiliency of the human spirit, and the strength that so often comes when life appears to be the most difficult. I can't thank all of you individually, but without you this book would not exist.

Growing up in a stepfamily with many people who nurtured me made my life richer, both for its loving figures and its challenges. Each person, in different ways, made my early years more rewarding than the word *step* has usually implied. I am grateful to those who were formally stepparents and those who stood in the parental role at times when one of my divorced parents was unavailable. I also cannot thank my parents, John W. Spackman and Ethel S. Farley, enough for their gracious handling of sharing their children. Neither of them, nor anyone in either family, Spackman or Farley, was disrespectful of the others, at least not in my presence! The loyalty and love my brother and I had for our parents and their families was never questioned nor challenged, nor were we ever made to feel guilty about our enthusiasm for both families.

The final writing of this book needed the help, guidance, and feedback from stepparents and stepchildren; their questions and challenges have proved invaluable. The examples set by so many of my own family who have raised amazing children in stepfamily structures and their willingness to talk about its joys and difficulties has certainly helped immensely in formulating my ideas. Tillman Farley, Susana Gonzales, and Audrey Christ-Farley and their shared children: you are all a gift and an example for all of us. Eugene and Linda Farley: Thank you for your openness in discussing the growth, growing pains, and joy of having a stepson added to a family which already had four boys, and then sharing the wisdom you and all five boys gained from Patrick Malunga's wonderful loving membership in the family. The whole family has been enriched by Patrick's presence, courage, and wonderful smile.

I also want to thank Clarissa Pinkola-Estes, who mentored me from the first day I became engaged in the process of understanding Jungian Analytic Psychology. Her teaching, guidance, and friendship has made this book possible, from its first dream to its last editing. Without her insights and patience, I never would have learned to hear any of the meanings and patterns of human experience in the metaphors and stories of myth and fairytale. Without this second language, which has so enriched my life, I might never have challenged my own misguided perception that stepfamilies were a new age phenomenon. As I studied the patterns in fairytales and myths which had endless descriptions of families with stepparents, I realized they were more than just descriptions of inner psychological processes; they were also recordings of the ways people have struggled for thousands of years with the ever changing landscape of human family systems.

I want to also thank the many friends who have supported me through the two years it has taken to get from chapter one to chapter fourteen. Many thanks to my husband, Tom Manning, his endless patience with weekends lost to my writing, , and his willingness to proofread for details my eyes did not catch. He has been a friend for over four decades, and has never seemed to falter in his belief I would get this done.

I so appreciate the friends and colleagues who also are stepparents, stepchildren, or both who read parts of this book and gave me honest and immensely helpful feedback as the chapters evolved. My special thanks to Joan Johannes, whose initial editing got this book from fourteen articles, some written years apart, to a place of cohesive flow for a book. Laura Klein, MD; Anne Cole, MSN; Patricia Bay, PsyD; Sarah Lincoln, LCSW; and C. J. O'Neill, EEd, many thanks not only for your professional insight and support, but also for your willingness to talk about your own experiences with stepfamily wisdom in your personal and professional lives. Sharon Carroll, for your patience with the changes as you tried to finalize the editing, many thanks.

Judy Selednik, sister-in-law, your ideas on visual imagery for book and presentations help me see the visual world from a new and appreciated vantage point. Michael Holtby, LCSW, whose lecture about his trip to China was almost interrupted by my reaction to the photo of the steps on the Great Wall of China which graces the front of this book, working with you has been just fun. Lara Newton, MA, of the Denver Jung Institute, and Lisa Jane Vargas of Sierra Tucson, thank you for believing in my work and organizing a place for me to present it while it was still in the early stages of development. The feedback from these and other workshop venues has nurtured the process as well as fine tuned it.

There are many more who have contributed to the concepts expressed in my writing. The many students and faculty, Deborah Bowman, PhD especially, at Naropa University, where I taught for over a decade, have challenged me in ways that allowed me to discard some ideas, and strengthen others. You are all special additions to my life: my stepfamily of choice.

About the Author

Eleanor Spackman Alden has been working with stepfamilies for over 40 years. After graduating from Earlham college with a double major in psychology and religion she began her professional work with these families in the poverty areas of Chester, Pennsylvania. There she gained a deep admiration and respect for families structured so differently from what was considered the norm at that time. Since then she has worked with thousands of individuals and families who have the word "step" attached to their relationships and continued to recognize that they had strengths and gifts not seen as readily developed in other family structures. Some also had difficulties that were unique to them, and they often were battling not only some of the individual problems each family has, but a culture which defined them as broken, and failed before they began.

The University of Washington in Seattle awarded her a Masters in Social Work majoring in Clinical Social Work, with an emphasis on research. She also received a Masters in Business Administration from the University of Puget sound with a major in management, and often contemplated the similarities between well managed business groups with high morale, and stepfamilies which were thriving.

In the 1980s she worked as a faculty member and Director of Behavioral Science at the Mercy Family Medicine Residency Program and was a member of the Society of Teachers of Family Medicine. She began a private practice in 1986, and has been seeing couples, individuals and families in this setting ever since.

As a senior adjunct professor in psychology at Naropa University for over a decade, she developed and taught classes and seminars on Jungian Psychology and Family Therapy and took a leave to finish this book.

Volunteer work has included being the Public Education Director of the Jungian Institute of Denver for several years, and serving as the President of the Jung Society of Colorado for almost a decade. She is trained in EMDR, hypnotherapy, group therapy, and works with people suffering from Post Traumatic Stress Syndrome.

Workshop presentations on Stepfamilies combine history, archetypal and depth psychology, family therapy, humor and common sense to engage audiences, and extend an invitation to change the shaming paradigm with which most of the culture views stepfamilies and enjoy the gifts they bring.

Index

W

Washington, George, 2, 73, 209

Z

Zeus, 25, 80, 82-88A

LaVergne, TN USA
16 November 2010

205035LV00001B/17/P